Resource management in developing countries

THEMES IN RESOURCE MANAGEMENT

Edited by Professor Bruce Mitchell, University of Waterloo

Already published:

John Blunden: Mineral Resources and their Management (Out of Print)

John Chapman: Geography and Energy

Paul Eagles: The Planning and Management of Environmentally Sensitive Areas (Out of Print)

R. L. Heathcote: Arid Lands: their use and abuse

Adrian McDonald and David Kay: Water Resources: issues and strategies

John T. Pierce: The Food Resource

Francis Sandbach: Principles of Pollution Control (Out of Print)

Stephen Smith: Recreation Geography

Forthcoming:

L. G. Smith: Impact Assessment defining a new role

D. S. Slocombe: Managing Resources for Sustainability

Peter H Omara-Ojungu

Resource Management in Developing Countries

Longman
Scientific &
Technical

Copublished in the United States with
John Wiley & Sons, Inc., New York

Longman Scientific & Technical
Longman Group UK Ltd,
Longman House, Burnt Mill, Harlow
Essex CM20 2JE, England
and Associated Companies throughout the world.

Copublished in the United States with
John Wiley & Sons, Inc., 605 Third Avenue, New York, NY 10158

First published 1992

British Library Cataloguing in Publication Data

Omara-Ojungu, Peter H.
  Resource management in developing countries.
  – (Themes in resource management)
  I. Title II. Series
  338.9009172

  ISBN 0-582-30102-5

Library of Congress Cataloging-in-Publication Data

Omara-Ojungu, Peter H., 1949–
  Resource management in developing countries / Peter H. Omara
  -Ojungu.
      p.   cm. — (Themes in resource management)
  Includes bibliographical references and index.
  ISBN 0-470-21799-5
  1. Natural resources – Developing countries – Management.
  I. Title. II. Series.
  HC59.7.O43   1992   76545
  333.7′09172′4 – dc20   91-24896
                                                                            CIP

Set in 10/12 Linotron Times

Produced by Longman Group (FE) Limited
Printed by Hong Kong

This book is dedicated to my father, the late Simairi Ojungu,
and to my mother, Imat Eresi Eki.

Contents

List of figures		ix
List of tables		xi
Acknowledgements		xiii
Foreword		xv

Chapter 1	**The field of resource management**	1
	Concepts in resource management	1
	The evolution of the field of resource management	5
	Summary	16

Chapter 2	**Approaches in resource management**	18
	Ecological approach	18
	Economic approach	27
	Technological approach	30
	Ethnological approach	34
	Summary and implications of the approaches	37

Chapter 3	**Poverty and its resource management implications in developing countries**	40
	Poverty in Uganda and its resource management implications	47
	Areas of study	48
	The respondents	48
	Poverty levels	51
	Indicators and effects of poverty	55
	Causes of poverty	56
	Remedial measures and responsibility centres against poverty	57
	Implications of poverty for resource management in Uganda	57

Contents

Chapter 4 Agricultural land management in developing countries   66
           Shifting cultivation   70
           Continuous rain-fed agricultural systems   75
           Irrigation agricultural systems   80
           The green revolution   84
           Causes and implications of declining agricultural
             productivity: a summary   85

Chapter 5 Resource management in mountainous environments of
             the tropics   91
           Introduction   91
           Resource management implications of mountain
             ecological dynamics   92
           Implications for resource management   102
           Resource development and management in mountainous
             environments   103
           Summary   119

Chapter 6 The management of marine and coastal resources   120
           Introduction   120
           The ecological dynamics of marine and coastal
             ecosystems   121
           Resource development in the coastal and marine
             ecosystems of the East African region   129
           Resource management issues and strategies in the East
             African coast   132
           Resource management strategy   144

Chapter 7 The management of urban resources in developing
             countries   152
           The land issue in urban areas   152
           The housing issue in urban areas   159
           Industrialization and environmental pollution   164
           Summary   173

Chapter 8 Perspectives on the future   174
           Salient trends   174
           The critical issues   178
           Prospects for the future   184

           References   198

           Index   209

List of figures

2.1 Component relationships in resource management: a conceptual
   framework 38
3.1 Poverty syndrome in developing countries 43
3.2 Poverty solution syndrome in developing countries 44
3.3 Political subdivisions (districts) of Uganda showing study area 47
3.4 The relationship between political instability, economy and
   poverty 60
3.5 Uganda: population density by district 64
4.1 Contribution of agriculture to economic growth 67
4.2 Decline in yield with continued cropping under shifting
   cultivation in forest environments 73
5.1 Ecological diversity and land use potential and practices in the
   Mount Kenya region 95
5.2 Air and soil temperatures on Mount Kenya in relation to
   elevation 96
5.3 Relationship between precipitation and eievation in the Mount
   Kenya region 98
5.4 Vegetation belts and zones 101
5.5 Relationship between free atmosphere, calculated air
   temperatures and soil temperatures in Mount Kenya altitudinal
   profile 109
5.6 Spatial relationship between rainfall and altitude in Mount
   Kenya region 110
5.7 Temporal variability in rainfall on Mount Kenya (1934–82) 111
5.8 Ecological zones of Mount Kenya 112
5.9 Trends in indigenous and exotic forests on Mount Kenya 115
6.1 Horizontal and vertical zonations in marine ecosystems 121
6.2 The East African coastal region 123
6.3 Oil exploration and refineries 137
6.4 Tanker routes in the East African coastal region 138

List of figures

7.1 Investment distribution of development plans in ESCWA
     countries   165
8.1 The poverty syndrome family loops   181

List of Tables

2.1 Trends in the ecological development of landscapes 21
2.2 Technical dilemmas and some social responses 32
3.1 Payment balances on current account, 1973–83 42
3.2 Overall balance of payments, 1973–83 42
3.3 Agro-ecological zones of Uganda 48
3.4 Respondent distribution by district 49
3.5 Respondent distribution by age group 49
3.6 Family size as % of total respondents 50
3.7 Income distribution amongst respondents 52
3.8 Relative poverty amongst respondents 53
3.9 Poverty related variables by district 54
3.10 Measures against poverty in Uganda 58
4.1 Past patterns of land use in developing countries by region, 1965 68
4.2 Changes in the nature of arable land and farming techniques 69
4.3 Occurrence of crops in the first and final years of the cropping phase in shifting cultivation systems in Zaïre. 75
4.4 Growth rates of agricultural production amongst some African countries, 1969–71 to 1977–9 78
4.5 Declining yields of continuous cropping in Nigeria 79
4.6 Deterioration in soil chemical and physical conditions with time under semi-intensive cropping in Senegal 79
4.7 Relative frequency of government and private sector control in the procurement and distribution of agricultural inputs in thirty-nine countries 88
6.1 Distribution of the mangroves in Kenya coasts 125
6.2 Estimated discharge of domestic sewage from major cities on the coasts 140
6.3 Conventions ratified by states of the East Africa region 145
6.4 Protected areas in the East Africa region 146
6.5 Threatened marine species of the East Africa region 148

List of tables

7.1   Net rural to urban migration in selected countries, 1950–70   155
7.2   Average annual growth rates (%) in Gross Domestic Product   166
7.3   Industrial production in Uganda   167
7.4   Principal industrial establishments in Ivory Coast   169
7.5   Principal industrial establishments in Abidjan and surrounding area 170
8.1   Current and projected population size and growth rates   190

Acknowledgements

During the preparation of this book, considerable assistance and encouragement were rendered by various people and organizations. The Ministry of Education, Uganda, provided research funds and travel grants to various countries including the Center for Technology and Development of Clark University, USA and UNEP library. During these visits, Makerere University willingly granted leaves of absence to enable me to collect data, complete further reading and start writing.

I wish to register my sincere gratitude to the Series Editor, Professor Bruce Mitchell, for the time and effort he personally devoted to editing of the manuscript. I am indebted to him for his constructive criticisms and informed advice often delivered in a most pleasant manner. A number of other colleagues read through one or more chapters, or discussed with me various aspects of the book at different stages. These include Professor Len Berry, Professor Victoria Mwaka, Dr John Kabera, Dr S. A. P. Owera, Dr Bob Ogwang and Professor Kalule Sabiti. Mrs Alladeen Balkiss typed the manuscript with cheerful smiles and wonderful speed and accuracy.

My wife, Miriam, was instrumental in compiling the literature and in helping with final editing. I am most grateful to her and to the children (Isaac, Emma, Linda and Bruce) for their love and encouragement and for leaving me with adequate time for preparing the book.

Finally, I take this opportunity to pay tribute to my brother, Mr Alfred J. Okot-Ojungu, for sponsoring my school education and for always giving education a high priority in his personal plans.

Acknowledgements

We are grateful to the following for permission to reproduce copyright figures and tables:

Erdkunde for fig. 5.2 (Winiger, 1981); Food and Agriculture Organization of the United Nations for tables 4.1 & 4.2 (FAO, 1965/1975), table 4.4 (FAO, 1980); McGraw-Hill, Inc. for fig. 4.1 (Kuznetz, 1964) material is reproduced with the permission of McGraw-Hill, Inc.; Soil and Water Conservation Society for table 2.1 (Odum, 1969); United Nations Environment Programme for table 7.4 (Briand, 1987), fig. 3.5 (GEMS, 1987); fig. 7.1 & table 7.5 (UNEP, 1987); University of Bonn for figs. 5.1, 5.5, 5.8 & 5.9 (Winiger, 1986)

Whilst every effort has been made to trace the owners of copyright material, in a few cases this has proved impossible and we take this opportunity to offer our apologies to any copyright holders whose rights we may have unwittingly infringed.

Foreword

The Themes in Resource Management Series has several objectives. One is to identify and to examine substantive and enduring resource management and development problems. Attention will range from local to international scales, from developed to developing nations, from the public to the private sector, and from biophysical to political considerations.

A second objective is to assess responses to these management and development problems in a variety of world regions. Several responses are of particular interest but especially *research* and *action programmes*. The former involves the different types of analyses which have been generated by natural resource problems. The series will assess the kinds of problems being defined by investigators, the nature and adequacy of evidence being assembled, the kinds of interpretations and arguments being presented, the contributions to improving theoretical understanding as well as resolving pressing problems, and the areas in which progress and frustration are being experienced. The latter response involves the policies, programmes and projects being conceived and implemented to tackle complex and difficult problems. The series is concerned with reviewing their adequacy and effectiveness.

A third objective is to explore the way in which resource analysis, management and development can be made more complementary to one another. Too often analysts and managers go their separate ways. A good part of the blame for this situation must lie with the analysts who too frequently ignore or neglect the concerns of managers, unduly emphasize method and technique, and exclude explicit consideration of the managerial implications of their research. It is hoped that this series will demonstrate that research and analysis can contribute both to the development of theory and to the resolution of important societal problems.

Peter Omara-Ojungu's book, the ninth in the Themes in Resource Management Series, is the first to focus exclusively on resource management and development in developing countries. Other books in the series have considered selective problems and strategies in developing countries, such as

Heathcote's book on arid lands, McDonald and Kay's book on water, Chapman's book on commercial energy systems, and Pierce's book on food.

Peter Omara-Ojungu's book covers a broad range of material. He introduces the field of resource management in the context of developing countries, and outlines basic ecological, economic, technological and ethnological aspects requiring attention. Appropriately, the pervasive issue of *poverty* is the central theme of the book, emphasizing that resource management and development cannot be separated from the need to address the acute poverty which overwhelms many who live in developing countries. He also highlights the relative importance of an *holistic or ecosystems approach and integrated approach* in dealing with resource management and development.

Drawing on examples from Africa, South East Asia and Latin America, he explores issues and problems related to agriculture, mountainous environments, marine and coastal resources, as well as urban resources (land, housing, industrialization). Mountainous and coastal areas are particularly significant. Not only are they sensitive environments, but also they are likely to be encroached upon as pressure grows in existing settled areas.

Peter Omara-Ojungu brings a variety of perspectives to a book on resource management and development in the Third World. Born in Uganda and receiving a B.Sc. from Makerere University and masters and doctorate degrees in Canada, he has held positions at Makerere University in Kampala, Uganda, the University of Nairobi in Kenya and in the University of Transkei. In 1985 he was one of two academics from Makerere University who were appointed on secondment to the Ugandan government Cabinet. He served as the Minister of Lands, Mineral and Water Resources. Thus, he has been involved in resource management and development as both an academic analyst and a policy maker.

The outcome is a book which not only draws upon the research literature, but also in many places reflects his direct experience in guiding resource management in a developing country. His views on poverty, difficulties of rural people and communities, and resource management and development deserve careful attention. The book is above all practical in its approach, and should be of interest to policy makers, resource managers, analysts, and students.

Bruce Mitchell
University of Waterloo
Waterloo, Ontario

January 1991

CHAPTER 1

The field of resource management

Resource management is a relatively new field of study. The newness of the field often presents communication problems. This chapter is designed to introduce the readers to the subject by equipping them first with underlying concepts in resource management and second with the evolution of resource management as a field of study.

Concepts in resource management

Resource management embodies several concepts the understanding of which provides an appropriate foundation for reading the rest of the content of this textbook. In this chapter only the outstanding concepts are examined in light of their application in the context of the Third World countries. Other concepts and terminologies are introduced in the remaining chapters of the text. Some other concepts such as resource appraisal, resource analysis, resource externalities are omitted from this text because they have been discussed in detail elsewhere (e.g. B. Mitchell, 1989; O'Riordan, 1971).

The concept of a resource

There are a host of definitions of a resource. None has gained universal acceptance. Instead, a set of definitions may be satisfactory at one time and thrown away later as perspectives on resources change. In his classical definition, Zimmermann (1951: 15) stated that 'resources *are* not, they *become*; they are not static but expand and contract in response to human wants and human action'. Thus a resource is not merely a tangible object but also a functional relationship that exists between people's wants, their capabilities and their attitudes towards the worth of an environment. B. Mitchell (1989) translated this rather philosophical view into an anthropocentric position and specified that often an object is first a neutral stuff and then, when human value is attached to it, it becomes a resource. For instance,

1

before the present uses of copper were discovered, all copper-containing rocks were not resources but mere 'stones'. But such stones may have been shaped into cutting knives by Stone Age man thus making the copper-containing rocks a resource for tool making but not for electric wires, copper plating, copper ornaments as we value copper for today.

Like Zimmermann (one of the fathers of resource management) Mitchell adopted a subjective, relative, cultural and functional viewpoint about resources. Their statements imply that the environment or parts of the environment are resources especially when they are considered to be capable of satisfying human needs. In other words, a resource must also be of value to people at any one time. In paraphrasing Zimmermann, Mitchell (1979: 1) stressed further that 'availability for human use, not mere physical presence, is the chief criterion of resources'. Availability in turn depends on human wants and abilities. But as we continue to care for the future generations, it must be accepted that all things or resources have value even if they offer no immediate utility to people. Other ecosystem components are also resources because of the functional roles they play in ecosystem stability.

Because of the subjective, relative and cultural context in which a resource is often defined, it is difficult to foresee a universally acceptable definition of resource as a concept. What seems clear by implication is that differences in value systems, aspirations and technology will mean that a neutral stuff to one culture at one time may become a resource in the same culture at some other time. For instance, until two decades ago, most members of the Banyankole tribe of western Uganda did not eat fish. Social stratification dictated the taboo with the belief that fish, hippopotamuses and other 'crawling' animals, together with roots and tubers which 'grow underground', were too inferior for the upper (ruling) class in the tribe. The tribal king could eat only 'dignified' foods from things that stand upright above the surface of the ground, such as millet, bananas, and the 'graceful' antelopes, duickers, deers, cows, etc. 'Inferior foods' of squirrels, edible rats, fish, cassava, potatoes, etc. were until the 1970s reserved for the lower class. In Papua New Guinea, similar effects of social stratification prevent certain sectors of the population from access to particular animal resources. Hyndman (1979) and Pernetta and Hill (1984) documented how women and children of the Wopkaimin of Western Province, Papua New Guinea, are excluded from eating certain larger game animals while the men are prevented by taboos from eating frogs, reptiles and small rodents, which are considered women's food. While such social segregation splits the exploitative pressure over different resources, it also complicates the problem of defining a resource.

These illustrations of the concept of resource should not be oversimplified, however, to imply that with time anything can become a resource to a community. Poisonous substances are neither neutral nor resources until their state is transformed, for instance, through industrial processing such as during the extraction of medicinal drugs from snake venom.

2

Finally, the stated functional significance of a resource implies that a neutral stuff may become a resource even if it serves only some but not all of the aspirations of people. For instance, the Kasubi Tombs, being the burial ground for the Kings (Kabaka) of the Baganda tribe of southern Uganda, are a symbolic resource with strong social and political significance amongst the Baganda. However, the burial ground does not play a direct economic role in the lives of individual members of the tribe. Therefore, the definition of a resource may also vary according to some more specific goals and aspirations of people.

Resource allocation

This is the spatial and temporal placing of resource uses (agriculture, soils, fodder, game park, fisheries) in a pattern that reflects the goals, priorities and aspirations of a community (B. Mitchell 1989). Under the communal grazing systems in Africa, areas of low agricultural potential are often set aside for livestock grazing by the local community. In such grazing land, other activities (agriculture, residential homes) are prohibited. But practices such as hunting, logging and apiculture (bee-keeping) which are compatible with livestock grazing may be permitted. Other examples of resource allocation are discussed further in Chapters 5 and 7 and also in B. Mitchell (1989).

In resource management it is intended that such resource allocation patterns do not result in unnecessary deleterious effects in the biophysical and socio-economic systems. Resource allocation should therefore influence the production, consumption and distribution of resources in a direction consistent with the local, regional or national development objectives. During resource allocation, trade-offs will be made with some 'costs' accepted to gain other benefits. For example, in the various swamp reclamation projects in developing countries loss of potential for local fishing in swamps is accepted for the gains of producing rice, fruits and vegetables and providing reclaimed agricultural land to the landless. Similarly, during the construction of the Kariba Dam (Zambia), large tracts of agricultural land were lost because of inundation. That loss was absorbable because the project promoted higher prospects for electrification, irrigation, fishing and navigation. But all effects of resource allocation cannot be well compensated. For instance the allocation of farms, formerly owned by Europeans, to indigenous Kenyans has led to threats of soil erosion, low productivity, food shortages and increasing levels of poverty within the Laikipia District of the Mount Kenya region (Chapter 5).

Resource development

Resource development is a more general term which incorporates the concepts cited above. In B. Mitchell's (1989: 4) words, 'resource development

3

represents the actual exploitation or use of a resource during the transformation of the neutral stuff into a commodity or service to serve human needs and aspirations'. Resource development will involve placing value, extraction and processing so that a neutral stuff becomes a resource to be used to meet human wants. Although for most resources the value is culturally, economically and technologically determined, other resources such as atmospheric oxygen possess biologically mandated and universal values.

Many examples of resource development exist in developing countries. In Egypt and the Sudan, the Nile water is diverted into channels for irrigation thus transforming desert soils into agricultural land. In tropical agriculture (Chapter 4), forests are cleared to allow cultivation or to provide timber for furniture, construction and for pulp and paper industry. In Thailand, through the Mekong Valley Project, large acreages of land are irrigated for rice cultivation while some of the same water is fed into locally made fish ponds. Rice cultivation and fish farming in Thailand are intended to reduce the problems of food shortages and malnutrition due to protein deficiency.

Resource management

Resource management is the broadest of all the cited concepts. It involves controls on the amount, quality, timing, availability and the general direction of resource development. Resource management strategies are designed to promote exploitation, enhancement and restoration of resources. According to O'Riordan (1971: 19) resource management

> may be defined as a process of decision-making whereby resources are allocated over space and time according to the needs, aspirations, and desires of man within the framework of his technological inventiveness, his political and social institutions and his legal and administrative framework.

Resource management studies are therefore concerned with allocation of resources and the biophysical and socio-economic milieu in which resources are or ought to be developed. Resource management examines strategies and technologies for resource development in order to sustain economic growth without causing unnecessary environmental impairment. Several examples of resource management strategies are discussed in the remaining chapters of this text. For instance, in Chapter 5 the resource management strategy in the Mount Kenya region includes application of agroforestry, terracing, mulching, contour farming, the Nyayo tea zone and regulations and restrictions on human settlement and forest clearing.

As a concept, resource management has been used within the last two decades in place of resource conservation because the latter is seen to be ambiguous and vaguely conceived, with great differences in views amongst its proponents. The term conservation retains an implicit streak or undertone of 'no use' (preservation), thus causing the misunderstanding that conservationists advocate no growth. In contrast, resource management is a more comprehensive and positive term which allows resource allocation to be dominated neither by the market forces nor by quasi-political forums but by a combination of and compromises in social, cultural, economic, ecological and institutional processes. O'Riordan (1971) confirmed this viewpoint by emphasizing that resource management is a process of decision making involving judgement, preference and commitment whereby certain desired resource outputs are sought from certain perceived resource combinations through the choice among various managerial, technical and administrative alternatives. Resource management thus becomes an essential national undertaking because all sectors of the national economy often depend on conditions and methods of resource utilization.

The evolution of the field of resource management

In both the developed and developing countries the evolution of resource management as a distinct field of study has been late and slow. Prior to the 1960s, aspects of resource management were studied in agriculture, forestry, soil science and wildlife conservation schools. In general it was only in the mid-1960s when some universities in the developed countries established resource management as a fully fledged course of study. By the 1970s a few universities in developing countries emulated this by conducting courses under such titles as land use and resource assessment, environmental science, resource development and conservation, environmental management or resource management itself. At these infancy stages, resource management courses had a poor conceptual structure with strong emphasis placed on issues of the day (pollution, soil erosion, deforestation). Little attempt was made to relate the issues to principles and concepts in resource management. In the developed countries the theoretical basis of resource management became more clarified through texts written by Zimmermann (1951), Firey (1960), O'Riordan (1971) and B. Mitchell (1989). Understandably none of these texts presented adequate analysis of resource management issues, problems and strategies in developing countries.

Several reasons account for the late arrival of the field despite the fact that human use and abuse of resources has been on stage for millenniums. One primary reason is that for a long time the nature of resources was ill-conceived. Resources were originally considered abundant and in single purpose terms, with no or few interlinkages within and amongst them. Perhaps the worst drawback has been the prolonged association of resources with what was commonly known as 'natural resources' (i.e. minerals, forests, land, fisheries, game animals). The concept of natural resources precluded other non-tangible especially common property resources such as air, climate, sunlight and historical monuments whose quantities and values could not be easily estimated using traditional economic frameworks. As a result, changes and damages to resources often passed without arousing public outcry. In the

1960s, however, fears of increasing resource scarcity, awareness of human ability to destroy, and inability to substitute for all resources prompted concerns from public and institutions associated with resource use. In developing countries, calls for resource management during the 1960s and 1970s were viewed as mixed up with concerns for environmental quality and limits on growth at a time when developing countries were hard pressed with needs for economic growth, provision of better facilities and conditions for education and health. As a result, governments in developing countries usually paid only lip-service to calls for more effective resource management. In any case in many developing countries, poorly developed mass media and monopoly of resource and environmental issues by government and international agencies prevented rapid diffusion of the news to the grass roots. Furthermore, most cities in developing countries were relatively small and less industrialized and were not exhibiting obvious symptoms of environmental deterioration. All these drawbacks were clouded by a general misconception that resources in developing countries were still abundant and urgent calls for resource and environmental management were viewed as unnecessarily conspiratorial and pessimistic. In the extreme the cry for environmental management was seen as a mere conspiracy of industrialized nations to restrain the growth and development of developing countries.

This section of the chapter presents a historical analysis of resource management as a field of study. The purpose of such an analysis is not only to review the history per se but also to prevent communities in developing countries from repeating the exact steps in history: the past should be known not for its own sake but in order to learn from and avoid bad experiences. Throughout this section, attempts are made to juxtapose concerns in industrialized countries against those in developing countries.

As a field of study resource management has evolved in response to shifts in the perceived values of land, labour, technology and capital. At various times resources have been conceived either as abundant or scarce and management concern responded to emerging crises associated with subsequent use of resources. On a global scale, pre-industrial perception of resources, their allocation and management differed from perceptions during industrial and post-industrial periods. In developing countries, periods of changing resource management issues and strategies may be analysed under pre-colonial, colonial and post-colonial periods. Features of resource management at the global scale and at a regional level may not necessarily be exclusive of one another.

Pre-industrial/pre-colonial period

In the pre-industrial period various communities had poor technology and therefore limited abilities for resource exploitation. Human numbers were relatively small and consumption patterns were less diverse and complex than in subsequent time periods. The human ability for resource appraisal and exploitation was poorly developed. Therefore in relative terms resources were scarce but in absolute terms they were abundant (unutilized and underutilized resources were plentiful). At this time a money economy was poorly or not developed. Bartering was the major means of transaction. Resource exploitation remained labour intensive and resources were allocated according to social norms, customs and traditions (O'Riordan, 1971). Each community had evolved a long-standing understanding of some aspects of the natural environment and resource use practices were in near harmony with nature. During good years and periods of abundance, population increased only to be checked by the subsequent and reciprocal pressure it imposed on resources. Damage caused by extreme fluctuations in nature (occurrence of disease epidemics, floods, drought) also helped to maintain equilibrium between resource demands and supply. Resource management techniques were largely developed in order to cope with physical limitations or fluctuations in the environment. High erosion rates on steep slopes, water scarcity in arid and semi-arid areas or rapid soil quality degeneration in humid tropical environments were some of the problems which frequently called for controls on levels of resource exploitation and traditional resource management measures.

In developing countries the period of absolute abundance but relative scarcity may be equated with the pre-colonial times even though many of the features cited above often stretched into the colonial and post-colonial times. In some communities in Africa, Asia and Latin America, resources are still relatively scarce because of limited technology but absolutely abundant because of underutilization (for example, amongst the Pygmies, the Aborigines of Papua New Guinea and pockets of the Indian communities in South America). For these communities a major resource management issue emerges:

> In view of their limited political and technological power and subsequent isolation, how can their own survival be guaranteed when more advanced communities increasingly encroach on them?

In retrospect, the issue facing the Pygmies, Aborigines and some American Indians today is the same issue that faced all communities in the developing countries when the colonization process was being advanced by relatively more powerful western cultures. But most fundamentally, their perception of resources and level of utilization support Zimmermann's (1951) contention that resources *are* not, they *become*; they contract and expand in response to human wants and cultural pressures.

It was during the pre-industrial or pre-colonial period that such resource management techniques as terracing, irrigation, transhumance and nomadism, use of fires, and shifting cultivation emerged in Africa, Asia and South America. Although at the time there were few organized and strong political institutions to guide and oversee the application of these techniques, in the Kingdom areas of Egypt, Mesopotamia, the Inca and in parts of Asia such political authorities must have prevented some environmental deterioration due to erosion.

Industrial or colonial period

During the industrial period, a major shift in resource management occurred. In Western Europe this was the period of great technological advance and societies' ability to unlock resources formerly hidden beyond human exploitation was enormously enhanced. Minerals could be obtained in large quantities from increasingly deeper mines, timber and other forest resources could be exploited *en masse*, fishing could be undertaken in increasingly distant and deeper waters and resource scarcity in one community was counteracted by importation from elsewhere. Increased technological power and mobility created an open system in which resource substitution and importation minimized the fears of scarcity. Resources were therefore perceived as being both absolutely and relatively abundant. During this period, according to O'Riordan (1971), social controls over resource appraisal and allocation gave way to the *laissez-faire* and the freedom of rights of the individual. Competition set the rules and economic principles dominated the resource allocation process. Large amounts of resources were exploited at commercial scales.

In developing countries resources rarely were perceived in practice as absolutely and relatively abundant by the indigenous community. Amongst these communities technological advancement, even during the colonial period, was slow. Even where technological development was relatively fast (such as in India), resources were not often perceived as absolutely abundant because of effects of high rates of population growth and escalating demand for more and diverse resources. Besides, social norms associated with land tenure and extended family systems did not free individuals enough to quickly extort resources for themselves in proportion to their accessibility to technology. In addition, technology remained relatively overpriced and was restricted to government farms and agencies, foreign settlers and a few wealthy members of the local communities.

Where acquisition of technology was backed by political power such as in pre-independence Kenya, South Africa, and colonial Zimbabwe, large-scale commercial exploitation by some individuals was undertaken. For instance, in colonial Kenya, White settlers operated large farms, plantations and ranches. On the whole this period witnessed a gradual blending of commercial extraction of resources (modern economy) based on a Western perception of resources with traditional subsistence practices. Government policies distinguished between cash crops for export and local subsistence crops. As implied, in areas of foreign settlers (Kenya, Zimbabwe, South Africa, Brazil), indigenous landowners were simply uprooted and often made labourers for the foreign landlords or pushed into areas of marginal productivity.

In developing countries, the colonial period introduced a growing and preferential emphasis on cash crops. Foreign cash crops, particularly coffee, cotton and tobacco, were introduced and grown for export. Therefore, for the first time communities in developing countries were expected to grow crops from which they might not directly or indirectly benefit. During this period labour was gradually withdrawn from food cropping, especially since mandatory taxation ensured that each family grew cash crops. The edging out of food cropping from the indigenous community increased dependence on foreign food commodities, ideas and resource development strategies. Grains such as millet, rice, wheat and maize became major food crops even for export trade. In Uganda, until the 1980s millet was basically a subsistence crop but its cultivation continued throughout the colonial period because it was an appropriate rotation crop in the cotton growing cycle.

The colonial institutions and power structures reversed the flow of ideas on resource practices. A centralized system of colonial government replaced and subordinated the indigenous grass roots approach which originally led to development of traditional resource use techniques amongst the pre-colonial communities. This meant resources were increasingly exploited with a Western perspective and often with little knowledge and consideration of the local ecology and environmental relationships. A glaring example is the imposition of arbitrary national boundaries in Africa, Asia and Latin America. One effect placed the pastoralists Karamojong and Turkana of East Africa in an almost never-ending war over cattle and grazing land. Under the traditional communal grazing system the Karamojong (Uganda) and Turkana (Kenya) pastoralists could roam the whole semi-arid area, thus reducing overgrazing problems and desperation for grazing land. After national boundaries were created, however, conflicts arose due to restriction of grazing within national boundaries.

The subordination of indigenous cultures together with increasing dependence on foreign decisions gave a green light to integrate the local communities into the international production system. Such dependence upon policies and decisions of the colonial masters also meant that certain projects were developed on a selective basis, often with little regard to the wants of the local people. Berry (1981) noted that the rural water supply projects surveyed or built in Tanganyika by the colonial administration from 1939 to independence (1961) were chosen on the basis of the following objectives:

1 to supply minor government settlements, such as prisons, labour camps and schools
2 to supply European farmers and other colonial outposts, such as missions
3 to encourage the introduction of cash crops including commercialization of cattle rearing in certain selected areas and labourers on plantations
4 as a reward and pacification of the African population, particularly the chiefs who co-operated with colonial authorities.

During the industrial period or the colonial period in developing countries, little knowledge existed and scant consideration was paid by the Western manager to the delicate linkages amongst different types of resources. Overuse and misuse of resources characterized the period. In developing countries the rights of the individual over that of the community were strengthened in some places as individuals began to buy and own formerly communal land. This revolutionary change was received differently in various countries. In the Lira region of Uganda, legislation allowing purchase of land by individuals generated resentment which in 1952 culminated in massive physical attack on government offices and officials by the local populace. The policy was abandoned thereafter and the traditional communal land use system was retained.

During the colonial administration, resource management policy in developing countries focused largely on the protection of a few public domains. In India, the British declared some forest areas as 'conservancies'. These were protected to maintain soil stability and control surface run-off. In other countries soil erosion control (by encouraging strip and contour farming, terracing and controlled burning of forests and grassland) was the major concern in the resource development policy. Throughout the colonial period, traditional practices and technologies were branded as primitive by colonial administrators. Little or no attempt was made to modernize or adapt traditional strategies to foreign strategies of resource management. The other significant and earliest resource management approach, introduced to developing countries by colonial administration, is wildlife management. Wildlife management became a widespread strategy for protection of flora and fauna throughout the developing countries.

In Africa, wildlife management was undertaken through four major strategies, namely creation of

1 national parks
2 game reserves
3 national reserves
4 forest reserves

By the time of independence in the 1960s, wildlife management had been practised for over twenty years in most African countries.

National parks

Lusigi (1989: 3), paraphrasing the International Union for the Conservation of Nature (IUCN 1982), noted that national parks are

relatively large areas where one or several ecosystems are not materially altered by human exploitation and occupation, where plant and animal species, geomorphological sites and habitats are of special scientific, educative and recreative interest or which contain a natural landscape of great beauty.

Large areas of land were set aside in almost every country in Africa to protect animal species and landscapes. The notable national parks today include the Serengeti National Park (Tanzania), Nairobi and Tsavo National parks (Kenya), and Murchison Falls and the Ruwenzori National Parks in Uganda. Almost all these parks were established in areas of low agricultural potential due to problems of drought and aridity, or tsetse fly infestation. In other cases parks were established in order to provide a buffer zone between warring tribes.

From the mid-1970s national parks in Africa began to face a number of problems which may threaten their viability:

1 Mounting conflict and competition from agriculture, human settlement and other resource practices. Human encroachment has been partly triggered by lack of compatibility between the prescribed values of parks and the resource development aspirations of communities in the park neighbourhood.
2 Unrealistic laws and regulations which allow park patronage to be monop-olized by foreign and urban tourists. For instance the regulations allow only visitors in motor vehicles to patronize parks. The majority of poor pedestrians who reside in the park neighbourhood are therefore excluded.
3 The majority of the poor inhabitants view parks as islands for foreign tourists and for the few wealthy people from urban areas.
4 For several reasons such as the high cost of maintaining tourist hotels and facilities coupled with widespread corruption, revenue from tourism has hardly benefited the rural community in Africa.
5 Deterioration in park management capacity (lack of fencing, poor vehicle maintenance and low morale of employees) together with international trade in ivory and rhino horns have aggravated poaching activities. Occasionally, in Kenya poachers engage security forces in a heavy military combat.

Although national parks provide an important strategy for the management of genetic resources, governments in developing countries must begin to distinguish between targeted and non-targeted beneficiaries from national parks development. Once this is done and the flow of benefits to park neighbourhood communities is guaranteed, the current threats on parks will become significantly reduced.

Game reserves

In Africa game reserves are most well developed in Kenya where the notable ones include Masai Mara, Samburu and Amboseli game reserves. In Kenya, game reserves belong to the county councils in which they are situated (Lusigi, 1978) and the proceeds from game reserves are meant to benefit the communities of the county. The game reserves strategy therefore has the element of modern resource management strategy which promotes community participation and benefit from resource development projects.

As with national parks, game reserves are threatened because benefits are not seen to accrue to the local people. Other problems include the following:

1 Much of the revenue generated is used for supporting county council facilities rather than community services such as schools, health centres, cattle dips and veterinary services.
2 The reserves are viewed as islands (for tourists and the urban rich) which unjustifiably occupy grazing and agricultural land.
3 The word 'reserve' is resented in those African countries where White settlement had occurred. For instance in pre-independent Kenya, most people of African origin were confined in what was called 'African Native Reserve'. The idea of reserves therefore leaves a negative and repulsive memory amongst many communities in Africa.

National reserves

National reserves are relatively large management (conservation) units where specified types of human activities are permitted while the area is simultaneously managed for optimum watershed, forestry and wildlife values. Human practices such as agriculture, logging for timber and livestock grazing are controlled in order to sustain natural qualities of resources.

National reserves throughout Africa have suffered some significant setbacks. In particular, political pressure has led to permanent allocation and encroachment of human settlement into national reserves. The reserves have often not had the management capacity to monitor and co-ordinate all activities within their boundaries. In addition, governments and mass media tend to give greater attention and publicity to national parks, leaving reserves with a rather inferior status. As a result, national reserve officials have had to succumb to the overwhelming political pressures for expansion of human settlement into the reserves.

Forest reserves

Like national parks, forest reserves are one of the most widespread and important resource management strategies introduced in Africa during the colonial period. In every country of Africa, forest reserves have been managed by a well-established department of forestry and backed by specific legislation on forest resources management. In fact the Departments of Forestry and Agriculture are the oldest government institutions which operate even at the county council level in almost all former British controlled territories.

As discussed in Chapter 5, the forest reserves throughout Africa had three major objectives:

1 To offer maximum forest protection to the catchment areas of the country.
2 To improve and sustain the productivity of forests as a source of timber and fuelwood. In many African countries plantations of softwood forest were established from imported species. In Kenya, forest reserves were also established as a source of fuelwood for the railway line running from Mombasa to Uganda.
3 To conserve areas of particular scenic value and public interest.

Throughout Africa, higher slopes (over 1,500m a.s.l. (above sea level)). of major mountains (Kilimanjaro, Elgon, Ruwenzori, Mount Kenya) have been gazetted as forest reserves.

Lusigi (1978) observed that the success of the forest reserve strategy can be attributed to the long-standing experience possessed by European colonial officials. Unlike wildlife management, forest management had a deeper foundation in European resource management. The colonial officials transferred the principle of sustained yield to African forestry management without much modification to the principle. Exotic softwoods were imported from Europe and propagated in many parts of Africa. Two effects occurred in African forestry:

1 Monoculture of pure stands of pines and eucalyptus were introduced in the place of traditional systems in which indigenous mixed forests are maintained in areas of communal grazing and hunting.
2 Together with peasant agriculture, the exotic softwoods replaced and caused the extinction of some indigenous species. As a result, there has been a significant lowering in species diversity and ecological resilience in the natural forests of Africa (Chapter 2).

The concept of wildlife conservation was one of the major contributions of colonial administration to resource management in developing countries. Its early introduction provided a basis for the management of other resources in developing countries. Many countries have gained substantial revenue from associated tourism. For instance, tourism is currently the leading earner of foreign currency in Kenya. In resource management such benefits underline the implications of technology transfer.

For a long time, however, the impact of colonial administration on patterns of resource utilization in developing countries has been underestimated. Wildlife conservation exerts a relatively remote effect on human communities. In other areas through agriculture, industry and government institutions, the colonial administration had a more direct effect on communities. In the preceding section discussion has shown how colonial administrations created major disturbances as they premeated the cultural fabrics, produced a new class of indigenous people (through religion, travelling, education and administration) and imposed a Western administrative and economic superstructure on to traditional resource use systems for over fifty years in each country. The effects of colonial administration are examined further in Chapter 5.

On a global level the events of the industrial period presented worrying concerns in industrialized and some developing nations. Misuse, abuse and overuse of resources generated several concerns:

1 Private gain did not necessarily lead to improved social welfare; in fact it often destroyed public benefits from resource development.
2 Resource scarcity was becoming absolute as people began to realize their ability to destroy the environment.
3 Big business and centralized economic power were blamed for environmental deterioration and the detriment of public good.
4 Methods of wise use of resources for the many rather than for the powerful and wealthy few had to be developed.
5 Sound management and wise use required training, rationality, and interaction amongst elected decision makers, professional experts and the general public.

These concerns rationalized the development of resource management as a field of study and forced many governments to enact laws for 'sound' management of resources. In developing countries these concerns rarely penetrated beyond the administrative bureaucracies. Thus, awareness of the deleterious consequences of economic growth based on an ever expanding use of technology was until the 1980s limited to the elitist few in government offices.

Post-industrial or post-colonial period

Mistakes of the industrial period strengthened the evolution of resource management during the post industrial period. When it was realized that private gains did not necessarily lead to enhanced public welfare, welfare economics was incorporated into resource management strategies. According to this theory, public intervention and political control are necessary to check the actions of private individuals. Public participation also began to play a significant role in resource allocation. During the post-industrial period, projects were established on a multiple use basis with environmental quality and dignity of life becoming major goals. Measures against all forms of pollution were legislated and environmental codes were developed to check pollution especially from industries. By the 1970s many universities in the developed countries started to offer resources management as a course of study and a major research field. In fact environmental issues became an interdisciplinary concern attracting engineers, agriculturalists, geneticists, economists, geographers, foresters, wildlife biologists and others. During this time resource management evolved to focus on the protection and enhancement of environment quality and the establishment of guidelines of public/ private use of such common property resources as air, water, landscape and historical monuments.

Developments in the post-industrial period took place when many developing countries had acquired independence from former colonial masters. In developing countries this period represents the post-colonial period. Although there were political and ideological differences amongst developing countries right from the time of independence, all of them inherited foreign administrative, economic and educational super-structures to which they later gradually introduced modifications.

During the post-colonial period, developing countries remained intergrated within the international economic system which linked them to foreign markets, technology and an economy based on cash exchange, export and mechanization. As a result, the post-colonial governments sought to increase the proportion of the population engaged in the cash economy in order to raise living standards. Investments in education and industry were significantly increased. But the overall preoccupation with growth in economy, in health and education facilities, and in provision of other social services robbed almost all efforts for protection and enhancement of environmental quality. As it were, developing countries continued to toe the line that would repeat mistakes generated by Western-style resource development. Thus it was not until the late 1970s that environmental concerns in developing countries were triggered by fears associated with effects of continuing rapid population growth, declining agricultural productivity, soil erosion, rising and unaffordable oil prices, fluctuating market prices, inflation, unemployment, poverty and the generally limited range of alternatives as neither agriculture, education, industrialization, nor political ideology presented any hopeful salvation.

Such fears were vividly expressed by Eckholm (1975), who showed how deforestation in Nepal caused a crisis characterized by poverty, severe soil erosion, frequent landslides and floods and farmland abandonment in the slopes of the Himalayas. At this time several researchers and international organizations, notably from West Germany and the USA, were involved in a number of research and development projects in Africa and Asia (Chapter 5). Their projects introduced a significant dimension to resource management: for the first time traditional technologies in Africa and Asia were promoted to gain significant acclaim among international resource specialists. This is of interest because these Western-based researchers came from a background which previously had ridiculed traditional resource practices in Africa and Asia as primitive. Whether the reappraisal was based on premonitions due to earlier attitudes or scientific objectivity, the efforts of the researchers introduced the need to re-examine and promote traditional technology and reappraise the transfer of technology from industrialized to developing countries.

The reappraisal of traditional technologies in Africa and Asia coincided in time with mounting public pressure in Europe and North America against the application of large-scale and complex technologies of the 'modern time'. In especially Canada, Europe and the USA, several pressure groups were formed to oppose 'modernity' and/or protect seals and other endangered species. Views on modern technology are discussed in detail in Chapter 2. But the important point about the backtracking trend is that its excitement among foreign researchers in Africa and Asia sometimes lent too much credibility to some traditional technologies.

Traditional technologies and resource practices in Africa and Asia are indeed less polluting and under low population density they induce limited environmental impacts. In many cases there is some implicit conservationist ethic in traditional technology. Baines (1982) described a situation in the South Pacific where a taboo exists on fishing in a defined area for an extended period after the death of a particularly important leader. The taboo is lifted when a memorial feast is held perhaps a month later. The build-up of fish stocks during the ban ensures a good harvest for the feast. He concluded that though this practice has a conservation effect it would be misleading to conclude that such practices are evidence of a fundamental conservation ethic built into South Pacific island cultures.

Traditional technologies were developed under different circumstances when human numbers and densities were small, aspirations and consumption patterns were simple and less diverse, population mobility was high and unutilized resources were plentiful. For instance, among the Micronesian communities of the South Pacific there is a system which enables them to manipulate groundwater and organic wastes to produce high yields of giant taro in a sandy and salty environment in which agriculture would normally be considered impossible (Baines, 1982). In many developing countries socio-economic situations have changed enormously since the 1960s. The level of poverty described in Chapter 3 not only alludes to the nature of socio-economic changes but also reflects the inability of some traditional systems to support contemporary resource development demands. As discussed in Chapter 8 and by the World Commission on Environment and Development (1987), the basic resource management issue in developing countries in this decade regards ways of raising and sustaining high levels of productivity without causing unnecessary environmental impairment. There is a growing belief amongst governments and researchers in developing countries that traditional practices alone cannot support current resource demands (Chapter 8).

These worrying developments justify the examination of resource management in developing countries today. It is an opportune moment to document issues, problems and strategies of resource management.

Summary

This chapter has reviewed the major concepts in resource management. Throughout the chapter, examples have been used to emphasize the point that 'things' are resources if often they satisfy human wants at specific times. Because of cultural and functional considerations, it is difficult to present a universally acceptable definition of a 'resource'. In defining other concepts in resource management, it has been demonstrated that sometimes only small distinctions separate one concept from the other but each concept embodies several factors and considerations.

The second part of the chapter reviewed trends in the evolution of resource management as a strategy for community development and as a field of study. Throughout the section attempts have been made to identify conflicts, parallels and intertwining events between systems of resource management in industrialized and developing countries. In certain cases the colonial process played a positive role. In other cases, it complicated the whole process of resource development in developing countries. Some of the worst effects of resource development arise from the nature of the international socio-economic system into which developing countries find themselves irreversibly absorbed. As a result, the new value and publicity given to some traditional technologies in Africa and Asia may be viewed as either premonitory and remorseful or too late.

CHAPTER 2

Approaches in resource management

This chapter reviews the major approaches in the general field of resource management. The review provides a foundation which is used in the rest of the text to bring existing issues, problems and strategies in developing countries into the context of resource management. In effect, this chapter provides an introductory background against which the state of the art in resource management can be evaluated. Because of the scattered literature on resources in developing countries and its general lack of direction, evaluation of the state of knowledge becomes an integral step toward introducing order and direction in the study of resource management.

Several approaches exist in the field of resource management. In this chapter only those broad approaches with distinct frames of reference are reviewed. The intent of the review is to present a detailed critique of all the approaches in order to gauge their viability.

At a broad level, resource management studies take the *physical* environment as one basic departure point, the *human* attribute as the other, and the *controls* on the interaction between the physical and human attributes as the third basic departure point. For organizational convenience the physical attribute is discussed under the *ecological approach*, the controls under the *economic* and *technological*, and the human under the *ethnological* approaches. Institutional arrangements as well as political and legal frameworks, which tend to relate to the organization of human communities, are considered as perspectives of the ethnological approach. Each of these approaches represents a broad area of knowledge organized around a common theme and method of study. Within each area of knowledge there may exist other well-organized resource-related perspectives, the details of which are beyond the scope of this text.

Ecological approach

The ecological approach to resource management is defined as the allocation and management of resources on the basis of an understanding of the functional components of the physical and biological environment, and the relationship amongst the components. The knowledge of elements and processes in a system and the relations among them is employed to safeguard humans' perceived long-term health of the whole environment. This definition is clarified below and in Chapters 5 and 6 by examining those concepts of ecology that are used in resource management.

Ecology is the study of the relation of organisms or groups of organisms to their environment (Odum, 1971). The science of ecology was developed mainly by botanists, zoologists and geographers. In geography, the ecological approach gained importance after Barrows (1923) proposed human ecology as the focus for geography. According to Barrows, geography should be concerned with the mutual relations between people and their natural environment (both physical and biological). He illustrated his viewpoint by stressing that the adjustment of people to landforms as elements of the natural environment rather than understanding the evolution of landforms was the concern of geography. Today, Barrows' views are strongly reflected in the ecological approach to resource management. For instance, the implications of Barrows's views are found in Barch's (1973) work where he stressed that effective resource management depends on definition of the system of ecological relationships and identification of structure.

The ecological approach is based on concepts associated with the behaviour and functional characteristics of ecosystems. Key concepts are community, succession and climax.

Community

Community in the ecological sense includes all the populations of organisms occupying an area (e.g. the mangrove swamp community). The community and the non-living environment (soils, bedrock and climate) function together as a unit within an ecological system or ecosystem (Odum, 1971; R. L. Smith, 1974). An ecosystem therefore results from the interdependence of the living and non-living components of the environment for a defined segment of space and time. Major (1951) stated that the ecosystem is similar to the term 'landscape' as used by geographers, but 'ecosystem' stresses biological rather than chronological and physical characteristics. The community concept is important in the ecological approach because it emphasizes life in an orderly manner. The concept demonstrates the dependence of an organism on the quality of the community of which it is part. The relevance of this concept to resource management is clarified by Odum's (1971: 141) assertion that 'the best way to control a particular organism . . . is to modify the community rather than to make a direct attack on the organism'. For instance, many of the tropical birds and other crop pests have had to migrate with successive forest clearance.

Succession

Succession involves the development of an ecosystem. In R. L. Smith's (1974: 258) words

> succession is characterised by progressive changes in species structure, organic structures, and energy flow. It involves a gradual and continuous replacement of one kind of plant and animal by another that is more complex.

Succession results from the modification of the physical environment by various processes including the organisms themselves. As the environment is modified, the habitat becomes less favourable to some organisms and they are gradually replaced by a different group of organisms more able to exploit the new environment.

There are two types of succession. *Allogenic succession* involves one community replacing another because of a change in the environment which was not produced by the community (plants) itself (e.g. effects on plants due to decrease in soil moisture as a result of improved drainage during land reclamation). *Autogenic succession* is a successional series in which one stage modifies the habitat in such a way that it is replaced by another stage. The trends in ecosystem development are summarized in Table 2.1, and specifically illustrated by examining serial succession of mangrove species in Chapter 6.

Ecosystem development demonstrates the basic conflict between the strategies of people and nature. For instance, Odum (1969:5) commented

> the goal of agriculture or intensive forestry now generally practised, is to achieve a high rate of production with little standing crop left or, in other words a high production/biomass efficiency. Nature's strategy on the other hand is directed towards the reverse efficiency, namely, high biomass/production ratio.

Because the concept of succession places emphasis on the consequences of environmental change, it is most relevant to resource management. For resources to be constantly available at reasonable costs, the nature and rate of environmental modifications must resemble the natural successional pattern. Unfortunately, in many developing countries the physical environment (resource base) is often easily modified by effects of rapid population growth, sudden influx of high-impact technology, and sudden changes from simple to complex and more demanding consumption patterns (Chapters 4–7). As a result, shortages of supplies occur, especially with vegetation-based resources (fodder, firewood, timber, grass for roof-thatching) and water resources. These modifications often create new ecosystems with poorer life-support capacity such as the currently expanding desert conditions in parts of Africa and Asia. In developing countries, such trends pose a greater threat than in industrialized countries because there is hardly any accumulated capital, technology or skilled manpower for averting environmental deterioration.

Table 2.1 Trends in the ecological development of landscapes

Ecosystem attribute	Developmental stages	Mature stages
Gross primary productivity (total photosynthesis)	Increasing	Stabilized at moderate level
Net primary productivity (yield)	High	Low
Standing crop (biomass)	Low	High
Ratio growth to maintenance (production/respiration)	Unbalanced	Balanced
Ratio biomass to energy flow (growth + maintenance)	Low	High
Utilization of primary production by heterotrophy (animals & man)	Predominantly via linear grazing food chains	Predominantly web-like detritus food chains
Diversity	Low	High
Nutrients	Inorganic (extrabiotic)	Organic (intrabiotic)
Mineral cycles	Open	Closed
Selection pressure	For rapidly growing species adapted to low density	For slow growing species adapted to equilibrial density
Stability (resistance to outside perturbations)	Low	High

Source after Odum (1969)

Climax

In theory, succession proceeds and finally slows down to an equilibrium or steady state. Equilibrium or steady state involves the maintenance of constancy or a high degree of uniformity in structure and functions of organisms or interaction of individuals in a community under changing conditions. This final stage produces a climax community; a mature self-regulating and permanent community (Russwurm and Sommerville, 1974; R. L. Smith, 1974). This terminal community is theoretically characterized by an equilibrium between energy input and output, a diversity of species, a well developed spatial structure, and complex food chains. These character-istics maintain the stability of an ecosystem. The tropical rain forests in Zaïre and Brazil are widely regarded as a climax community.

For resource management, the important implication of climax arises from the concept of stability and from the subsequent need to identify critical factors that contribute to stability. Stability implies constant supply of resources from one generation to another. Because vegetation plays a significant role in maintaining land quality, it is possible that certain vegeta-tion communities or species will be more effective in restoring and maintain-ing resource use stability than others. For instance, in agroforestry several plant species (e.g. grevillea robusta) can coexist with a variety of crops in addition to being sources of fuelwood, timber and livestock fodder (Chapter 5). Changes from one community to another (e.g. from forest to grassland ecosystem) may therefore relate directly to environmental instability due to increased rates of soil and moisture loss (Chapter 4). Indeed the ecological concepts permit the study of elements and processes and changes in components and stability of an ecosystem. For instance, in Chapters 5 and 6 ecological components and processes are analysed in order to demonstrate the vulnerability and resource potential of mountain and coastal ecosystems in the tropics.

For practical purposes, the climax concept is questionable. It has not been proved that succession ends in a climax community. R. L. Smith (1974: 272) writes

> Even in the so called climax communities stability is never really achieved. Self-destructive biological changes are continually taking place, even though slowly. Trees grow old and die and may be replaced by new trees of a different species . . . Thus the idea of the climax is rapidly coming to mean those more or less stable and long-lived communities that develop late in succession in the absence of disturbance.

Smith's idea of a climax seems not to be directly relevant to resource management because resource use itself constitutes environmental disturbance. Yet when humans are considered as an 'ecological dominant', their dependence and role in ecosystem development make it imperative to conceive of a climax attained in spite of or because of human influence. Firey (1960) named such a climax community as anthropogenic climax, that is a climax that results from 'particular association of plants and animals which is able to perpetuate itself in a habitat throughout the course of a given pattern of human activities' (Firey, 1960: 25). In agricultural villages in Africa, Asia and South America, the anthropogenic climax is characterized by scattered fruit trees (mangoes, oranges, bananas), cultivated crops (coffee, sugar cane, rubber, cassava), scattered remains of indigenous forest species and occasional plantations of exotic forests (e.g. eucalyptus).

The other concept used in association with climax in the ecological approach is that of *species diversity*. Species diversity is a measure of ecosystem stability (Sheard and Blood, 1973). In game park management, greater diversity provides park users with a variety of plants and animals. In the management of National Parks in Africa, wildlife experts have argued that wildlife population reflects the types of changes in climate, water, soils, vegetation, interrelationships among species, diseases and levels of human impact (Lusigi, 1978). In the ecological approach, a low number of species implies a high stress on an ecosystem. For instance, severe grazing acts as a stress and reduces the number of grass species to a few palatable ones. The concept of species diversity is therefore used in resource management to evaluate effects of human-induced or natural stresses on an area (Nelson and Byrne, 1966). For resource management, the important implication of these generalizations is that environmental deterioration is more likely when species diversity is low. What is not clear, however, is the upper limit to species diversity. Until it is clarified, the concept will continue to present operational problems because environmental deterioration may also be caused by high species diversity.

The resource management strategy in the ecological approach

The methods used in the ecological approach are well documented by Dansereau (1957 and 1975), McHarg (1966), MacKintosh (1974), Kitchen Cameron (1976), and Lusigi (1978). The overriding concern amongst these researchers and relevant to resource management is the allocation of resources in a manner that minimizes environmental 'impairment'. Technically, 'impairment' begins when volumes of extracted resources exceed a calculated carrying capacity of an area. In the ecological approach the resource allocation strategy involves:

1 ecosystem inventory to determine community zones (e.g. open water, swamps, mixed forests)
2 identification of natural processes that lead to stability and determination of the limited factors (e.g. slope, alkalinity, watertable, altitude and external factors)
3 analysis of inventory data to evaluate the functional significance of the ecosystem components
4 recommendation of alternative uses based on the established functional significance (e.g. potential intensive use areas, sensitive areas, recreation areas).

In the ecological approach, the ecosystem or community forms the management unit. In many developing countries drainage basins and sub-basins, administrative districts, and electoral constituencies may form the management unit. According to Firey (1960), a set of resource uses in a management unit must remain in 'some degree' of equilibrium with that environment. For instance, extraction rate must balance regeneration rate. Therefore the object of the ecological approach is to attain and/or maintain such equilibrium within a management unit. Such an objective ensures sustained yield of resources over long periods of time and can therefore cater for the needs of present and future generations.

The concept of *sustained yield* has been widely used, especially in forest and wildlife management. Sustained yield can be defined as a strategy which maintains productivity at a level which is acceptable, beneficial and relatively constant on a long-term basis. The concept rests on three assumptions (Raup, 1964):

1 resources are scarce
2 resource use requires a stable and regular flow of resources
3 no alternative supply from outside or from within a nation's capital resources.

While the sustained yield concept has merit as a policy objective in resource management, its underlying assumptions raise some questions. The assumption of a stable flow of resources can be appreciated because it gives rise to a degree of certainty as to the course of development over time. For most resources the assumption is realistic only when it emphasizes controlled removal of resources so that extraction is balanced by regeneration. However, due to relatively rapid rates of environmental deterioration in environments such as mountain slopes, swamplands, and other sensitive and marginal lands, a stable flow of resources may not always be possible. For instance, on the easily eroded slopes of Mount Kenya, deferred and rotational grazing management techniques may preclude objectives of continuous grazing in already damaged sites (Chapter 5). The first assumption regarding resource scarcity seems to have no readily perceivable analogue in the ecological approach. The third assumption introduces the idea of a closed economy and therefore precludes the influence of international or inter-regional trade and technology on provision of alternative sources of resource (Chapter 1).

In spite of those limitations, resource use policies based on the concept of sustained use of resources should reduce fears of abuse and overuse of resources, problems most prominent today in developing countries. To avoid these problems, sustained yield policy depends on knowledge of biophysical carrying capacity of an area. In livestock grazing under modern management in Kenya, Zimbabwe, and ranches in Argentina, for instance, biophysical carrying capacity is used to balance livestock numbers with a sustained supply of suitable vegetation. This is why biophysical information, currently in poor supply, is urgently needed in developing countries.

The concept of *carrying capacity* is discussed in detail and critically by Mitchell (1989: 155–73). The concept basically means the regulation of resource demands within the capacity of an ecosystem so that extraction is balanced by regeneration. While the concept of carrying capacity is particularly useful in undertaking environmental impact assessment or other physically oriented research, it has also been questioned. In using the concept, foresters have been blamed for resolving problems on the basis of technical considerations without adequate appreciation of alternative societal goals (Bultena and Hendee, 1972). Wagar (1974) argued that the term obscures an essential distinction between technical issues and value choices. He noted that the statement of 'carrying capacity includes the assumption that unacceptable consequences will occur if use is permitted at a higher level. Defining what is acceptable, however, is a value choice rather than a technical issue' (Wagar, 1974: 274).

The definition of resource management stated in Chapter 1 introduced value judgement in the process of resource management. Until the 1960s, the ecological approach was thought to give little attention to public consider- ations and values. Values are now included in some studies using the approach. In the study of forests and wildlife in Africa, Lusigi (1978) emphasized the need to incorporate local community interest. McHarg (1966), for instance, developed a model which consists of six stages:

1 Ecosystem inventory, including identification and arranging the communi- ties in gradients from succession to climax.
2 Description of the natural processes and an assessment of the extent to which people affect the ecosystem.
3 Limiting factors which maintain the ecosystem complex. These include external factors such as the transformation of a fresh water body to salt water through river channel deepening and widening.
4 *Attribution of value*, that is for what do people consider the ecosystem valuable?
5 Determination of prohibition and permissiveness to change, assess ecosys- tem tolerance to change, how much development can occur on a marsh without destroying its role of water equalization, emergency flood storage or wildlife habitat.
6 Identification of indicators of stability or instability.

The model helps in selecting areas suitable for development and their relative tolerance to human activities.

More recently, the ecological approach has made significant contributions. As indicated in Chapter 8, the approach has been used for the development of the UNEP *state of the environment reporting*, and the *World Conservation Strategy* formulated by the International Union for the Conservation of Nature (IUCN). Furthermore, the approach has helped in the development of *environmental impact assessment*.

Environmental impact assessment is rapidly gaining use even in developing countries as a 'legislative or policy-based concern for possible positive/ negative, short/long term effects on our total environment attributable to proposed or existing projects, programs or policies of a public or private origin' (Mitchell and Turkhein, 1977: 47). Dorney (1977: 184) summarized the functions of environmental impact assessment as to

1 identify and articulate the environmental goals and objectives of the project as related to the overall goals of the project
2 identify human concerns
3 describe the proposed action or impact
4 describe alternatives
5 describe what changes will occur without intervention
6 describe the nature and magnitudes of environmental effects
7 in any weighting or aggregating process of various environmental factors, provide a clear statement as to the procedure followed and a clear

indication of the values incorporated into the solution or recommended action

8 identify remedial action

9 identify any positive results that can be developed by direct or indirect spin-off from the project

10 identify any trade-offs necessitated

11 develop a baseline inventory capable of conversion to a monitoring system.

Environmental impact assessment can therefore be used to minimize disruption to the environment by proposed projects and to ensure that environmental consideration is given adequate attention in relation to attention paid to economic and technological aspects. In developing countries operationalizing environmental impact assessment will remain troublesome for some time because of the following factors:

1 The high costs involved. Impact assessment requires an additional budget from the already overburdened financial situation of developing countries. It requires more data and better knowledge of the natural environment system. Such data and skills are in inadequate supply in developing countries. However, a humble initiative can be made by legislative action that compels large commercial ventures and industries to incorporate environmental impact assessment in their operations.

2 Lack of a common guideline and standards. There must be a standard procedure by which the assessment is undertaken and assessment reports prepared so that reliable and replicable decisions can be made on the state of the environment *vis-à-vis* development projects.

3 Once the impact statement is acceptable it may not be easy (because of poor institutional capacities) to utilize the assessment results to contribute positively to resource development.

While several concerns, requiring explicit attention, can be expressed, environmental impact assessment is an important strategy for ensuring sustainable development of resources.

In general, the ecological approach has been applied selectively for some resources and only in certain areas. For instance, the ecological approach has been applied more widely in managing national parks, forests and soils than other resources in developing countries (Chapters 1, 5 and 6). This has been because the management goals emphasize preservation and protection of plants, animals and soils in these areas. In game parks, the ecological approach is used to monitor environment quality change and to assess environmental impacts of proposed and existing developments. The reason for limited application of the ecological approach to managing other resources is that for a long time the ecological approach was thought to advocate 'no growth'. However, the current view in resource management is that ecology acknowledges the necessity for growth and development but does not accept the view that environmental degradation is an unavoidable companion of growth and development.

Economic approach

The essence of economic activity is the removal of materials from the environment, their transformation by production and consumption and their eventual return to the environment. (Mills, 1975: 23)

The economic approach in resource management is based on the premise that resources are scarce and therefore that resource users have to make a choice and optimize their use of resources. Thus to obtain a resource a user must forego some other resource uses. Such considerations, according to the economic approach, lead to a rational allocation of resources which is possible in a free, competitive market economy. In a free, competitive market situation, the objective of resource allocation is to achieve *economic efficiency* by minimizing production costs (labour and capital input) and maximizing monetary profits. The market value of resources will determine which resources are to be selected for use.

To achieve the stipulated economic efficiency (maximum profit), economic theory depends on a number of assumptions. These assumptions are discussed in detail elsewhere (Firey, 1960; O'Riordan, 1971) but may be summarized as

1 production factors are freely substitutable for one another in achieving a desired level of output (e.g. replace land by labour)
2 demand can be identified and consumer preferences for different uses are known and can be compared
3 benefits from resource uses can be quantified in monetary terms
4 resource use has no external effects on the physical environment and economic situation.

These assumptions are not all tenable. As a result, the economic approach often is used to provide an ideal against which present practices can be compared. Limitations to the economic approach arise largely from the argument that not all resources are similar to market goods. For instance, there is no readily perceivable substitute for aesthetic resources nor is there a means of accurately quantifying or substituting pleasure derived from a beautiful landscape. Some goods such as visual beauty, unique ecological habitat and historical monuments are subjective and personal in their value and cannot easily be evaluated in the market-place. On a long-term basis, even pricing the tangible resources (timber, minerals) becomes difficult.

The challenge posed by the critics of the economic approach stimulated research in especially the non-quantifiable (intangible) resources. Methods of estimating the monetary equivalence of these resources have been proposed (Leopold and Marchand 1968; Fines, 1968; Pearse, 1968).

'Willingness to pay' or 'contingency evaluation' is a technique widely used today to determine demand and consumer preference (R. C. Mitchell and Carson, 1989). Sewell and Bower (1968) identified water resource demand as that amount of water or water-related services for which individuals are willing to sacrifice other resources rather than go without the water. They then calculated the price of that amount of water to establish individual 'willingness to pay'. However, O'Riordan (1971) cautioned that when applying 'willingness to pay' as a measure, due consideration must be paid to existence of *externalities* (effects external to a project), intangibles and collectivities as they relate to technology, public policy, social taste and nature of the biophysical system.

In applying the economic approach to certain specific resources, a number of problems may be confronted. In mountain resources, morphology and the sensitive nature of mountain slopes may raise production costs beyond the point where economic efficiency is achieved (Chapter 5). This is one reason why mountainous environments attract such practices as tourism and recreation which often require relatively low capital investment. On the other hand, in the Drakensburg ranges of South Africa, mining and recreation facilities with relatively high profit returns are undertaken on the basis of economic efficiency. In either case emphasis on economic efficiency in developing countries has promoted pressure on such long-established practices as selective logging, nomadic pasturalism and shifting cultivation which fetch relatively low returns but require large tracks of land (Chapter 4). It must be pointed out, however, that high production costs today are partly a result of past neglect and perception of certain resources as being of little use for purposes other than satisfying demands at 'primitive' levels of development. Until recently in the tropical coastlands, there were few competing uses and consequently few regulations were developed concerning production practices or resource rehabilitation in coastal areas of developing countries. Current regulations (pollution and sedimentation control measures) and effects of inadequate regulations in the past have combined to increase production costs for such activities as mangrove forest clearance, navigation, fishing, recreation and mining in coastal areas of developing countries (Chapter 6).

Again in sensitive environments, such as steep mountain slopes, environmental deterioration leading to severe erosion, landslides and general slope instability can be relatively fast while regeneration may be slow. As a result, it is difficult to substitute freely most resources without additional high cost (e.g. replacement of fertile soil loss by fertilizer use is costly unless erosion rates are first brought under control). Many developing countries lack elaborate technology for erosion control. Finally, the strong emphasis placed on economic efficiency makes it easy for developing countries to neglect concerns for environmental degradation, restoration and protection, for fear that these concerns will divert attention and resources from the revered economic growth, fight against disease, and illiteracy.

In spite of the limitations cited, economic motivation has dominated resource use and management policies in developing countries. In these countries the economic approach is responsible for the current rapid shift from subsistence to market-oriented economy. Plantation and cash agriculture, industry, commercial forestry and ranching have assumed increasing importance in many countries as these are seen to provide a ready answer to rapid accumulation of foreign currency and subsequent national development.

Economic efficiency, at least in theory, is met when benefits outweigh or justify the costs. In the economic approach, *benefit-cost analysis* is the oldest and most commonly used technique of resource allocation. The technique is based on the premise that a desired objective is achieved by choosing the lowest cost alternative of a number of alternatives designed to meet the objectives (Ciriacy-Wantrup, 1971).

The underlying assumption of benefit-cost analysis technique is that the desired objective is known. Sewell (1973) cautioned that resource management objectives or goals are usually general, multipurpose, implicit, ever changing and often vague. While this reservation is reiterated by many (Suchman, 1967; Weiss and Rein 1970; Mitchell and Ross, 1974) and the criticism is realistic, it should rather be directed to goal formulators and not to the technique. In many developing countries, costs are considered only in order to initiate or maintain a project but often not to gauge project performance or its environmental impact.

A fairer criticism of benefit-cost analysis arises from the implicit assumption that benefits are quantifiable and that benefits from one resource can be isolated from those of other resources. Pearse (1977) argued that if two or more simultaneous uses yield greater benefit than one use, then resources must be used on a multiple basis. Sargent (1969) adds that in a multiple use situation the proper use of the benefit-cost technique is to determine which of the two alternatives is better after surveying a range of other possible alternatives (Chapter 7).

The other underlying assumption of the benefit-cost technique is that the overriding resource management objective is economic efficiency. In the 1970s many resource management goals in industrialized countries were to establish acceptable environmental quality or to achieve redistribution of income. When the latter goal is adopted, proponents of the economic approach submit that income redistribution can be incorporated by the beneficiaries compensating the losers. But how can compensation be operationalized simultaneously with maximization of private gains? In any case, in developing countries often corruption and lack of fair-play makes it difficult to envisage losers being compensated (Chapters 3 and 7).

However, the complex nature of resource management decisions makes it difficult to foresee any widely acceptable and appropriate technique. As long as this situation remains unchanged, benefit-cost analysis will continue to provide a yardstick against which current decisions can be measured. In any case and from a materialistic viewpoint, some of the highest standards of living in the world today have been achieved through adherence to the premises of the economic approach. Thus to counteract some of the criticisms of the approach, one can argue that environmental damage has occurred because all costs have not been evaluated in the market-place. For instance, the price of an automobile has never included costs of air pollution, health hazards, smog damage to crops and general discomfort, all of which may result from the production and use of cars. Neither have crop prices included costs of soil conservation. The problem with developing countries is that due to low capital accumulation, resources quickly become unaffordable even after slight increases in cost. Furthermore, it seems benefit-cost analysis functions best where resource practices are organized on the basis of stipulated guidelines. This is often lacking in developing countries.

Technological approach

The effective application of the economic approach has been enhanced greatly by the development of technology. Technology not only has aided the achievement of economic efficiency but also is expected to reduce the fears of resource depletion and the urgent need to cut down economic growth and consumption. The close association between technological development and economic development is noted by Rosenberg (1974) and amplified in development policies of all developing countries. Rosenberg defined technological progress as a process which consists of changes in production method and allows more output to be produced from a given volume of labour and resources, or allows a given output to be produced with a smaller volume of labour and resources.

A salient objective of technological development has been the mastery of nature. As a result, in industrialized countries there has been strong emphasis on understanding the 'laws of nature' so that nature can be manipulated to the satisfaction of human material needs (Zimmermann, 1964). Improving the material basis of human life should, according to this approach, reduce or eliminate social conflict. This viewpoint is most prominent in industrial societies, societies that strive to produce as much and as efficiently as possible by renewing the instruments and organizations of production in accordance with technological progress (Aron, 1974).

In developing countries, however, technological development has been slow and piecemeal. As a result, some resources were not developed till recently. Dry farming techniques in semi-arid zones, and land reclamation in swamps and tsetse fly infested areas were undertaken only in the 1970s and 1980s in many countries of the tropics. Similarly, research and the use of 'new inputs' such as fertilizers, artificial insemination facilities, hybridized seeds and livestock are only beginning to be applied outside government experimental farms. At the same time there are a number of resource development activities which either have been deferred or neglected until appropriate technology is acquired (e.g. deep sea fishing, surveillance of marine traffic and pollution (Chapter 6), oil exploration in the Western Rift Valley of Uganda and industrial processing of several minerals into finished products). As a result, an impression has been created that resources in developing countries are still underdeveloped. This impression has in turn strengthened the wish for more sophisticated technology amongst governments in developing countries.

The faith in technology as a promoter of economic growth led to employing technological feasibility as a criterion for resource allocation. Given the range of technologically feasible alternatives, the use which minimizes costs is selected. In developing countries, some resource use problems such as floods and drought are 'solved' technically and respectively by building dams and irrigation projects. In the management of landslides in Nepal, suggestions have been made that technology can be employed to effect artificial drainage through excavation of ditches, galleries, borings and pumping from shafts or drilled wells.

As with the economic criteria discussed earlier, the reliance on technological feasibility has been criticized for ignoring the interdependence amongst resource processes and particularly the social impact of engineering projects (Leiss, 1970; Clarke, 1974; Roszak, 1974). The mastery of nature has caused or threatened the extinction of many species. In discussing the health effects of human-made lakes, Stanley and Alpers (1974) attributed increased rates of crime, alcoholism, and psychosomatic diseases to the resettlement scheme preceding the construction of the Kariba Dam in Zambia. Leiss (1970) further argued that technological progress distorts the process of social analysis by making social change appear to be largely dependent upon technological change. This is an important observation for developing countries where resource development problems are more often due to poor social and infrastructural arrangements than to lack of technology.

Because of increasing fears about technology, five schools of thought have evolved with views formed around the conception that most of the technology used today is polluting. In developing countries, a further argument is that existing technologies are more relevant to the needs and environment in industrialized countries. The views from each school of thought are summarized in Table 2.2. In many countries of the world, effects of the technological approach relate to the fact that technology promotes large-scale, rapid and efficient extraction of resources. Such operations may involve road construction, slope undercutting, excavations using heavy trucks and machinery, and extensive clearance of forests. These operations may accelerate environmental deterioration. However, from a positive viewpoint, technology has helped to minimize and reduce fear of environmental deterioration and resource scarcity. Experience from industrialized societies has shown that anti-pollution technology has been cost-effective in terms of health, property and environmental damages avoided and it has made many industries more profitable by making them more resource-efficient (World Commission on

Table 2.2 Technical dilemmas and some social responses

Technical dilemma	Price response	'Fix-it' response	'Away-with-it' response	Alternative response	Radical political response
1 Pollution	Pollution inevitable and worth the benefit it brings	Solve pollution with pollution technology	Inevitable result of technology; use less technology	Invent non-polluting technologies	Pollution is a symptom of capitalism, not of poor technology
2 Capital dependence	Technology will always cost money	Provide the capital; make technology cheaper	Costs of technology are always greater than its benefits; use less	Invent labour-intensive technologies	Capital is a problem only in capitalist society
3 Exploitation of resources	Nothing lasts for ever	Use resources more cleverly	Use natural not exploitable resources	Invent technologies that use only renewable resources	Wrong problem: exploitation of man by man is the real issue
4 Liability to misuse	Inevitable, and worth it	Legislate against misuse	Misuse so common and so dangerous, better not to use technology at all	Invent technologies that cannot be misused	Misuse is a sociopolitical problem, not a technical one
5 Incompatible with local cultures	Material advance is worth more than tradition	Make careful sociological studies before applying technology	Local cultures better off without technology	Design new technologies which are compatible	Local culture will be disrupted by revolutionary change in any case
6 Requires specialist technical elite	Undertake technical training schemes	Improve scientific technical education at all levels	People should live without what they do not understand	Invent and use technologies that are understandable and controllable by all	Provide equal chance for everyone to become a technical specialist

Table 2.2 (Cont.)

Technical dilemma	Price response	'Fix-it' response	'Away-with-it' response	Alternative response	Radical political response
7 Dependent on centralization	So what?	No problem, given good management	Decentralize by rejecting technology	Concentrate on decentralized technologies	Centralization an advantage in just social systems
8 Divorce from tradition	This is why technology is so powerful	Integrate tradition and technical know-how	Tradition matters more than technical gadgets	Evolve technologies from existing ones	Traditions stand in the way of true progress
9 Alienation	Workers are better fed and paid; what matters alienation?	More automation needed	Avoid alienation by avoiding technology	Decentralize; retain mass production only in exceptional cases	Alienation has social, not technical, causes

Source Cross et al (1974)

Environment and Development, 1987). In developing countries, technology is being increasingly used to rehabilitate areas damaged by severe erosion, to restock ranches with better livestock breeds, to evolve new crop varieties and to promote less damaging resource use methods (e.g. proper road construction, agroforestry, slope terracing, rangeland management). Research using technology provides further hope of resolving more intricate environmental problems including even those problems arising from the use of inappropriate technology. In particular, several countries (India, Malaysia, Brazil, Kenya, Nigeria) have undertaken significant surveys aimed at determining land use potential and agro-ecological zones. These surveys will promote more appropriate allocation of resources.

Ethnological approach

Fundamental issues of resource management are the allocation of resources, the setting of priorities, the determination of emphasis and the making of choice (O'Riordan, 1971). Questions relating to these issues are beginning to receive increasing attention in developing countries. The nature and significance of the public interest in resource appraisal were usually assumed or inferred but not specifically considered by governments in developing countries. Ecological, economic and technological considerations tended to be more dominant but they often ignored some aspects of the social worth of resource inputs and outputs. Hence, Firey (1960) suggested that *public consent* be incorporated in resource allocation and management everywhere.

The ethnological approach stipulates that cultural differences in part influence the way people perceive and use the resources of their environment. The use of a resource is therefore related to specified cultural themes and perception of resources. In North America, Firey (1960: 27) identified four main cultural themes (success, efficiency, progress and democracy). Regarding perception, he stated:

so pervasive is the role of culture in fixing people's perception and manipulation of natural phenomena that different populations, though occupying the same habitat, may have literally different resources. (Firey, 1960: 27)

Thus for a resource to be used, it must be valued on the basis of a people's cultural themes (Zimmermann, 1964). This is an important consideration in developing countries where conflicts between competing tribal interests often result in costly failure and abandonment of government projects. Among some lowland communities of Uganda, mountains are feared because they are believed to harbour supernatural spirits and diseases brought about by the spirits. In such areas, mountain resources are often left unexploited and never cared for and any known mountain community is sometimes associated with immoral acts such as cannibalism and sorcery. The neglect and careless exploitation of some resources may partly be a result of such attitudes and beliefs.

The other significant perspective of the ethnological approach is institutional arrangements. Various definitions and aspects of institutional arrangements have been discussed by B. Mitchell (1989: 242–62). Craine (1969) and Kaynor and Howards (1971) noted that institutional arrangements are a composite of administrative structure, laws, politics, financial provisions, customs and behaviour organized to deal with problems of life in society. According to Fernie and Pitkethly (1985: vii) institutional arrangements are important because

all resource problems – overpopulation, hunger, poverty, fuel shortages, deforestation – are fundamentally institutional problems which warrant institutional solutions. The success or failure of resource management is intrinsically tied up with institutional structures – the pattern of agencies, laws and policies which pertain to resource issues.

In Chapter 1 it was stated that almost all developing countries inherited colonial administrative structures, laws and policies. As demonstrated in Chapters 6 and 7, there are several resource management issues in developing countries for which legislation is either lacking or inadequate. In most cases existing legislation needs re-examination and updating to avoid overlaps, fragmentation and confusion of responsibilities as between fisheries resources and wildlife in East Africa (Chapter 6). Effective institutional arrangements help in co-ordination of various interests and timely action during resource development thus reducing costs emanating from effects of duplication, negligence and conflict of responsibilities.

The ethnological approach offers *cultural consistency* as a criterion for resource allocation. The approach involves judgement of the degree of conflict or conformity with politics, law, tradition or expected modes of behaviour and the nature of institutional arrangements. For resources in developing countries, this approach calls for the development of resources on the basis of local community guidelines and priorities. Environmental deterioration in many developing countries is sometimes blamed on inappropriate management methods designed with the outside rather than the local community in mind. This is because often politics tend to play a major part in resource allocation. As a result, some communities tend to have greater political power than their less fortunate counterparts. Therefore ignoring any local culture easily can lead to lop-sided resource development.

In almost all developing countries, a transient semi-culture is emerging amongst the 'educated' class and often conflicts arise between resource decisions of the 'uneducated' and those of the ruling 'educated' class. For instance, in the energy policies in East Africa, electricity and biogas alternatives are often favoured by the educated. However, among the rural poor there are serious problems of sanitary controls during the use of cowdung and other waste matter in biogas plants. Charcoal and fuelwood are often preferred by the rural poor. Because of suspicion in which the 'educated' are often held, new techniques and innovations generally take too long to be adopted by rural farmers, the majority of whom are 'uneducated'.

The methods used in the ethnological approach attempt to assess the direction and magnitude of public attitudes and preferences regarding a given resource use issue. One of these methods is attitude scaling, encompassing differential scales, summated scales, cumulative scaling, and semantic differential. The application of this approach is described by Priddle (1971). A major problem with attitude scaling techniques is that respondents do not have freedom of expression because the items to which they respond and the relative weights of items are predetermined by interviewers. The interviewer in turn has limited chances of learning anything new from the respondents. Schiff (1971) realized a further danger of assuming attitudes and behaviour are synonymous.

A more widely used method in developed countries involves *citizen participation* in the decision-making process. In 1972 the United States Forest Service created a study team which developed a conceptual framework for identifying processes basic to any public involvement. The framework is discussed by R. N. Clark and Stankey (1976) and consists of five interdependent processes:

1 Issue definition: the legal, administrative and environmental constraints within which resource managers operate; and the range of possible alternatives.
2 Collection of data: soliciting public input by letters, petitions, reports, form letters and public hearing.
3 Analysis of data: display of the nature, content and extent of input without judging the relative value of inputs.
4 Evaluation: input is interpreted and weighed by decision makers.
5 Decision implementation: involves feedback to public.

During the 1980s the Kenyan government evolved the District Focus strategy. Through each District Development Committee, projects for the district are identified and requests for funding are submitted to the government headquarters in Nairobi. Because of local participation in project decision, the strategy has stimulated enormous grass-roots enthusiasm and goodwill in development efforts of each district.

Public input is especially important in undertaking *social impact assessment*. In developing countries social impacts of human-made lakes have revealed the need to incorporate social variables in the planning and management of development projects. Adams (1985), Kalitsi (1973), Scudder and Colson (1972) and Scudder (1966) studied environmental impact of the Kainji (Nigeria), Volta (Ghana), Kariba (Zambia) and the Aswan High Dam, respectively. The social impact of these dams includes social disruption during the resettlement of large number of families, loss of prime agricultural land, loss of fishing prospects for downstream communities and social problems of adjusting to the new area of resettlement. For instance the Kariba Dam was completed in 1958 and by 1963, a lake covering 5,180 km² had formed (B. Mitchell, 1989). This area was previously occupied by some 57,000 Gwembe Tonga people who had all to be resettled (Scudder and Colson, 1972). As mentioned earlier in this chapter, the Kariba Dam resettlement programme resulted in increased rates of crime, alcoholism and psychosomatic diseases (Stanley and Alpers, 1974).

Because public involvement requires analysis of the complex issues and large volumes of data, the content analysis technique has been recommended (R. N. Clark and Stankey, 1976). Content analysis identifies opinions offered for, against and about the issue, along with the reasons given to support the views. The limitations of this method include time involved and the difficulty of ensuring that public input is relevant to the issue in question. Furthermore, the fact that the alternatives proposed by the public are eventually ranked by decision makers makes it necessary to study the attitudes of the professionals themselves. Such a study should focus on the manner in which goals are set, strategies identified and alternative solutions scanned. In developing countries public participation is still rare and may not be widely practised until the ruling elite begin to accept that one can know what is good for him or her without having been to school.

Summary and implications of the approaches

Resource management is a decision-making process in which optimal solu-
tions regarding the manner, timing and allocation of resource use are sought within the economic, political, social and institutional framework (O'Riordan, 1971). This statement implies that the different approaches described cannot be deployed independently for a satisfactory allocation of resources. Firey (1960) noted that an attempt to achieve anthropogenic climax usually violates the conditions for cultural consistency and economic efficiency. Ideally, the goals of each approach should be considered and balanced against each other to achieve a degree of ecological possibility, economic gainfulness, technical feasibility and cultural consistency. Many resource-related studies (biomedical, aesthetics, natural hazards, environmental impact assessment) tend to combine features of all these approaches. In Chapter 8 the discussion shows how a strategy of increased growth and sustainable development pulls together ecological, economic, technological and social considerations.

Each of these approaches can be applied over space and time with varying degrees of emphasis. For instance, immediately on acquiring political independence, it was necessary for developing countries to emphasize economic growth in order to provide facilities for education, health and other forms of national development. But as mounting problems of environmental deterioration begin to threaten economic growth, it is imperative that an integrated approach is adopted to arrest the situation and sustain growth and development.

Figure 2.1 is a conceptualized framework for an integrated approach to

Approaches in resource management

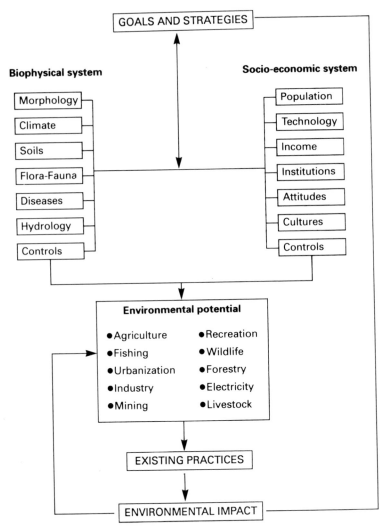

Fig. 2.1 Component relationships in resource management: a conceptual framework

resource management. Ecological considerations form the biophysical system. Cultural considerations of population, technology, institutional arrangements, attitudes and perceptions form the socio-economic component. The interaction between the biophysical and socio-economic systems determines the resource potential of an area. The choice from a range of potential practices depends on goals and strategies as influenced by technology and income levels. Once adopted, resource practices will cause some environmental impacts. Depending on their magnitudes, the impacts will affect environmental potential and induce a re-examination of goals and strategies so as to harmonize the relationships between the biophysical and socio-economic systems.

Figure 2.1 is therefore a summary which attempts to balance the goals of the major components of the resource management system and to describe the interrelationships between the components. Specific linkages (e.g. between deforestation and soil quality or between population growth and human health) are considered in the rest of this book. What is important from the framework is that appropriate resource management requires detailed information on elements of each component. In addition, environmental impact assessments have to be incorporated as an integral part of the resource development effort so that environmental degradation is checked before it becomes irreversible. Initially these suggestions appear costly and unaffordable in developing countries but in the long run prevention is better than cure.

CHAPTER 3

Poverty and its resource management implications in developing countries

One of the fundamental issues of resource development in developing countries relates to the existence of widespread and persistent poverty. Absolute poverty is overwhelmingly concentrated in the rural areas, although a significant proportion of the urban population also fails to meet its basic needs. It was estimated that by 1980 over 780 million people (excluding people from China) were living in absolute poverty (World Bank, 1982a). In other words, nearly one in four people in the world were in poverty. This chapter will first discuss poverty at a global scale and then illustrate the global picture with the poverty situation in Uganda.

Absolute poverty in developing countries in characterized by inadequate provisions of food, shelter, clothing, drinking water, sanitation, health services, educational facilities and opportunities for employment. These problems are especially widespread in countries that frequently experience violent political changes. All these, together with lack of freedom to participate in decision-making processes and to enjoy human rights, have weakened the physical and mental well-being of the poverty-stricken individuals in developing countries. In fact, lack of material well-being seems to corrode individual interest and initiative in community affairs so that the poor individual becomes increasingly isolated and powerless. The ultimate result of poverty is manifested in complex ways. Often it creates insecure and unstable relationships between people and their national governments, between resource practices and environmental capacity, and amongst neighbours in search for survival.

In operational terms, poverty in developing countries is associated with low levels of income and consumption per head, low gross national production, poor employment opportunities and a degenerating economic base as land becomes increasingly scarce and unproductive and as the labour force is unable to sustain consumption demands. This poses a great worry because in resource management, innovative and well-motivated individuals are needed to adopt, sustain or initiate the required management techniques. Amongst poor communities the question of basic survival becomes so preoccupying that little or no effort is spared for activities (soil conservation, re-afforestation) whose benefits are slow to come.

In the post-colonial times, a major reason for persistent poverty amongst developing countries has been the poor balance of payments and lack of foreign exchange. In relative terms the economies of many African, Asian and Latin American countries have been characterized by increasing deficits and heavy debts. Tables 3.1 and 3.2 indicate that all non-oil producing countries in the Third World have experienced increasing deficits in billions of US dollars ever since 1973. In some countries large deficits have occurred even when remarkable growth in exports had been achieved. In Tanzania between 1975 and 1980, exports grew by 71 per cent but imports soared by 96 per cent (Berry, 1981; World Bank, 1980). It is this trade imbalance, involving larger expenditure on imports than exports, that poses a most critical constraint to resource development in developing countries. The imbalance causes a contraction in the foreign exchange reserve so that developing countries are unable to purchase necessary inputs for agriculture, health, schools, etc. This leads to frustration, the effects of which extend over other resource-related activities (e.g. little care for game park management, or soil erosion control).

Several reasons combine to account for large deficits in the economy of developing countries. For most developing countries 50 per cent of export earnings come from agriculture. World market values of agricultural produce often decline, while prices of imported goods keep rising. In mineral-dependent countries such as Zambia, Zaïre and Botswana, downward fluctuations in world prices of minerals similarly result in larger deficits. For both agriculture and minerals, greater production usually requires more use and renewal of imported inputs. As the volume of inputs declines, production of exports decreases and poverty is entrenched. Indeed, in most developing countries recent increases in export values are due more to higher prices than to actual improvement in production. Many developing countries see that the remedy to scarcity of foreign exchange is increased production and volumes of export while cutting back on imports (by pursuing import-substitution policies).

A second reason for the larger deficits relates to the price of oil. Since the mid-1970s, the price of oil and other forms of energy has witnessed an absolute upward thrust. As a result, non-oil developing countries have had to utilize over 50 per cent of their foreign exchange for the purchase of oil. Although expenditures on oil declined since 1981 (World Bank, 1983a), costs of oil imports have remained higher than before the mid-1970s.

A third reason is that consumption patterns in developing countries have changed enormously in response to an increasing proportion of the 'educated', the travelled and the rich and affluent in the population structure. Of significant concern is that higher consumption (sometimes over-consumption) of increasingly diverse and voluminous commodities is beginning to typify

41

Table 3.1 Payment balances on current account, 1973–83 (in billions of US dollars)

Region	1973	1974	1975	1976	1977	1978	1979	1980	1981	1982	1983
Non-oil developing countries	−11.3	−37.0	−46.3	−32.6	−28.9	−41.3	−61.0	−89.0	−107.7	−86.8	−68.0
Oil exporting developing countries	6.7	68.3	35.4	40.3	30.2	2.2	68.6	114.3	65.0	−2.2	−27.0
Industrial countries	20.3	−10.8	19.8	0.5	−2.2	32.7	−5.6	−4.01	0.6	−1.2	16.0

Source World Bank (1983b)

Table 3.2 Overall balance of payments, 1973–83 (in billions of US dollars)

Region	1973	1974	1975	1976	1977	1978	1979	1980	1981	1982	1983
Non-oil developing countries	10.2	1.1	−4.1	8.0	9.5	16.0	12.6	−1.4	−10.6	−32.2	4.0
Net oil exporters	1.2	1.5	0.3	−0.7	0.6	0.1	4.1	3.5	0.7	−9.6	0.6
Net oil Importers	9.0	−0.4	−4.4	8.6	8.4	16.6	7.9	−5.3	−13.2	−27.6	0.2

Source World Bank (1983b)

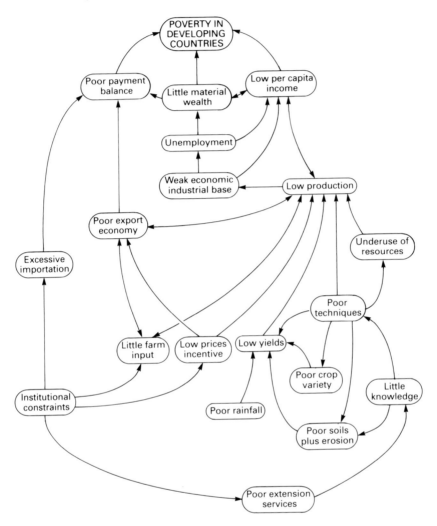

Fig. 3.1 Poverty syndrome in developing countries

urban communities. This has resulted in unwise allocation of foreign currency on luxury and often non-essential material possessions (remote control videos). As foreign currency is diverted to such urban demands, the rural poor is deprived, strained and becomes less innovative and productive.

Such consumption patterns have resulted in unfair demands on meagre capital resources and frequently in blatant corruption in the civil service of almost all developing countries. In addition, there are large inter-ministerial debts, diversion of funds to hitherto unplanned expenditures, poor financial accountability and control and widespread '*supply of air*' (supply of no goods) against colossal withdrawals of funds from the treasury. This trend means

Poverty and its resource management implications in developing countries

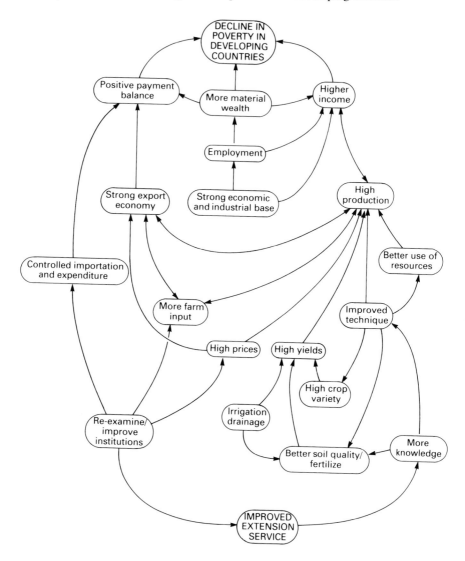

Fig. 3.2 Poverty solution syndrome in developing countries

projects and priorities previously budgeted for cannot be funded, neither can new projects nor expansions of existing facilities and services be supported. Often in such cases projects for rural areas are sacrificed, thus further entrenching rural poverty.

The consequences of large deficits are to create a chain of effects characterized by growth in tension among the rich and poor regions. Because of large deficits and limited, if any, foreign exchange, shortages exist in raw materials, spare parts, industrial and agricultural inputs, building materials and transportation facilities. In a few countries in Africa and Asia, extreme situations have been experienced whereby essential commodities (salt, soap, sugar, medicine) disappeared into illegal and expensive black market systems. All these, coupled with shortages of fuelwood, agricultural land and building materials, cause real frustration at a national level.

Amongst the rural poor these developments have led to low productivity, low income per capita and low expenditures on food, health and clothing and increasing tendency for rural-urban migration. It is estimated that in South East Asia about 500 million people live below the poverty line (World Bank, 1983b). In Africa a large proportion of the rural population may not have access to money for up to three months of each year. The other reasons for low levels of income include little diversity in economic base, low work-hour per head, greater emphasis on subsistence production and poor distributions and opportunities for non-farm employment.

Figures 3.1 and 3.2 summarize the causes and 'solutions' to the poverty problem. The methodology is simple but analogous to the medical practice of diagnosing the problem by probing questions (trouble-shooting) and prescribing the medicine. In this case the problem is poverty. By working backward, causes are identified from the obvious (e.g. low income) to the rather detailed or hidden (e.g. little knowledge). Each cause then represents a potential intervention or treatment point. Solutions are actions that reverse the cause of the problem, that is literally the opposite feature of each cause (intervention point). Figure 3.1 presents the casual relationships in a poverty syndrome while Figure 3.2 presents a linked set of 'solutions'. A case study, presented in the next section of this chapter, illustrates the application of the diagnostic approach to the poverty situation in Uganda. Although not all the intervention points identified in Figures 3.1 and 3.2 are repeated in the Uganda case study, the general features of the cause, indicators/effects and remedies are quite similar.

Although such a diagnostic-prescriptive approach may oversimplify the process of decision making, it becomes quite helpful where research facilities are poor or where quick overview of resource development problems and tentative counteractions are required.

Whatever the cause, poverty and the associated low purchasing power limit the scope and rate of industrial growth, thus accelerating unemployment. Communities living in absolute poverty become much more vulnerable to calamities as they are remote and harder to reach and their priorities are directed primarily to basic survival. While poverty provides a sound call for resource management, often preoccupation with basic survival leads a community to equate environmental management concerns with denial of growth and development.

What remains a drawback is a way to integrate poverty concerns into the general resource management and development strategy in developing countries. Unless this question is answered, newly established environmental management institutions or ministries may be rendered ineffective, especially as inevitably they have to struggle for jurisdictional powers with longer established government departments. Experience in East Africa points to the following avenues as a departure point for alleviating poverty:

1 Decentralization of power structures so as to transfer some power from urban to rural areas and increase public participation in decision making. Recent literature strongly recommends this departure, although it has to be supplemented by other measures. In Kenya this is being effected through the District Focus Policy (see Chapter 7).
2 Increased rural industrialization with greater preferences for small-scale industries using local raw materials.
3 Expansion of rural employment opportunities and rural economic base by
   (a) improvements in production and sales of arts and crafts
   (b) diversification and intensification of agriculture
   (c) job creation in environment-based community projects such as dams, rural water supply, afforestation, pest control, soil conservation, irrigation management and general self-help schemes.

Because of the nature of economies in developing countries, solutions to most of environmental problems lie in changes made in the rural countryside. In the first place, the direction of flows of decision-making power and capital needs to be reversed. In most cases, development measures originate from the top in cities while capital continues to flow from the rural areas to the cities. This leaves the rural areas unnecessarily dependent on action occurring in the urban areas. In particular, the current flow of capital has lowered the purchasing power of the majority of the rural poor to a level where many now do without essential commodities.

Through government intervention, capital can be transferred to the rural poor directly through job creation in rural industries or indirectly through subsidizing costs of education, farm inputs and energy costs or by development of recreation activities and state function facilities in rural townships. These measures should be supplemented by promoting commercial livestock keeping, fishing and other money-earning rural projects. Attempts have to be made to ensure much higher capital inflow into the rural areas if the pre-1970 labour force quality is to be recovered.

Raising the purchasing power of the current rural poor requires changes in consumption ethics both within the rural and urban areas. For rural communities, a public education programme is necessary and it must encourage greater expenditure of peasant income on essential commodities such as housing, clothing, salt, soap, medicine and farm inputs. In urban areas, definite policy measures must be taken against the consumption race in which luxury goods exhaust the national revenue and precipitate 'foreign currency sickness' throughout the national fabrics.

To supplement rural capital build-up, research must be sponsored to provide insights and solutions to environmental problems in rural areas. For instance, research is required to develop local seed varieties that will increase

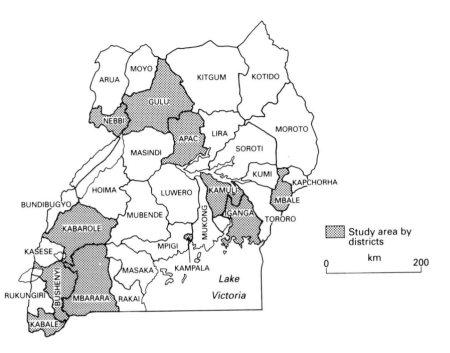

Fig. 3.3 Political subdivisions (districts) of Uganda showing study area

yields without depending too much on pesticides, water and fertilizers or other inputs with negative side effects on the environment. Research associated with 'dry farming' techniques in Kenya has successfully evolved crops (peas, maize) that can withstand prolonged drought, mature rapidly and are relatively resistant to local diseases. The next section of this chapter illustrates the salient points raised here with a case study of poverty in Uganda.

Poverty in Uganda and its resource management implications

Research was conducted in eleven out of thirty-three districts in Uganda in 1986–87 (Figure 3.3). The primary objective was to understand the nature and magnitude of poverty in Uganda and to assess how poverty conditions affect efforts to manage Uganda's resources. The specific objectives were

1 to describe the levels of poverty in selected areas of northern, eastern, central and western Uganda
2 to identify the perceived indicators and cause of poverty amongst the Ugandan populace
3 to identify the perceived effects, remedies and remedial responsibility centres in Uganda
4 to relate the poverty situation to resource management needs in Uganda.

47

Areas of study

Uganda can be divided into three major agro-ecological zones:

1 the coffee–banana zone, consisting of the southern half of Uganda or the Lake Victoria Basin (south of Lake Kioga)
2 the cotton–finger millet zone, consisting of the areas north of Lake Kioga
3 the semi-arid pastoral zone, comprising mainly Karamoja and pockets in Mbarara districts.

In selecting areas for research, each of the three agro-ecological zones was considered and represented. In 1986–7 security considerations and accessibility to respondents were also considered. The districts shown in Table 3.3 and Figure 3.3 were chosen. Because of security considerations, the semi-arid pastoral zone of Karamoja was not included.

Table 3.3 Agro-ecological zones of Uganda

District	Agro-ecological zone
Apac	Cotton – Finger millet
Bushenyi	Coffee – Banana
Gulu	Cotton – Finger millet
Iganga	Coffee – Banana
Kamuli	Coffee – Banana
Kabale	Not clear cut
Kabarole	Coffee – Banana
Kampala	Coffee – Banana
Mbale	Coffee – Banana
Mbarara	Coffee – Banana/pastoral
Nebbi	Cotton – Finger millet

The respondents

A total of 1,142 respondents, selected from the combined list of tax payers and co-operative society members in the eleven districts, was interviewed in order to address each of the objectives already outlined (Table 3.4).

The following were the respondent characteristics: age, family size, land tenure and literacy.

Age

Because of problems of food, health and general survival hardships in developing countries, many people especially in rural areas become 'old' and weak at a relatively early age. In classifying respondents into age groups, this fact was borne in mind and only four age classes were considered appropriate. The first age class begins at below 25 to reflect the age when most people take up responsibility as household leaders.

Table 3.4 Respondent distribution by district

District	Respondent number
Apac	103
Busenyi	92
Gulu	63
Iganga	104
Kamuli	117
Kabale	84
Kabarole	91
Kampala	164
Mbale	86
Mbarara	126
Nebbi	112
Total	1 142

Table 3.5 indicates that the majority of respondents (73.9 per cent) are between the age of 25 and 55. This age bracket is a most productive one in terms of participation in community affairs, personal drives to conquer poverty and rendering support to dependants. The table also reflects the relationship between age group and personal declaration of poverty, and it correlates age group with generalized (small or large, see Table 3.6) family sizes. A large number (91.6 per cent) of young respondents (below 25) admitted being poor in spite of having relatively small families. These are people in their formative stage in household responsibility: with no accumu-lated wealth or any well-established mode of wealth acquisition. Age groups above 25 years have large families but with a lower number of poor people. The large family size amongst respondents over 55 years arises from the incorporation of grandchildren and other young members of the extended family to replace sons and daughters who have grown and become independ-ent of the parent family. This complex tradition has helped to sustain large families across the age groups above 25 years. The 41–55 age group shows a significantly lower proportion of poor people. This is the age of material accumulation due to achievements over the years as caused by an increasing family labour force. Above 55 both the effects of ageing and incorporation

Table 3.5 Respondent distribution by age group

Age group	% of total respondents	% declared poverty	Family size
Below 25	7.6	91.6	Small
25–40	37.4	81.3	Large
41–55	36.5	84.1	Large
Over 55	18.5	84.1	Large

of new dependants lead to gradual decline in accumulated wealth. It can therefore be deduced from these findings that in Uganda a satisfactory standard of living supported by accumulated wealth comes relatively late into a family and lasts for a relatively short period of time.

Family size

Table 3.6 shows the size of families amongst the respondents and the proportion of respondents within the family size brackets. Table 3.6 shows that large families are common in Uganda. For instance, 38.7 per cent of the respondents have a family size of six to ten persons, 16.5 per cent have a family size of eleven to fifteen members and 6.1 per cent of the respondents reported having over twenty dependants in a family. As indicated in Table 3.9, the districts of Apac, Gulu, Iganga, Kamuli and Nebbi, where poverty is more pronounced, have generally larger families while in low-poverty areas such as Kampala and Bushenyi smaller families are found. The reason for this is that where better medical facilities have led to low child mortality rates (e.g. in Kampala) parents feel more secure about child survival. This feeling together with effects of affluence amongst low poverty areas set a limitation on the number of children per family while the converse causes more children to be desired in the high poverty districts with high child mortality rates. In especially the urban areas of Kampala and Mbale, both a mother and a father in a family may, in many cases, have a good education and can appreciate how to improve the quality of life in the family through family planning. In contrast, in the majority of cases in rural Uganda, only the father may have attained education and he becomes constrained by the prevalent anti-family planning attitudes in rural areas. These factors create spatial differences in family size in Uganda.

Table 3.6 Family size as % of total respondents

No of persons in a family	% of total respondents	Qualitative grouping
1–5	33.5	
6–10	38.7	Small
11–15	16.5	Large
16–20	3.8	Very large
Over 20	6.1	Excessive

There is a complex causal relationship between poverty levels and family size. Because over 70 per cent of the respondents are poor, a strong statistical correlation exists between family size and level of poverty. The correlation implies that poverty is more entrenched in large families. However, when family size is correlated with income and level of material possession, only a weak statistical correlation is indicated. Indeed in Uganda, many of the wealthier men have significantly large families often with two or more wives. This is because additional wives and children are acquired as one becomes wealthier rather than during the formative period before one has accumulated some wealth. Such large families become self-supporting due to the large base for a labour force. However, most of these large families tend to complain of land shortage because each entitled member expects to inherit plots of land. This implies an explosive situation in time as large families continue to be sustained.

Land tenure

The majority of respondents (85.4 per cent) own land while 14.6 per cent are landless squatters. Of the people who own land, 76.3 per cent acquired land through subdivision of the family land. The majority of respondents (94.7 per cent) from Apac, Gulu, Nebbi and Mbarara districts inherited their land from the parents while in the remaining districts 61.3 per cent of the land was purchased from outside the parents' land. In Kampala district, almost all the land (97.1 per cent) is purchased from non-family landowners.

In general, districts with low population densities (Apac, Gulu, Nebbi, Mbarara) tend to have larger plots (over 3 hectares) of land per family. There was no positive statistical correlation between plot size and income or material possession. This is because it is the productivity of land as enhanced by climate and agricultural practices (rather than plot size per se) which influences the degree of poverty.

Literacy

It is generally believed that the level of literacy influences the degree to which one would understand government policies, adopt new techniques and amass a range of alternative strategies for survival. According to this research finding, 77.5 per cent of the respondents can read in both vernacular and English. This literacy rate is much higher than the national literacy rate. The reason for the high rate is that most of the respondents are male who are knowledgeable tax payers and members of the co-operative societies. Literacy rate was not correlated with other variables of poverty (income, material possession, etc.) because there was no significant statistical difference in literacy amongst the respondents.

Poverty levels

In the research, analysis of poverty levels was carried out at the district and family unit levels. At these levels, districts or families either exhibited a high, average or low incidence of poverty. The criteria used to assess poverty during the interview were income, material possession and personal declaration of poverty.

Income

In 1986–7 when the interviews were conducted, an average family whose annual income was between 50,000 and 100,000 shillings (USh) was able to lead a decent life and to afford most of the basic domestic needs of the family. Respondents were therefore divided into those whose annual income was inadequate to support family (i.e. below 50,000 UShs), those who had adequate annual income (50,000–100,000) and those families with over 100,00 UShs (see Table 3.7).

Table 3.7 Income distribution amongst respondents

Below 50,000 UShs	Inadequate income
50,000–100,000 UShs	Adequate income
Above 100,000 UShs	Not poor

On the basis of the three income categories, 34.1 per cent of the respondents had inadequate income, 37.3 per cent had adequate income for basic needs and 28.6 per cent were categorized as not poor. This categorization was evolved purely on the basis of the conditions which prevailed in Uganda at the time. For instance the 37.3 per cent with adequate income were those who could meet only their basic requirements (i.e. reasonable house, even grass-thatched, some hoes, reasonable clothing, evidence of good feeding and food supply and some few backyard livestock or poultry). In this category luxury items, such as cars, radios, sofa sets or large herds of cattle, are completely lacking and were not considered as part of the basic domestic needs. In general, the income needs of the Ugandan family fluctuate considerably with ever changing inflation and cost of living. For instance by 1989 the 100,000 UShs was much lower in purchasing power than in 1986–7.

Material possession

A monetary economy and banking system are much more developed amongst the urban elite than among the rural peasants in Uganda. Throughout the rural area, monetary savings are made in the form of cattle and such backyard livestock as goats, sheep, pigs and poultry. The sales of these are often supplemented by sales of bananas, fruits, grains and arts and crafts. Possession of these items in addition to a house, food supply, furniture, bicycles, radios, cars, land, etc. reflected the degree of poverty or wealth in a family.

On the basis of material possession amongst all the respondents, 58.2 per cent had a poor material basis, 28.6 per cent had average, and 13.2 per cent had a good variety of material possession. But 64 per cent of those registering good material possession were from the urban area of Kampala. On a district basis, Apach, Gulu, Mbarara and Nebbi had a poor material basis. Mbarara is a district where most respondents had large herds of cattle but with poor housing conditions, domestic amenities and frequent absence of backyard animals, fruits and grain stores. Iganga and Kamuli districts showed an average level of material possession because of good household amenities, good backyard animals, bananas and fruits but the respondents reported very low income and many personally admitted being very poor. As a result, statistical analysis showed a weak relationship between poverty rating and material possession amongst the districts.

Personal declaration of poverty

In order to reduce the personal bias of the researcher, respondents were asked whether in their opinion they considered themselves and their family poor, average or not poor. There was a general tendency, especially in Iganga, Kamuli and Apac, for respondents to declare themselves poorer than the observed conditions of the family household. This is because amongst some rural communities in Uganda it is considered conceit and bad omen to declare oneself rich, and the punishment is for God to withdraw His gifts from the conceited.

Table 3.8 Relative poverty amongst respondents

District	Personal declaration %	
	Poor	*Not poor*
Apac	85	15
Bushenyi	52	48
Gulu	78	22
Iganga	92	08
Kamuli	85	15
Kabale	57	43
Kabarole	48	52
Kampala	31	69
Mbale	50	50
Mbarara	83	17
Nebbi	60	31
Average	65.6	33.6

Across the districts, 71.8 per cent of the respondents personally declared themselves poor while 28.2 per cent stated they were not poor (Table 3.8). According to Table 3.8, Bushenyi, Kabale, Kabarole, Kampala and Mbale have relatively high numbers of people who are not poor. It was observed during the interviews that actual household cash income is higher in Mbale, Kabarole and Kabale mainly because of cross-border trade with neighbouring countries. Bushenyi is one of the few districts in Uganda where rapid economic development involving modern ranching, farming, trade and accumulation of household amenities had started especially since 1981. Kampala, being the capital of Uganda, has the largest number of people who are categorized as not poor.

On the basis of the three criteria, the districts of Uganda can be classified into high, average and low poverty districts (Table 3.9).

High poverty districts

The districts of Apac, Gulu, Iganga, Kamuli, Mbarara and Nebbi form the high poverty districts. In these districts over 65 per cent of the respondents personally admitted to being poor. The research results further showed that a large proportion of the respondents have incomes below 50,000 shillings, poor housing, poor material possession and generally large families. In addition, these are districts where medical facilities, schools, water supply and access roads are most poorly developed. In many families, seasonal food shortages are common especially between the months of December and March. There is a general weak statistical correlation between poverty level and the size of land holding per family. The districts of Apac, Gulu and Mbarara have relatively large plots of land which can be further subdivided to heirs according to traditional inheritance systems. These are also districts where population densities are relatively low but where harsh climatic variability, relatively low soil productivity and poor agricultural inputs have kept levels of farm productivity low. The other high poverty districts of Iganga, Kamuli and Nebbi have relatively small plots of land per family because of higher population densities. The plots here are adequate for the basic family needs but little to no land is available for subdivision to heirs.

Table 3.9 Poverty related variables by district

District	Poverty rating	Family size	Income level	Literacy level	Material possesion	Family land
Apach	High	Large	Low	High	Poor	Large
Bushenyi	Average	Average	High	High	Good	Small
Gulu	High	Large	Low	Low	Poor	Large
Iganga	High	Large	Average	Average	Good	Large
Kamuli	High	Large	Average	Low	Average	Adequate
Kabale	Average	Small	Low	High	Good	Small
Kabarole	Low	Average	High	Average	Good	Small
Kampala	Low	Small	High	High	Good	Small
Mbale	Low	Large	High	High	Good	Small
Mbarara	High	Average	Low	High	Poor	Large
Nebbi	High	Large	Low	Low	Poor	Large

The average poverty districts

This includes the districts of Bushenyi and Kabale where family size is relatively small but the households have good material possession. Both Bushenyi and Kabale farmers operate relatively small plots of land with frequent cases of land fragmentation. Their incomes are boosted, however, by application of modern farming techniques (land terracing, dairy farming and production of bananas and vegetables for sale in Kampala markets) with a strong commercial orientation. As mentioned earlier, Kabale has benefited much from border trade with Rwanda. In the two districts, population density is high and family landholding is therefore small and often inadequate for family needs. There is need for more land. Outward migration to cities and to other less densely populated rural areas is quite common, especially among the youths.

Low poverty districts

With the exception of Kabarole, the two districts of Mbale and Kampala form the major urban centres in Uganda. The 'City advantage' helps in supporting high income, good material possessions with relatively small family sizes. Most respondents in Kampala are non-farmers although in Mbale 63 per cent of the respondents own small plots of land. The farmers around Kampala and Mbale have the advantage of a nearby urban market, good climate and very productive soils. Kabarole seems to have benefited much from the border trade with neighbouring Rwanda. It has a large flow of cash income but only average material possession and small land holdings per farmer.

Indicators and effects of poverty

When asked to state conditions which indicate that one is poor, the respondents gave a multiplicity of indicators. Below is a classification of the several indicators. The classification reflects the complex problem of defining poverty and the vicious cycle in the poverty phenomenon.

1 *Income*
   - low income
   - no savings
   - low purchasing power
   - unable to pay tax
2 *Material possession*
   - no land
   - poor/no housing
   - little land
   - no livestock
   - poor dressing
   - no food reserves
3 *Education*
   - illiteracy
   - low level of education
   - poor/no skill

4 *Employment*
   - jobless
   - working as porter
   - low promotion opportunity
5 *Social*
   - limited social interaction
   - no wife/children
   - resort to theft or crime
   - unpresentable
   - too dependent
   - resort to begging
   - low morale
   - unable to meet social obligations
6 *Health*
   - sickly
   - thin, weak, lazy
   - poor feeding and nutrition
   - poor sanitation.

Many of these conditions were well reflected in the personality and household conditions of especially those respondents who declared themselves poor. In the context of the diagnostic approach outlined earlier in this chapter, income, material possession, education, employment, social and health factors become intervention points. The antidote of poverty therefore becomes the opposite of the poverty indicator (e.g. no land = more land; sickly = improve health) as indicated in Figure 3.2.

Causes of poverty

Both biophysical and socio-economic problems were blamed for persistent poverty in Uganda.

Adverse variability in rainfall conditions leading often to prolonged drought greatly affect crop and livestock production in Uganda. Failure of rain during the planting and weeding period is quite common in northern Uganda. This has respectively caused low harvests and excessive crop losses, especially during the 1979/80 growing period. Respondents in Apac, Gulu and Mbarara districts also reported large losses of livestock in the yearly dry seasons. The 1979 drought which lasted for up to five months in Mbarara was blamed for the loss of nearly 50 per cent of the livestock in the area that year. In addition, rainfall variability creates general uncertainty amongst farmers thus inducing them to gamble with crops whose requirements (for weather and soil) and harvest values are still little known to farmers.

Poor soils and land shortages are the other factors which lower crop production. Although many areas of Uganda have fertile soils, the districts of Apac, Gulu, Mbarara and parts of Iganga have large areas of lateritic soils whose inherent productivity is between moderate to low (Chenery, 1954). But throughout Uganda, soil productivity is on the decline because of continuous cultivation without applying manure or fertilizers.

Land shortage is becoming a significant problem in all parts of Uganda. The situation is most acute in areas of high population densities where families are forced to survive on less than 1 hectare of land. In areas where pastoralism or mixed farming is the primary source of living (Apac, Mbarara, Bushenyi, Mbale, Iganga, Kamuli, Kumi, Soroti and Karamoja), pastoral land is rapidly being encroached upon by cultivation.

In addition, biological factors also cause both pre-harvest and post-harvest crop losses. Ever since the onset of political instability in Uganda in 1971, agricultural modernization programmes were abandoned. The subsequent inadequate use of agro-chemicals has led to re-emergence of crop diseases and pests which previously had been brought under control. In addition, the general insecurity that prevailed since 1971 did not provide conditions conducive to proper maintenance of crop storage facilities. As a result large amounts of millet, sorghum, maize, groundnuts and beans have been lost during storage.

The respondents further identified eight major socio-economic factors which they believe to cause poverty. The relationship between each factor to poverty in Uganda is similar to what was discussed earlier in the introductory remarks to this chapter. The factors are ranked according to the number of respondents who mentioned them:

1 inflation, high cost of living and black marketing
2 shortage of agricultural inputs including seeds
3 insecurity to life and property
4 poor pricing and marketing systems
5 large family sizes and land shortage
6 poor education and lack of extension service
7 social evil (stealing, looting, land conflicts)
8 labour shortage.

The ranking system employed has one major drawback. While it gives an overview picture of the most and least burning concerns among all the 1,142 respondents acting as a group, it plays down the local significance of individual factors. For instance, in Mbale, Kabale and Bushenyi districts where land fragmentation is common, social evil associated with conflicts over land is ranked third to inflation (ranked first) and insecurity (ranked second).

Remedial measures and responsibility centres against poverty

Table 3.10 presents a list of remedial measures, their effects and associated responsibility centres as mentioned in respondents' responses. From Table 3.10 it is evident that remedial measures to poverty should be centred around improvements in agricultural productivity, pricing and marketing. This reflects not only the fact that agriculture is the mainstay of families in Uganda but also the limited range of alternatives open to peasants in Uganda. Remedial measures and their effects were quite vivid in the minds of respondents, but there was generally low personal motivation and confidence in accepting responsibility to tackle even household poverty. This is reflected in the fact that government is held responsible for effecting almost all remedial measures against poverty. Where it is not the government, the village community and private firms are held responsible but not often the family or an individual. The family or individual remains detached with too low a morale to initiate community programmes or projects.

Implications of poverty for resource management in Uganda

Many observers, comparing Uganda with other countries in Africa, conclude that Uganda has abundant natural resources. In many parts of Uganda, climate allows for crop growth throughout the year. The soils are generally of high productivity. Coffee, cotton, tea, tobacco, bananas, fruit and many

Table 3.10 Measures against poverty in Uganda

Remedial measure	Effects	Responsibility centre
1 Provide and subsidize costs of agricultural inputs	Increase production	Government
2 Provide credit facilities	Improve production, purchasing power and rural commerce	Government, banks and co-operative societies
3 Provide human and animal drugs	Improve health and livestock output	Government
4 Diversify production to include brick-making	Improve income and counteract disease, pest rainfall vagaries	Government, village communities, and the family
5 Provide irrigation and swamp reclamation	Counteract rainfall variability	Government
6 Improve employment opportunities	Improve income, material possession and social status	Government and private firms
7 Industrialize even in rural areas	Provide jobs, local market and cheaper implements	Government and private firms
8 Provide rural extension services	Encourage better land utilization cropping and crop storage	Government
9 Mass education	Know government policy, cropping regulations	Government
10 Improve transport and communication facilities	To reach and convey rural products	Government
11 Improve marketing systems	Easy and cash sales of produce	Government
12 Double/treble producer prices	More incentive income and production	Government
13 Review land tenure system	Provide land for the landless	Government and village community

types of vegetables grow well and easily in various parts of Uganda. Where agricultural potential is relatively low, livestock is predominant. In addition, there are deposits of copper, tin and phosphates, and oil prospecting has begun within the floors of the Western Rift Valley. As a result, many people believe that the current low level of economic development is temporary because it is a result of political instability rather than the state of natural resources. It is true that political instability and associated insecurity has set Uganda back and has made it difficult for development efforts to be consistently applied. In particular, the instability allowed population growth to outstrip growth rates of agriculture, industry and infrastructural development. Consequently, the balance between resource supply and demand is so adverse that there is relative resource scarcity in Uganda. But if politics is to blame, it must also be true that a sound economic performance based on proper utilization of resources is one way of resolving and avoiding political problems. The relationship between political instability and poverty and other resource use problems is presented in Figure 3.4.

In Uganda, as elsewhere in developing countries, natural resources have been major assets in

1 generating revenue to support the establishment and expansion of industries, roads, health, education and employment facilities
2 improving the local purchasing power for manufactured goods and for various other services
3 providing raw materials for industries and construction works and food for human and animal consumption
4 providing security against dietary, economic and ecological imbalances.

In spite of those central roles, problems exist with use, management and life support capacity of Uganda's natural resources. These problems manifest themselves in widespread poverty throughout Uganda and increasing fears of environmental deterioration. Environmental problems in Uganda arise from a lack of a consistent policy to assess and restore the state of the environment. It was only in 1987 when the Ministry of Environment Protection was established; that agency is still organizing itself to face the jurisdictional intricacies of environmental issues.

The resource management problems in Uganda are illustrated below by a discussion of the trends and issues associated with arable land, forest, water and livestock resources.

Arable land

Land has become increasingly scarce in Uganda since 1970. In the 1960s the national per capita landholding was 2.5 hectares (Jameson, 1970). Earlier research by the author in the foothills of Mount Elgon placed the average land holding in Bulucheke sub-county at 1.4 hectares (Omara-Ojungu, 1977). Many areas in Kabale, Rukungiri, Mbale, and parts of Mengo, Masaka, Jinja and Iganga districts have families who own less than 1 hectare of land. This is accurate because by the 1970s, Langlands (1972) discovered that many areas in these districts had per capita landholding below the national average.

Where land shortage is a problem such as in Mbale and Kabale districts, land fragmentation poses the other drawback to agricultural productivity. The scattered plots are difficult to operate because they are small, distant and cannot be easily protected from agents of crop loss.

Land management issues in Uganda relate largely to problems of agricul-

Poverty and its resource management implications in developing countries

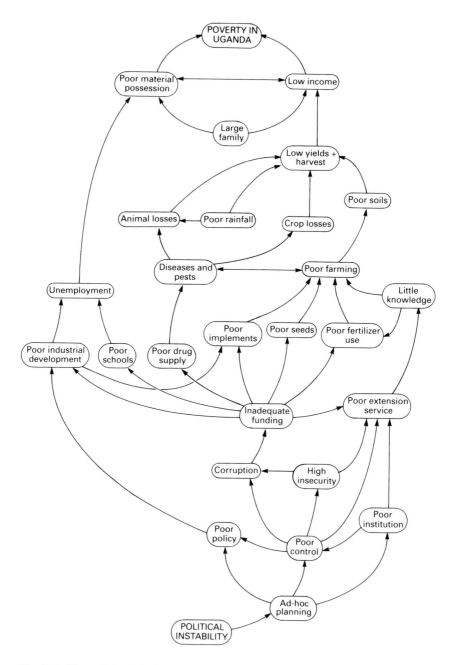

Fig. 3.4 The relationship between political instability, economy and poverty

tural productivity. In Uganda, agricultural areas can be divided into two groups:

1 Those in which a possibility still exists to extend areas under cultivation as in most parts of northern Uganda.
2 Areas where crop production requires new methods of farming because of high population pressures.

Between 1970 and 1980, the following trends seem to have occurred throughout Uganda:

1 A decline in agricultural production while population growth rate exceeded growth in agricultural production.
2 Stagnation in agricultural exports and in the 1970s a decline in food production.
3 A shift from local cereals to rice and maize flour, thus increasing external food dependency.
4 Displacement of traditional cash crops by potatoes, matoke, maize, pineapples.
5 Commercialization of traditional food crops (millet, pigeon peas, ground nuts).

Thus, a major issue of agricultural land is declining productivity. The causes of declining agricultural productivity include the following.

1 Little planning and research are devoted to deliberately improving agricultural production.
2 Misallocation of development investment where more funds are available for large-scale schemes (plantation, ranching). The smallholder farmer whose produce supports almost all other sectors of the economy continues to rely on family labour, soils, climate, rudimentary tools and personal initiative.
3 General neglect of the agricultural sector with exception of coffee, the main foreign currency earner.
4 Current marketing systems, inadequate and irregular supply of inputs and poor credit facilities seem to lower the incentive of farmers.

Livestock keeping

For a long time and especially since the livestock census in 1966, cattle were the most abundant livestock in Uganda. With increasing pressure from agriculture, the number of cattle has progressively declined throughout Uganda. Hamilton (1984) noted a significant increase in the pig population, especially after the 1970s. In Lira and Apach districts the poultry population has also increased. Several reasons account for the reduction in cattle population:

1 decrease in the area of grazing land

2 decline in the quality of pasture due to overgrazing and climatic aridity
3 re-emergence of diseases and cattle stealing which hitherto were brought under control
4 prolonged dry season and associated water shortage.

These trends are not healthy for areas such as Karamoja, where cattle is the major source of livelihood and in other areas where cattle provide the only buffer or insurance against poor crop harvest and galloping prices of goods.

The forest resources

Prior to the introduction of agriculture in Uganda, the whole of Lake Victoria Basin, the shoulders of the Western Rift Valley, and the high mountain regions were forested. The rest of Uganda had wooded savannah except in the drier regions of Karamoja, where thickets were dominant.

Ever since the introduction of agriculture, areas under natural forest have been on the retreat. The areas of natural forest and of government forest reserves have declined significantly (Hamilton, 1984). By the late 1980s the Ugandan landscape consisted of scattered tree species and a few government-owned forests. Forests have been destroyed by many agents such as the following:

1 Smallholding farmers in search for cultivation land, and building material.
2 Charcoal and brick-making activities.
3 In the 1960s large numbers of trees were also lost while eradicating tsetse flies and establishing ranches and plantation agriculture.
4 It is also possible that high concentration of elephants due to agricultural pressure may have caused massive tree destruction.

The overall reduction of tree cover has far-reaching environmental implications. Forests help to maintain soil fertility, prevent soil erosion and reduce climatic aridity by regulating water supply. The present droughty conditions must be partially a result of forest destruction. Furthermore, the destruction of forests and trees has created serious shortages in fuelwood and construction timber. As a result several other effects have ensued:

1 Distance travelled for fuelwood collection has increased.
2 In many places, dwelling houses have become smaller as building poles become scarce and much shorter in length.
3 In Kabale district, straws of sorghum and other crop residues are now used for fuel. This may lead to undercooking many foods and other associated health problems.

As the landscape loses its protective cover, soil erosion sets in and local wind speeds may increase so that buildings fall victims of gusty winds.

Water resources

Two significant changes have occurred in the water resource situation in Uganda since the early 1970s. These are changes in water supply for domestic use and changes in the fisheries industries.

Domestic water in Uganda is obtained from surface water in local depressions, lakes, swamps and rivers, and underground water. Many of the local depressions have become either filled with erosion sediments or are cultivated. The natural waterways to some of these depressions and man-made dams have been cultivated so that less than adequate water reaches these reservoirs. The result is that even the unsilted depressions can no longer hold water from one rainy season to the next. The shores of Lake Kyoga are so choked with erosion sediments that lake water is hardly accessible, except where there are rocky shores.

Many swamps are now reclaimed for the cultivation of rice, fruits and vegetables. It is possible that excessive loss of water from reclaimed swamps may accelerate the lowering of water tables so that wells and springs will dry out prematurely. All these developments have increased the distance travelled for collecting drinking water. As water becomes increasingly distant, water consumption per family is reduced and resticted to essential roles such as cooking and drinking. Domestic utensils and children may not be washed, thus posing important sanitation problems. Furthermore, many domestic livestock depend on family water. With water scarcity, poultry, goats and other animals begin to go without drinking water.

Fisheries

Research undertaken by Makerere University students and my personal survey of the fishing industry reveal the following:

1 Since 1980 the number of fishing vessels, nets and fishermen has substantially increased in Lakes Victoria, Kyoga, Albert and George.
2 There are already indications of over-fishing as evidenced by large numbers of young fish in a catch, decreasing volume of fish catch per day and gradual withdrawal from and abandonment of fishing villages.
3 The actual diversity of fish species in Lakes Kyoga and Victoria has been significantly reduced. Today the dominant species in Lake Kyoga are the Nile Perch and Tilapia. Because of the voracious nature of the Nile Perch, other fish species have retreated to the River Nile and are now fished from waters near the Lake Kyoga arms. In effect these are endangered species.

Although every resource has specific reasons for its present state, there are some general limitations which appear to have affected renewable resources of Uganda. In the mid-1960s when governments and organizations in developed countries were beginning to tackle environmental quality problems, Uganda was understandably more concerned with pressing needs for rapid economic growth, provision of better facilities, and conditions for education and health. Departments of agriculture, forestry and parks and wildlife undertook piecemeal conservation measures against soil erosion, deforestation and preservation of wildlife in Uganda's national parks. In the 1970s no plans were established to manage natural resources. In recent times Uganda is faced with fears associated with effects of widespread poverty, rapid deforestation, expansion of more arid conditions, accelerating erosion, decline in quality of grazing land, excessive fishing, water shortage and human encroachment into ever marginal and sensitive environments.

These problems are often blamed on rapid population growth. It is true that between 1959 and the early 1980s, Uganda's population doubled; being 6.5 million in 1959, 12.6 million in 1980 and over 13 million by 1985. It is also true that the high population growth rate of 2.6 per cent signals the danger of excessive demands on ever contracting resources and the need for family planning in Uganda. Figure 3.5 shows population distribution in the various districts of Uganda by 1980. The figure also shows that more than 30 per cent of Uganda has become crowded into population densities exceeding 200,000 km². High human numbers seem to present the pressure on resources when consumption patterns are not realistic and corruption is rampant.

The other cause of deteriorating resource quality and quantity in Uganda relates to lack of research and data for planning purposes. It is important for research to

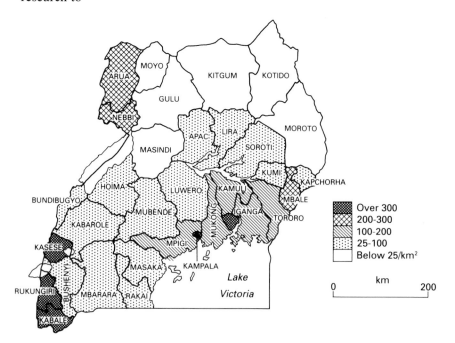

Fig. 3.5   Uganda: population density by district
   Source GEMS (1987)

1 map, survey and measure the supply and demand on renewable natural resources
2 determine alternative allocation of resources so as to identify the best place, time and function of a given resource
3 study effects of social, legal, ecological and technological factors on the utilization of resources
4 assess the impact of specific resource allocation decision (e.g. dams, industry and ranches).

In the absence of research, resources are easily abused, overutilized or even underutilized.

The effects of deteriorating resources seem to hit the rural communities most and reinforce poverty. Rural poverty in Uganda is caused largely by low productivity of resources. Unless the effects of low productivity are resolved, proper management of resources will remain low keyed, and appear unjustifiably costly or it may be seen as a conspiracy of the 'well-to-do' against the emergence of the rural community out of poverty. There is need today to transfer capital from urban to rural areas through job creation in rural industries, subsidies in costs of education, farm inputs, energy costs and re-orienting the job market so that less technical jobs are made available to the uneducated or less educated persons. These measures should be supplemented by promoting better standards of livestock keeping, fishing and other money-earning rural projects. Without greater inflow of capital into rural Uganda, poverty will continue to reduce the quality of labour force so that even simple resource management measures may become too cumbersome to undertake.

CHAPTER 4

Agricultural land management in developing countries

In the context of resource management, agriculture may be defined as the manipulation of ecosystem components in order to increase productivity of those elements which people require for the satisfaction of their wants. Crops, livestock, weather, soils and biological organisms are the primary ecosystem components which support agriculture. The actual manipulation of ecosystems involves combining appropriate weather, soil preparation methods, planting patterns, disease and pest control, weeding and harvesting time and methods, and genetic modifications of domestic plants and animals. It is implicit from this statement that the degree of ecosystem manipulation will vary from place to place and from one level of technology to another.

In order to satisfy human wants, agricultural systems must fulfil the following criteria:

1 *Productive*: yields in calories must exceed energy expended in raising crops.
2 *Qualitative*: produce must be nutritive enough to eliminate dietary ineffi-ciencies and diseases.
3 *Economic*: crop sales must cater to the financial and material needs.
4 *Stable*: yields must be dependable on a yearly basis so that food, industrial raw material, employment and income needs are met.
5 *Environmentally enhancing*: agricultural systems (cropping and grazing subsystems) must not result in insect plagues, disease epidemics, soil erosion and such forms of environmental deterioration as lowering water table, drought, surface water pollution, salinization, alkalinization and flooding.

These five criteria are most appropriate in assessing the quality and impact of agricultural systems in both the developed and developing countries.

Agricultural land in developing countries is the most important resource for almost all forms of development. In all countries, save mineral-rich countries, revenue from agriculture supports the establishment and expansion of industry, roads, health and educational facilities. In non-oil and mineral poor developing countries, agriculture accounts for over 50 per cent of the Gross National Product, 80 per cent of export earnings and 70 per cent of land underutilization. In addition, the livelihood of over 60 per cent of the population in developing countries relies on agriculture (World Bank, 1982a). Thus, in developing countries agriculture is most valued because

1 it contributes savings most needed for overall national development
2 it supplies food and industrial raw materials
3 it supports local purchasing power for manufactured goods
4 it provides employment and security against dietary inefficiences.

Figure 4.1 illustrates the contribution of agriculture to economic growth. The

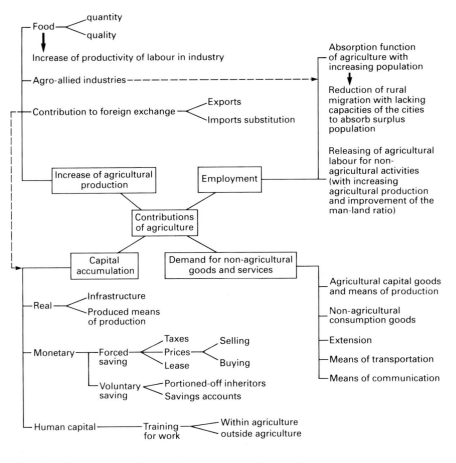

Fig. 4.1 Contribution of agriculture to economic growth
   Source Kuznetz (1964)

figure demonstrates that agriculture affects food supply, industry, trade, income, labour quality, employment, resource demands and consumption and rural–urban migration. As demonstrated in the rest of this book, agriculture influences critical intervention points for economic growth and development. Patterns and opportunities for agriculture in developing countries vary from place to place depending on weather, soils, technology, crop and animal diseases as well as on such socio-economic factors as pricing, marketing and development policies. As a result, it is difficult to paint accurately a general picture of agriculture in developing countries as a whole. However, from a short-term perspective one can say that agriculture in developing countries continues to rely on weather, soil conditions, and manual or non-mechanized labour. On a long-term basis, as discussed below, agricultural patterns appear to have evolved as a result of changing ecological and socio-political history. These factors together with effects of ever-rising population pressure are responsible for spatial and temporal variations in the character of agriculture in developing countries.

Table 4.1 shows past patterns of land use in five major regions of developing countries in 1965. During this period both arable land and permanent pasture occupied, on the average, 30 per cent of the total land area in each region. The table also indicates that agriculture in China, South and South East Asia, and in Near East and North Africa relied more on

Table 4.1 Past patterns of land use in developing countries by region, 1965

	China	South and South East Asia	Near East and North Africa	Africa south of Sahara	Latin America
Percentages of total land area					
Arable land	11	24	7	7	6
Permanent pasture	18	11	17	32	24
Forested land	8	35	5	27	48
Other	63	30	71	34	22
Total	100	100	100	100	100
Of which: potentially cultivable land		2	4	3	3
Irrigated land as percentage of arable land*	68	21	24	1	8
Area sown in a given year as percentage of arable land:					
Irrigated	147	110	75	100	75
Non-irrigated		95	50	40	50

Sources FAO (1965, 1970).
Note * Information from the FAO Yearbook (1965), Table 1. Only potentially cultivable land in countries specifying such land is included

irrigation than it did in Africa south of the Sahara and Latin America (this situation has not changed much). Since 1965, agriculture has expanded into marginal arable lands in almost every developing country. In many developing countries, agricultural characteristics have changed from

1 traditional labour intensive systems to increasingly capital and technology intensive (e.g. in Kenya, Zimbabwe, Thailand, parts of Sudan, Malaysia)
2 traditional long-fallow systems to little or no fallowing during intensive perennial cultivation
3 dependence on roots, tubers (cassava, sweet potatoes, arrow roots) and tree crops (coconuts, bananas, leaves, wild fruits) to dependence on seed (grain) crop cultivation (rice, millet, sorghum, wheat, coffee, cotton, etc.)
4 purely subsistence to dual subsistence and/or market-oriented farming.

Other broader changes in the nature of arable land and farming techniques are depicted in Table 4.2. According to this table, arable land in Africa south of the Sahara and Latin America increased by 24 per cent and 30 per cent respectively between 1962 and 1985. This was a much higher increase than in South East Asia (6 per cent) and the Near East and North Africa (11 per cent). Similar increases are seen in the area sown, irrigated and in the use of

Table 4.2 Changes in the nature of arable land and farming techniques

	South and South East Asia	Near East and North Africa	Africa south of Sahara	Latin America
Percentage increase of arable area, 1962–85	6	11	24	30
Area sown within a year as percentage of arable land				
1962	100	56	42	54
1985	121	64	52	60
Irrigated land as percentage of arable land				
1962	21	24	1	8
1985	32	26	1	10
Kilos of fertilizer per hectare sown (nutritive content)				
1962	6	11	1	12
1985	80	51	7	64
Number of tractors per 1,000 hectares sown (adjusted for differences in size)				
1962	0.4	1.7	0.3	5.0
1985	4.1	3.6	0.6	8.0

Sources FAO 1965, 1970

fertilizers and tractors. In general Africa south of the Sahara showed minimal growth in the application of irrigation, fertilizers and tractors.

These changes have taken place within the context of specific agricultural systems. In developing countries three main types of agricultural systems exist:

1 shifting cultivation
2 continuous rain-fed agricultural systems
3 irrigation agricultural systems.

Each system is analysed from the point of view of resource management.

Shifting cultivation

Shifting cultivation is one of the oldest methods of resource exploitation developed to replace hunting and gathering. It is a traditional resource management technique developed by pre-colonial communities in Africa, Asia and Latin America (Watters, 1971; FAO, 1957; Conklin, 1963). Although shifting cultivation has been called by various names (e.g. bush fallow, forest fallow, rotational bush fallow or semi-permanent cultivation), there is general agreement that it is characterized by

1 rotation of fields rather than crops
2 clearing by means of fire
3 little use of draft animal, manuring and capital
4 use of human labour mainly
5 short periods of occupancy alternating with long fallow period
6 use of simple tools (sticks and hoes)
7 emphasis on subsistence cropping
8 occasional but not always a shift of homesteads.

The term can therefore be used to denote a cultivation system in which the length of the fallow period exceeds the cultivation period. Ruthenberg (1971) associates shifting cultivation with a cultivation frequency of not more than 30 per cent. A cultivation frequency greater than 30 per cent therefore characterizes a semi-intensive to intensive rain-fed cropping system. Cultivation frequency is the length of the cropping phase in years divided by the total length of the cultivation cycle (crop years divided by fallow years) expressed as a percentage. According to Ruthenberg, permanent cropping has a cultivation frequency of 70 per cent. For example, in Northern Uganda by the 1960s, mixed cropping of cotton, beans and maize were being grown in the first year of forest clearance. The following year millet, peas and sesame were cultivated in the same plot. In the third year potatoes, sesame and ground nuts were cultivated after which the land was fallowed for up to five years. In this case, the cropping phase is three years followed by five years of fallowing. This gives a cultivation frequency of 60 per cent. According to Ruthenberg this is a semi-intensive cropping system. About the

1940s, fallow periods in Uganda would last up to ten years thus giving a cultivation frequency of 30 per cent which characterizes the shifting cultivation system.

In shifting cultivation, small patches of land are cleared out of secondary (usually) or primary forest, leaving the largest trees standing. Felled vegetation is burned at the onset of rains and the crops are planted with minimal soil preparation. However, today the use of ox-drawn ploughs in many parts of developing countries ensures a higher level of soil preparation. After one to three harvests the plot is abandoned and the site is allowed to regenerate its vegatative cover (FAO, 1957). The length of the fallow period varies depending on pressure on the land but in parts of Papua New Guinea fallow periods range between three and ten years. This is often too short a period to allow the regeneration of forest vegetation so post-fallow cultivation often takes place after bush rather than forest regeneration. Site abandonment is due to deteriorating soil productivity, weed build up or pest-epidemics. Due to longer fallow periods, shifting cultivation in the tropics engages twice the land area (33 million km²) used by temperate continuous cropping systems (Manshard, 1974) with much lower yields per hectare than in the temperate regions. This is one reason why a change from shifting to intensive cultivation is necessary to reduce land shortage or meet rising consumption demands due to population increase.

According to the National Research Council's estimate, in the 1980s shifting cultivation supported more than 240 million people in Africa, Asia and Latin America. These people live at or near subsistence levels (National Research Council, 1982). Shifting cultivators need large acreage of fallow land and the carrying capacity varies considerably according to technology, crop preferences and potential productivity of the land. Carrying capacity for shifting cultivation varies between a low of four through forty to two hundred people per km² in areas of high population densities (Manshard, 1974). In the past when population pressure was low and consumption per capita was less complex or minimal, every shifting cultivator possessed adequate land for his or her needs. Previously cultivated sites could be allowed sufficiently long fallow periods to permit forest regeneration and soil fertility restoration. Subsequent post-fallow firing would unlock additional large quantities of chemical nutrients stored in felled vegetation. Crop yields were therefore relatively high and sustainable. In this context, shifting cultivation was an appropriate technique of resource management.

Today the effects of expanding population pressure, consumption patterns and externally created market forces have exposed inherent limitations of shifting cultivation. In many parts of the developing countries, fallow periods have been reduced to less than five years (D. Brown, 1971). Such premature fallowing leads to low crop yields and soil erosion, plus persistence of pests, weeds and crop diseases. As a result, shifting cultivation has given way to more intensive and continuous cultivation in areas of high population densities. The attendant resource management problem is that the shift to intensive farming may become necessary before the cultivator has acquired appropriate skills for intensive farming. Changing to new techniques perceived as untested also creates uncertainty which ultimately affects agricultural production in a community (Chapter 5). One of the symptoms of such transitional uncertainty is the dualism between traditional methods and modern or 'foreign' methods of resource development (nomadic pastoralism vs. ranching or smallholder cultivation vs. mechanized plantation). In the dualism, traditional methods are seen as culturally and ecologically more appropriate. The argument for modern methods is the higher production levels associated with the use of farm machines, fertilizers, irrigation and higher yielding crop breeds. Shifting cultivation was therefore originally developed in a situation where labour rather than land was the limiting factor.

Environmental implications of shifting cultivation

The environmental impact of shifting cultivation results basically from the replacement of a closed and relatively stable vegetation by bare or cultivated ground. During the fallow period (pre-cultivation phase), perennial climax vegetation dominates as weeds and herbaceous annuals are suppressed almost to non-existence. In the post-fallow period, a crop community of relatively low biomass composed largely of annuals takes over the cultivated site. The burning and cultivation lead to rapid consumption and reduction of the ground litter layer, and a reduction in rate of mineral return to soil as less dead matter litters the soil surface. Because the cultivated landscape of grain crops and legumes resembles the savannah landscape, it is likely that the rate of soil mineral return in the savannah region deviates only slightly from pre-cultivation rates. This contrasts markedly with the larger reduction in post-fallow rates of mineral returns in a tropical rain forest. In time, however, there is a general decline in both organic and inorganic nutrients in the soil.

Several processes predate such ultimate decline in soil nutrients. Burning causes selective differentiation in soil nutrients. Norman (1976) found that due to burning in the tropics nearly all of the nitrogen and sulphur from the incinerated vegetation is lost to the atmosphere as oxides but that total amounts of phosphorus, potassium, calcium and magnesium tend to increase. Burning and cultivation further cause a replacement of the massive root system of the fallow period by a shallow and weak root system of the crops. All of these, together with effects of increased erosion as surface soil is exposed to rain splash and sheet flow, gradually deplete soil nutrients.

Land preparation and cultivation also create conditions favourable for the gradual proliferation of crop weeds, pests and diseases. Under pre-cultivation conditions, radiation levels of forests near the ground are low because of shading from canopy and other well-adapted undergrowth. In the savannah zone competition for light near the ground level is intense and the surface soil is fully dominated by the more aggressive grass species with well-

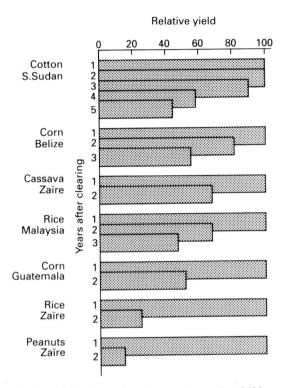

Fig. 4.2 Decline in yield with continued cropping under shifting cultivation in forest environments
Source Ruthenberg (1971)

developed roots. These conditions exclude weeds and other less competitive species from fallow land. After clearing, arable weeds which are more demanding of light, weakly competitive but with aggressive growth rates begin to invade the cultivated site. Norman (1976) noted that at the first cropping phase weed density is low but increases rapidly during the subsequent cropping phases. Early weed density may be due to effects of fallow vegetation roots before they ultimately decay away. In shifting cultivation often the same crop species or related species are repeatedly planted during the cultivation period. This raises the probability of an increase in specific crop weeds, pests and diseases over the period of cultivation.

These various factors contribute in varying proportions to gradual environmental deterioration and subsequent decline in crop yields with each new cultivation year. Figure 4.2 shows the decline in yield with continued cropping of various crops. Cotton in the Sudan shows a gradual decline from the first to the fifth year of cultivation while rice and peanuts in Zaïre and corn in Guatemala show drastic declines in yields within only two years of cultivation. From Figure 4.2 it is implicit that the length of the cropping period and shifting frequency may vary according to crop type and crop combination. For instance, in Malaysia reasonable yields of rice are possible even in the third year of cultivation while in Zaïre a much more significant decline in yields of rice occurs early by the second year of cultivation. Shifting cultivators adjust to pre-fallow decline in soil productivity by changing crop combinations and sequence of planting before finally shifting to rotate crop fields.

Management techniques under shifting cultivation

Many authors (Conklin, 1963; Norman 1976) state that in a shifting cultivation system the cropping patterns are complex with a varied assembly of crop species grown in a single cleared plot or by a single cultivator in one cropping season. Most likely this is true only in the tropical rain forest zone where high moisture, little seasonal variations in moisture and temperature and the high pre-cultivation soil fertility permit the growth of diverse crops. In his study of the Philippine rain forest, Conklin (1963) described one of the highest crop diversities within a single clearing. It seems that where moisture periods are short and levels low (as in parts of the savannah), or where soil fertility and temperatures (high altitude) are low, crop diversity is progressively reduced. For instance, monoculture occurs under shifting cultivation in the highlands of Mexico, South East Asia and Papua New Guinea where corn, upland rice and sweet potatoes are the dominant crops respectively (Norman, 1976).

Shifting cultivators, because of limited space in the cleared site, generally attempt to exploit microclimatic variations within a clearing. Natural or human-made mounds, beds, ridges, shades and sunny areas are each assigned a suitable crop species. The crop patterns thus reflect a near mimicry of the local natural environment based on a sound knowledge of that environment and of individual crop requirements. Such multiple cropping has the advantage of cushioning against effects of extreme climatic fluctuations (floods, droughts and disease outbreak). Multiple cropping is a labour-saving technique which also provides security against dietary deficiency. The Ngbaka people of the Central African Republic are known to grow a combination of sugar cane, sweet potatoes, manioc, maize, tobacco, sesame and groundnuts. These crops are further supplemented by fish, bushmeat, fruits and other wild leaves, thus boosting the nutritive value of local foods.

To undertake multiple cropping, the cultivator must be able to make assessments of

1 site (slope, weeds, local diseases, moisture, soil)
2 crop genotype, combination, sequence of planting
3 required length of fallow period.

The selection of crop combination and sequence of planting is particularly important as soil productivity declines progressively during subsequent

Table 4.3 Occurrence of crops in the first and final years of the cropping phase in shifting cultivation systems in Zaïre

	Forest fallow		Savannah fallow	
Crop	First crop	Last crop	First crop	Last crop
Bananas/plantains	44.1	16.7	0	2.7
Millets/sorghum	—	—	16.7	7.7
Corn	11.8	8.3	3.8	0
Cassava	8.4	41.7	3.2	36.2
Peanuts	—	—	14.3	5.0
Legumes	—	—	10.0	14.5
Yams	5.9	8.3	0	1.9
Sweet potatoes	—	—	7.4	5.0

Source Norman (1976)
Note Figures are percentages of number of observations made. Only the figures for first and last occurrence in one type of fallow for one crop may be compared

cultivation phases (Table 4.3). In Uganda the most important subsistence and cash crops of cotton, millet, coffee and bananas are planted in the first year of clearing when conditions are at their best. Towards the third year of cultivating a cleared site, crops such as cassava, sweet potatoes, peas and sesame, which are able to compete with weeds, and yield moderately well under poor soils, are grown. Cassava also suits the eve of land abandonment because it requires less weeding and it is often not the major food crop in the diet except during periods of bad weather or famine. Table 4.3 also shows how cassava and yams become dominant at the last cropping phases.

The appropriateness of shifting cultivation as a resource management technique therefore depends on controlled burning of a selected cultivation site, careful manipulation of cropping tactics, timely abandonment of the cultivation site and adequate length of the fallow period. In areas of low population densities and abundance of land, relatively high soil productivity can be sustained in the long run, especially amongst shifting cultivators outside the humid tropics. In the tropics, heavy leaching makes it difficult to sustain cultivation of soils without fallowing.

Continuous rain-fed agricultural systems

Numerous socio-economic pressures have forced a gradual change from shifting to sedentary continuous cultivation. In this section, the discussion is focused on the nature and resource management problems of continuous rainfed agricultural systems. For simplicity, all agricultural systems which depend on rainfall other than irrigation waters and whose cultivation frequencies range from 30 to 70 per cent are here grouped under continuous rain-fed agriculture. According to Ruthenberg (1971), a cultivation frequency of 30 per cent draws the line between shifting cultivation and semi-intensive rain-fed cropping while a frequency of 70 per cent is typical in permanent intensive rain-fed systems. In semi-intensive systems, a short fallow phase follows the cropping phase. However, the fallow period is often too short to produce any significant differences in natural soil nutrient regeneration between semi-intensive and permanent intensive rainfed systems. Hence both systems share the common feature of not relying on natural rates of biogeochemical nutrient restoration.

Continuous rain-fed agriculture is a system in which the fallow period ranges from less than five years to no fallowing at all. In developing countries continuous rain-fed systems are practised by over 30 per cent of the population where population densities range above eight people per sq. km. The system is widespread throughout the Third World, especially in densely populated areas such as the lowlands of South and South East Asia (India, Java, Malaya), pockets of dense settlements in northern Nigeria, the Lake Victoria Basin of East Africa, and the densely settled foothills of Elgon in Uganda and the Usambara mountains in Tanzania. In South America continuous rain-fed agriculture exists in the fertile valleys of the Andes (Okigbo and Greenland, 1977; Norman, 1976).

Although an apparent association exists between the emergence of continuous rain-fed agriculture and population growth, researchers seem to detect a chicken-and-egg problem regarding a causal relationship between the two. Boserup (1965) held the view that intensification of agriculture was a result of population increase rather than vice versa. However, many reciprocal events probably are responsible for agricultural intensification in developing countries: initially, population pressure and changes from simple to more complex consumption patterns caused the abandonment of shifting cultivation in favour of continuous rain-fed cultivation. As time passed, increasing emphasis on farming efficiency and subsequent sedentarization of settlements ultimately increased farm output and reduced fears of food shortages. Population growth thus began to depend on higher agricultural production, little outward migration of population and effects of improved health facilities. Other effects associated with application of compost manure and fertilizers, new land reform measures and farmer-incentive promotion also contributed in some degree to subsequent sustenance of continuous cropping systems.

Today continuous rain-fed agriculture in Africa, Asia and South America is characterized by

1 rotation of crops rather than crop fields
2 less than adequate fallow period
3 reduced crop diversity in each plot at any one time
4 increasing adherence to regular crop geometry (row cropping)
5 sedentary settlements especially in nucleated villages
6 some application of compost manure, fetilizer, mulching and other forms of soil conservation methods

7 clear-cut rather than selective logging in cultivated sites
8 increasing use of draft animal and tractor power
9 increasing emphasis on cash/export crops
10 smallholder farms operated by a family unit.

Continuous rain-fed agriculture is therefore a step away from shifting cultivation. It emerged in order to increase agricultural production so as to meet ever changing socio-economic demands involving exchange of commodities both within and outside national boundaries.

Issues and problems in rain-fed agricultural land management

Agricultural areas in developing countries may be divided into two groups

1 those in which the possibility still exists to extend the area under cultivation by opening up new areas, improving marketing and transport systems, extending irrigation and drainage systems
2 areas where crop production must depend on new methods of farming technology because high population pressures have caused increasing reduction in per capita landholdings.

It is in the first group that shifting cultivation is possible while high rates of population growth are rapidly absorbing many countries into the latter group.

The effects of population increase together with rapid changes in consumption patterns exert the most significant impact in every type of agricultural system in developing countries. In almost all developing countries population growth rates have exceeded growth in agricultural production since the mid-1970s (World Bank, 1983b). Under shifting cultivation systems, rapid increases in population lead to a reduction in fallow period and subsequent decline in soil fertility. High pressure on land plus inadequate fallowing transforms the ecosystems into a savannah-like system consisting of grass annuals plus some perennial grass and scrub vegetation. Such vegetation is incapable of withdrawing nutrients from deeper soil profiles nor can it return sufficient organic matter to the soil system. The result is a progressive decline in crop yields. In pastoral systems, high population leads to overgrazing and destructive potential of pastureland. Amongst the Karamojong and Turkhana pastoralists of East Africa, land shortage has created desperation for pastureland, leading to cattle theft and invasion of neighbouring cultivating communities.

Where continuous cultivation exists, increasing land pressure leads to intense subdivision and fragmentation of landholding. In almost all farming systems in developing countries, rapid population growth tends to lead to increasing costs of agricultural production and hence to widespread low productivity of these systems. Nash (1973) observed that as a result of increasing population within largely subsistent agricultural systems, grinding poverty, massive unemployment, drift to cities, and a pervading atmosphere

Table 4.4 Growth rates of agricultural production amongst some African countries, 1969–71 to 1977–9

4+	3–4	2–3	1–2	0–1	0
Kenya	Cameroon	Benin	Botswana	Ethiopia	Angola
Malawi	Ivory Coast	Burundi	Chad	Gabon	Congo
Swaziland	Rwanda	Central	Guinea-	Gambia	Ghana
		African	Bissau		
		Republic	Lesotho	Guinea	Mauritania
		Liberia	Madagascar	Somalia	Mozambique
		Upper Volta	Mali		Togo
		Zambia	Mauritius		Uganda
		Zimbabwe	Niger		
			Nigeria		
			Senegal		
			Sierra Leone		
			Sudan		
			Tanzania		
			Zaïre		

Source FAO (1980)
Note average annual growth rate in volume as a percentage

of unrest and irritation conducive to peasant risings, religious millennialism, and the empty-eyed apathy of those whose social circumstances make a mockery of hope.

Since the 1960s, the following trends became common amongst all agricultural systems of many developing countries.

1 There was a decline in growth rate of agricultural production and in the 1970s the population growth rate exceeded agricultural production. Table 4.4 shows the growth rates of agricultural production for some African countries. Most of these countries had annual population growth rates of 2.5 to 3.5 per cent. With the exception of Kenya, Malawi, Swaziland, Cameroon, Ivory Coast and Rawanda, the rest of the African countries registered less growth in agriculture than in population.

2 There was stagnation in agricultural exports so that the share in world trade with developing countries also declined. This created serious foreign currency shortage.

3 In the 1960s per capita production of food crop recorded encouraging increases but declined in the 1970s (World Bank, 1983a). As a result, commercial importation of food grains became rampant and competed with other essential commodities (medicine) for the already dwindling foreign currency reserves.

4 Especially in Africa, a shift occurred in consumption from local cereals to wheat and rice, thus increasing external food dependency. Although being increasingly grown locally in many developing countries, these crops

Table 4.5 Declining yields of continuous cropping in Nigeria

Five-year cropping period	Peanuts (kernels kg ha⁻¹)	Millet (grain kg ha⁻¹)	Sorghum (grain kg ha⁻¹)
1931–35	1 015	920	540
1936–40	785	455	330
1941–45	700	320	105
1946–50	320	545	90
1951–55	510	330	Discontinued

Note in the above experiment, manure was applied to other plots; its effect is discussed later.

require more labour and better techniques than the usual crops of millet, sorghum or maize (corn).

Declining agricultural production is the most serious problem in agricultural land management in developing countries. Trends in crop yields in many countries are similar to the situation shown in Table 4.5. This table indicates a decline in peanuts (50 per cent decline), millet (70 per cent decline) and sorghum (80 per cent) between 1931 and 1955 in continuous cropping systems in Nigeria. Much of the decline in crop yields is due to deterioration in soil productivity as most of the continuous cropping systems do not apply adequate manure and fetilizers. Table 4.6 shows the changes in soil chemical composition during ninety years of continuous cropping. The table indicates that within twelve years of cropping almost 30 per cent of organic matter is lost. Tables 4.5 and 4.6 emphasize the need for constant application of manure and fertilizers in order to sustain agricultural production at levels which will meet consumption demands and requirements for natural ecological resilience.

Table 4.6 Deterioration in soil chemical and physical conditions with time under semi-intensive cropping in Senegal

Duration of cropping period from original forest clearing (years)	Organic matter			Mean available soil water (%)	Cations (MEQ 100 g soil⁻¹)		
	Carbon (%)	Nitrogen (%)	C/N ratio		Ca	Mg	K
0	16.5	0.90	18.3	4.1	5.0	1.7	0.07
3	13.8	0.79	17.5	4.7	2.7	1.2	0.02
12	11.6	0.68	17.0	3.7	2.2	1.0	0.04
46	6.8	0.43	15.8	2.8	1.4	0.5	0.04
90	5.0	0.35	14.3	3.3	1.0	0.5	0.04

Source Mouttapa (1974) after Suban, no reference

Irrigation agricultural systems

On a global scale, irrigation systems evolved almost as early as agriculture itself. Irrigation emerged in response to situations where crop-water demand exceeded the supply of rain water. In ancient times human communities in the Tigris, Euphrates, Nile and the Hindu valleys sustained agriculture through irrigation of field crops. Today 10 per cent of the world's cultivated land is irrigated with the significance of irrigation in agriculture varying from country to country. Amongst the developing countries, 100 per cent of all cultivated land in Egypt is irrigated while in Peru 75 per cent, Iraq 45 per cent, Mexico 41 per cent and Pakistan 38 per cent of the cultivated land is irrigated (FAO, 1968). Almost all other countries of the Third World practise irrigation agriculture with the significance of irrigation gaining increasing importance in areas of erratic and/or inadequate rainfall. Especially in dryland farming countries, there has been a natural tendency for people to see in irrigation the best hope for improving agricultural production.

In this section, attention is focused on what an irrigation system is, its potential, performance and problems in the context of resource management in developing countries.

Definition of irrigation

The term 'irrigation' has been defined from various points of view but few definitions are clear and all-embracing. For instance, C. Clark (1970) defined irrigation as the application of water, by human agency, to assist the growth of crops and grass. This definition portrays a general picture without bringing to light the fact that in irrigation systems, inadequacy of rain or ground water makes water a more critical constraint on agricultural production than even land. In defining the word irrigation, comparisons should be made between supply and crop demand for water. This point was realized by Ruthenberg (1971) who defined irrigation as those practices that are adopted to supply water to an area where crops are grown, so as to reduce the length and frequency of the periods in which a lack of soil moisture is a limiting factor to plant growth. Although this definition is specific, it is still not all-embracing enough to cover key words which resource managers look for in irrigation. From the point of view of resource management, irrigation may be defined as a practice in which people deliberately supply water and store surplus water in a controlled manner so as to supplement rain or ground water and thus sustain or improve crop production in a cultivated field. This practice may take place in arid, semi-arid and even in humid areas. It is not accurate to conceive of irrigation as a practice unique to areas of general moisture deficit. Irrigation is practised in such humid areas as southern Uganda, Mexico and South East Asia to supply water at critical times during the plant-growth continuum. Sensitivity to crop-water requirements and adoption of irrigation helps to extend the cropping phase across drier seasons and thus to improve overall crop production and diversity.

Irrigation water may be obtained by

1 regulating the flow or damming of rivers and streams
2 pumping ground water through wells
3 direct withdrawal from natural stream flow

On the fields, water is supplied to the crop by flooding, spraying or by channels (canals). In developing countries irrigation is practised in both small- and large-scale farming systems. In smallholder farms, irrigation water may be supplied from farm or village reservoirs (e.g. Nigeria, South Africa, Cameroon, Mexico). In the Indian subcontinent, human or draft animal power together with simple mechanical devices (e.g. the Persian Wheel) are employed to withdraw water. Today, however, there is an increasing use of electric or internal combustion motors for pumping water especially into large-scale farming systems (sugar, tea plantations). Examples of large-scale irrigation systems are found in the Sudan (Gezira Scheme for cotton, sorghum, lubia bean), Kenya, South and South East Asia (major river basin programmes in the Ganges, Mekong in Thailand, the Irrawaddy supplying water for rice, sugar cane and upland crops). In India there also are several places which use tube well systems to supply water for a wide range of crops and livestock.

Issues and problems in irrigation agriculture

Since the Second World War, investment in irrigation projects in Africa, Asia and Latin America has been on the rise. During this period, growth in population and socio-economic pressures pushed agriculture into increasingly marginal lands. Especially in the savannah zone, high rates of evapotranspiration prevent rain-fed cropping in the many areas that receive less than 760 mm of annual rainfall. Large parts of the savannah are experiencing rapidly expanding agriculture. This shift together with increasing emphasis on better levels of farm production, forced many countries to invest in irrigation projects.

In developing countries, irrigation would provide a salvation as it is expected to

1 reduce crop-growth dependence on weather
2 reduce seasonal variations in crop yield, thus increasing overall production and supply reliability
3 support greater variety of crops
4 ensure a more intensive succession of crops.

According to the attitudes and actions of many governments, it seems as if there has been little grasp of the fact that supply of irrigation water is only one of the many prerequisites for agricultural development. This misunderstanding was soon to be demonstrated as irrigation projects began to fail in one place and succeed elsewhere. The Mubuku irrigation scheme in Uganda, the Perkerra, Wei Wei, Galole and Tavlota in Kenya and the Mbarali in Tanzania have all not recovered their costs (Chambers and Moris, 1973). In contrast, some of the projects in Mexico have demonstrated the important positive role of irrigation: only 0.5 per cent of all irrigated farm units produce 32 per cent of the total value of agricultural production, whereas 50 per cent of all rain-fed farms produce only 4 per cent of total agricultural value (Stavenhagen, 1969). Other cases of irrigation in Asia are discussed in Chapter 5.

The majority of irrigation projects involve large and costly structures such as diversion dams, storage reservoirs and canals. Because of their high costs, it is the state rather than individual farmers which finances and administers most of these projects in developing countries. These large structures tend to attract much political attention and their establishment often has been influenced more by political considerations than ecological and economic reasons. As a result many irrigation projects operate without adequate baseline data on stream flow regime, soil conditions, evapotranspiration rates, land capability, systems of local land tenure, and other social influences on innovation diffusion. The projects thus become islands with little or no co-ordination of their development plan with conservation of the watershed above the project and other irrigation-related services (research stations, seed farms). These drawbacks together with a host of other problems make it difficult for irrigation projects in developing countries to be fully productive. Kovda (1977) summarized four fundamental errors in planning and implementing irrigation projects in developing countries:

1 Disregard of the implications of the natural soil situation in each country, the level and quality of irrigation water, the salinity of the soil up to the ground water-table, and natural conditions of drainage.
2 Construction of shallow instead of deep drainage in order to reduce cost of irrigation projects.
3 Because of little control of water supply, there is often oversupply and flooding.
4 Little or no action taken to reduce water loss by seepage and evaporation from reservoirs, canals and crop fields.

The costly consequences of such problems have made irrigation agriculture in developing countries most inefficient. Garbrecht (1979) estimates that only 40 per cent of the diverted water actually reaches the crop field. Furthermore, not all the irrigated fields may be cropped and not all crops sown are harvested. As a result, potential irrigation water productivity does not always justify the cost of irrigation projects. Arnon (1981) illustrated the 'irrigation syndrome' with experiences from the Plain of the Punjab and the Sind region of West Pakistan. This area is drained by the Indus and its five tributaries. More than 70 per cent of the 30 million people there live on farming and only 50 per cent of the river flow is used to irrigate 90 million hectares. Despite the enormous potential for lucrative agriculture, the majority of people live in poverty and depend on imported food. Arnon (1981) attributed the problems to poor drainage, leading to waterlogging and salt accumulation in irrigated fields. Elsewhere in western Nigeria, Tanzania, Kenya, the Tigris and the Euphrates, the problems of poor irrigation management are compounded by poor land tenure systems and farming practices involving low-yielding seeds and no fertilization. As the canals lose water by seepage, less and less water is delivered to the field during each season. Because of under irrigation in the summer salinity problems are accelerated. In low rainfall climates, high evaporation rates and lack of thorough leaching may bring about undesirable accumulation of salts in the crop root zone. Conditions favouring salt accumulation include

1 high natural salt concentration in the groundwater
2 high salt concentration in irrigation water
3 inadequate supply of irrigation water so that little leaching occurs
4 hydrological conditions such as a high water table that retards or prevents leaching.

Periodic heavy irrigation is therefore necessary to leach away salt concentrated in the root zone. Indeed, development of high water tables and salinity has rendered inoperative even initially successful irrigation projects.

There are, however, some irrigation projects which have shown remarkable success and provide encouraging lessons for further investments in irrigation in other parts of the Third World. The Gezira irrigation scheme in the Sudan is a prime example of a successful project. In the Gezira and other successful projects, production efficiency is due to

1 well-organized production systems (crop selection, input supply, rigid adherence to planting, collecting and marketing schedules)
2 careful site selection and preparation (fertile soils, flat terrain, stable water supply)
3 strict social controls on settler farmers without curtailing individual initiative (land rental by family rather than ownership, additional land acquisition depending on performance in the existing farm)
4 rigid adherence to precise management controls (planting dates, recommended crops and farming techniques, continuous monitoring of projects)
5 farmer incentives and settler services (credit facilities, bonus for production, research station, seed farms, provision of fertilizers, pesticides, cultivation machinery and technical supervision).

In the successful projects, there is usually a steady rise in yield and an increase in area irrigated by each tenant. As a result, large numbers of settlers are supported by these projects. For instance the Gezira Scheme has some 70,000 settlers who farm over 720,000 hectares (Millikan and Hapgood, 1967). The other successful irrigation scheme with similar features is the Mwea Irrigation Scheme in Kenya (Arnon, 1981).

In summary, irrigation projects in developing countries often are still confronted with many problems. Their performance often is poor and cannot justify the heavy financial burdens they exert. There is no doubt that the size and scope of these projects present problems just as much as other social factors discourage investments in new irrigation projects. There seem to be brighter prospects in medium- or small-scale irrigation projects, especially when these draw on lessons from both the successful and unsuccessful projects.

The green revolution

Associated with the need for more efficient use of agricultural inputs and higher farm productivity is the term green revolution. The green revolution was launched in the 1960s in order to increase food production through more efficient use of water, fertilizers and hybrid crop seeds. Prior to the green revolution, several attempts had been made to increase crop yields among especially countries which were net importers of food grains. A major concern at the time was that varieties of maize, wheat and rice imported to developing countries fared poorly because of foreign soils, pests, diseases, climatic conditions and farming techniques. Even when fertilizers were applied to varieties of wheat and rice which had been grown traditionally in developing countries, the grain heads often became too heavy for the tall, spindly stalks thus causing the plants to fall over (Moran et al, 1986). The grains were therefore difficult to harvest and were vulnerable to spoilage and pests.

To promote the green revolution, crop geneticists, in the 1960s, helped to produce and propagate high-yielding varieties (hyv) of such cereals as wheat, rice, maize, millet and sorghum. The goal was to evolve hyvs which could mature faster than native varieties but which were also less vulnerable to local climatic conditions, diseases and more adaptable to a wider range of environmental conditions. The hyvs were cultivated in conjunction with more use of water and fertilizers in order to increase food production and undermine high costs and shortages of food in grain importing countries. In addition other international institutions such as the International Institute for Tropical Agriculture (IITA) in Ibadan, Nigeria established programmes to develop and improve indigenous tropical roots such as cassava, yams, sweet potatoes and aroids-taro.

By the early 1970s, the green revolution had produced some notable impacts in South America, Asia and Africa. In the 1960s, 90 per cent of the Mexican wheatland were planted with hyvs and average yields per hectare were doubled (Ojala, 1972). In Indonesia, hyv of rice was introduced in 1967. By 1969, 190,000 hectares were grown with hyv in the dry season and in the wet season of 1970/71, 306,000 hectares were under hyv. Throughout the developing countries, there was a general increase in areas planted to new varieties of wheat and rice. Considerable increase in yields of rice occurred in especially Asia. Some countries such as the Philippines attained self-sufficiency in rice within five years (Arnon, 1981). There was also a significant spread of hybrid maize in Africa and the rest of the Third World. However, in many countries, the spread of maize was slowed down because of poor seed supply. Other notable effects of the green revolution include improvements in farm income, employment prospects, nutrition and water use efficiency.

However, the green revolution has not been a total success. In most developing countries, a significant decline in per capita food supply has occurred since the mid-1970s. Worse still, the hyvs have displaced other traditional crops with higher nutritive value (e.g. fruits, vegetables, dairy products and high protein pulses). As a result food crop production in especially African countries has failed to meet the demands of a rapidly increasing population. The other problem is the high cost of production associated with hyv farming. Large supplies of fertilizers, efficient water management and considerable improvement in farming techniques are required to sustain the revolution. Arnon (1981) noted that the high volume of fertilizer used in hyv farming, in particular nitrogen, tends to increase the vulnerability of crops to a large variety of pests and diseases at all stages of crop growth. This leads to large inputs of chemicals for crop protection which ultimately increases overall cost of production per unit of land.

Although hyv farming in Asia caused a significant increase in the use of family and hired labour per unit of land, there has been a general decrease in labour efficiency per unit of output. In addition, advantages derived from the hyv farming accrued more to owners of farms than to tenant farmers and to owners of larger farms than of smaller farms.

In the few countries where the green revolution has been successful, the revolution became a catalyst of change. It led to agricultural modernization and improvements in rural standards of living. More inputs, increased use of mechanical power, improved techniques of farming (seed-bed preparation, accurate planting dates, spraying and judicious application of fertlizer) have all resulted in higher yields and income and more investments in industrial development. In most other countries, the revolution suffered set-backs and from the mid-1970s grain production either declined or became erratic, and the growth, that occurred prior to this period could no longer be sustained.

Causes and implications of declining agricultural productivity: a summary

The major issue in agricultural land management in developing countries is declining agricultural production and subsequent weakening of economic development potential. Between 1970 and the 1980s, several factors combined to cause significant constraints for agricultural development. During this period, industrial growth remained between 4 and 7 per cent, domestic saving grew by 3 per cent, the number of children in school grew by 4 per cent, and population growth rate averaged 3 per cent (Meier, 1984). The per capita demand of a fast growing population pushed total resource demand well above 3 per cent. As a result, many countries were turned from having an export surplus to an import situation regarding food. Because agricultural production has not kept pace with demands, a series of other problems, such as rural-urban influx, shortages of foreign currency, diseases, inefficiency in farming and development policy implementation, and low work-hour per head have grown. In addition, large human numbers have led to smaller non-economic farms, more landless people and lower output per head.

The other factor is that in many developing countries, the technological revolution in agriculture has only just begun. During the colonial period, research was confined to export commercial crops (rubber, coffee, cotton, cocoa). Even with food crops, research on exportable grains such as wheat, maize, and irrigated rice received more attention than subsistence crops of millet, non-irrigated rice, sorghum and sesame. During the post-colonial period, little planning and research were devoted to improve agricultural production. In many developing countries agricultural training and research remained conservative and elitist with premature emphasis on topics such as crop genetics and hybridization, agricultural mechanization for large-scale production systems, etc. It is not that these topics are unimportant in themselves but that they appear premature where such fundamental questions of location, quality and availability of agricultural land, effects of land tenure and reforms on agricultural production and spatial and temporal changes in crop demands have not been adequately addressed.

Two consequences are discernible from such an elitist approach:

1 even the most well-structured agricultural modernization proposal eventually fails to be implemented because of inadequate knowledge of land capability or of local response to new measures for agricultural modernization
2 a false impression is given that research is too new an innovation to be understood by everyone except the researchers themselves.

In Nigeria almost every major crop has been assigned a prestigious research institution within the last twenty years but agricultural production has not improved much (P. Adeniyi, 1984: personal communication). Even where such research undertakings are producing prolific information (as in Kenya), the actual findings are ploughed back more into government experimental farms and large-scale commercial establishments (plantations) than into the more widespread smallholder farms in rural areas.

Because of slow technological evolution and poor institutions and extension service, agricultural production in developing countries has remained most vulnerable to fluctuations in weather and disease epidemics. In the 1970s, climatic shifts leading to drought and poor rainfall patterns contributed to drastic declines in crop yields and famine devastated human life and settlement in the Sahel region of Africa. Countries such as Chad, Somalia, Ethiopia and parts of Kenya and Sudan frequently experience serious food shortages. The West Pokoth district of Kenya continues to rely on food relief supplied from other districts and church organizations within Kenya.

Furthermore, there is often a misallocation of development investment, with more funds provided for large government schemes (irrigation projects, ranching and plantation agriculture). The smallholder farmers whose produce supports almost all other sectors of the economy continue to rely on family labour, natural potentials of soils and climate, rudimentary farming tools and personal initiative (Chapter 3). Although the number of progressive and wealthier farmers has been on the rise since the 1970s, the greater bulk of agricultural production still comes from these relatively neglected farmers. Many of the government farms, established in the 1950s as demonstration centres, are badly in need of rehabilitation and modernization. These trends have reduced the prospects of expanding or setting extension service networks and have forced farmers in many countries to concentrate more on food crops for survival than on cash crops.

The problem of declining agricultural productivity became even more of a concern because of additional effects of disruptive wars and civil strife. Since the 1970s in many countries of Latin America, Africa and parts of Asia, effects of political instability due to *coups d'état* have deprived several communities of the opportunity to utilize capital and experiences accumulated over the years. These *coups* and associated new political outlooks and policies cause sudden discontinuity in resource development trends. In Uganda, the effects of political instability since 1972 turned back the clock and set Uganda back in its development by several years. The subsequent wars of 1979, 1985 and 1986 to the present time have resulted in little export production, off-season cropping in disturbed areas and widespread starvation and malnutrition.

But perhaps the worst drawback for agricultural productivity in developing countries is associated with poor terms of trade and inadequate incentives given to farmers: low official producer prices, uncertain marketing systems, inadequate and irregular supply of agricultural inputs, little participation especially of the rural farmer in decisions affecting agriculture and poor credit facilities for the farmer.

A review of twenty-seven agricultural projects undertaken by the World Bank (1980) noted the almost overriding importance of producer prices in affecting production outcome and production levels, often cutting across the quality of technical packages and extension services. Seven out of nine projects implemented under favourable prices achieved or surpassed their production objectives, 13 out of 18 under unfavourable prices failed to do so. In many developing countries producers receive only a fraction of the world market prices of major export crops. The larger fraction of the money goes to the national government as payments for export taxes, marketing board levies, and excessive marketing costs. These low prices discouraged further expansion of farm produce and contributed to the limited share of the Third World in global markets. Prices of food crops are also low. In many developing countries Produce Marketing Boards legally control the basic price of foodstuffs. Governments therefore set and regulate consumer prices. Because of urban-biased policy-makers, prices of imported wheat and rice are becoming steadily cheaper than domestic staples (World Bank, 1983a). In many countries this has presented problems for sales of locally produced cereals (millet, sorghum, maize).

The other reason for declining productivity is inadequate and irregular supply of agricultural inputs. In spite of government subsidies, agricultural inputs continue to be overpriced, in short supply and unaffordable by many farmers in developing countries. The inadequate supply of inputs comes about because currencies in developing countries are so devalued that governments find it difficult to raise sufficient local currency to pay for importing large quantities of inputs. Because of subsequent high demand and import effects of a devalued currency, costs of inputs often remain sky high. As a result it is often the government, rather than the private sector, which procures and distributes agricultural inputs (Table 4.7). It is probable that better supply conditions are possible if private individuals play a greater role in procuring agricultural inputs. At least individuals do not have to wait for government budgeting and allocation, all of which often suffer from cumbersome bureaucracy. All these drawbacks make it difficult for farmers in developing countries to increase production beyond subsistence levels.

Even where subsistence production is widely preferred, the average family still usually suffers from nutritional deficiencies in calories, proteins and vitamins. In the pre-harvest period in Kenya, 25–30 per cent of the rural families consume less than 60 per cent of the estimated needed calorie requirements and over 25 per cent of the children suffer from some form of malnutrition (World Bank, 1975). Undernutrition and malnutrition are important causes of low labour productivity in developing countries. 'An avoidance of effort is the body's natural defence mechanism when suffering from under or malnutrition' (Arnon, 1981: 8). Furthermore, it seems that

Table 4.7 Relative frequency of government and private sector control in the procurement and distribution of agricultural inputs in thirty-nine countries

Item	Percentage of countries			
	Fertilizer supply	Seed supply	Chemicals supply	Farm equipment supply
Government control	64	61	47	42
Private sector control	11	11	17	22
Mixed government and private sector involvement	25	28	36	36
Total	100	100	100	100

Source World Bank data files

traditional feeding composition and style can no longer sustain the greater vigour and endurance required in today's labour (whether as a farmer or factory worker). This is probably why many researchers have reported declining labour productivity in developing countries.

The same disappointing picture is also true of commercial production for cash. By the end of the 1970s, agricultural exports were less than during the 1960s. In the 1970s export production in Africa decreased by 1.9 per cent in comparison to production in the 1960s (World Bank, 1983b). This is a serious situation because in many developing countries production for export accounts for the bulk of commercial agriculture. Furthermore export crops are the major source of foreign currency used for the purchase of all imported inputs vital to the overall economy. With the exception of mineral-rich developing countries, commodities such as coffee, cotton, tea, sisal, rubber and cocoa account for over 75 per cent of the total value of exports (McPherson, 1968). What is worrisome is that many developing countries still rely on a single crop or a narrow crop range for their foreign exchange earnings. Arnon (1981) observed that in Chad cotton accounts for 80 per cent of the country's exports, in Ghana, cocoa accounts for 60 per cent of exports, in Gambia and Senegal ground-nuts account for 90 per cent of exports and in Malaya rubber accounts for 60 per cent of exports. In most of West Africa and Latin America, three commodities account for 90 per cent of their exports. All these make the overall economy of developing countries highly vulnerable to fluctuations in weather, market prices and crop disease epidemics.

The effects of low agricultural productivity and poverty make it exceedingly difficult for a farmer to think beyond mere survival. Yet increasing pressure on land under poor farming techniques continues to set the stage for environmental deterioration. The most common problems under all agricultural systems in developing countries are increasing run-off erosion, weeds, crop pests and diseases, and fuelwood shortage. As consumption pressures cause the extension of the cropping phase and a shortening of the fallow period, run-off erosion becomes a major factor in declining crop yields. Under continuous rain-fed systems, the soil surface remains exposed to arable conditions for the main part of the year. A number of ecological changes take place. Pereira et al. (1967) noted that infiltration capacity of soils in Kenya decreases with increasing periods of cultivation. According to his measurements, infiltration decreases to 94 per cent after one year of cultivation and to 75 per cent after four years of cultivation under continuous cropping. Poor infiltration leaves excessive run-off water which enhances dangers of soil loss.

Agricultural systems in developing countries therefore require techniques that can handle both problems of water retention and soil loss. Research at the International Institute of Tropical Agriculture in Nigeria recommends surface mulching as an effective technique for conserving moisture and reducing soil loss in the humid tropics. Throughout the humid Lake Victoria

Basin of East Africa and in the Mount Kenya Region (Chapter 5), mulching (using banana leaves and fibre, coffee husks and other crop residues) is widely practised. Norman (1976) has cautioned, however, that mulching may not be effective in drier regions where in any case the mulch material is scarce. Research is still required to provide a comprehensive appraisal of techniques already in use such as contour bunds, terraces, graded furrows, agroforestry and several cropping techniques. Because little attention is given by extension workers to promote these techniques, farmers tend to adopt a technique only in areas where a land shortage problem is acute rather than as a day-to-day prelude to sustained crop production.

Many farmers in densely populated areas of developing countries have relatively small landholdings, often under 3 hectares. In a number of cases the holdings are scattered or fragmented. Furthermore, land is often communally owned and traditional land inheritance systems do not give enough leverage and security to a farmer. These factors make it difficult for 'a progressive farmer' or government to invest in programmes that would stimulate higher production without prior institution of new land reform measures.

As indicated in Chapter 7, land reform is one of the neglected measures in agricultural development in developing countries. Calls for land reforms come up repeatedly without being responded to. This may imply that governments in developing countries do not appreciate the positive claims made about land reforms. Perhaps recommendations for land reforms would appear more practical and attractive if, in addition to the items in Chapter 7, a land reform package incorporated credit facilities, provision of agricultural inputs, extension services and improvements in rural infrastructure. In this way, agricultural production will be perceived as a commercial investment.

Finally, declining agricultural productivity has a direct effect on industrial development because both agriculture and industry complement each other. Poor agricultural output means insufficient raw materials and underdeveloped markets for manufactured goods. In the end, import substitution policies will fail because industries cannot adequately supply manufactured goods for the nation. It is therefore imperative to increase complementarity rather than competition between agriculture and industry.

CHAPTER 5

Resource management in mountainous environments of the tropics

Introduction

The recent times have witnessed a growing dependence of many countries on mountain resources. In industrialized nations, the reason for the rapid shift of emphasis is similar to what Hart (1968: 1) said of Britain:

> As more and more of lowland Britain disappears beneath bricks and mortar, steel and concrete, tarmac and asphalt, so the upland areas, underpopulated and underdeveloped, must gain greater importance both for the physical and for the spiritual nourishment of the people.

In developing countries, expansion of resource use into mountain slopes is a result of declining productivity of previous agricultural lands and rising population and socio-economic pressure from within and outside the mountain regions.

But the new demands on mountain resources are ill-timed in many parts of the world. For a long time resource development in mountainous regions received only marginal concern from governments and researchers. Even within the field of resource management, mountain ecosystems are often treated with only passing remarks. As a result, significant and often irreversible environmental deterioration has occurred in many mountain regions.

Several reasons account for the relative neglect of mountain ecosystems. Especially in Africa, there has been a long-standing tradition which associates mountains with danger, catastrophism and the supernatural. The Bagisu and the Lango people of Uganda, the larger Kikuyu ethnic group of Kenya, the Chagga of Tanzania and several other tribes in Africa attribute the origin of their tribes to ancestors who lived in caves in mountain peaks. Similarly, the early Greek culture, the Christian religions (Noah's flood and Mount Ararat and Moses and the Ten Commandments on Mount Sinai) and Eastern Buddhism all identified mountains with scenes for supernatural events. These myths together with the catastrophic nature of mountain geomorphological processes (snow avalanches, landslides, earthquakes) and the relatively detached locations of many mountain regions, helped to reinforce scepticism about human habitation of mountains.

The other reason for the neglect is the long-standing dualism between the principles of resource conservation and economic growth. Until late in the 1960s in developed countries and the 1980s in developing countries, conservation was considered the antithesis to the revered economic growth. As a result, it was difficult to extend appropriate resource management measures to areas considered peripheral to core resource use areas in lowlands. Other such marginal areas as marshlands, coastal zones and semi-desert fringes were also mostly neglected until the 1970s.

The apparent lack of attention left many mountain ecosystems with a paucity of data, sketchy and scattered literature and severe effects of soil erosion, landslides, floods, sedimentation of bottomlands, deteriorating water quality, outward migration and farmland abandonment.

The purpose of this chapter is to describe the relationship between mountain ecodynamics and resource development and management. It surveys resource management experiences in various parts of the developing countries and focuses on Mount Kenya to provide an insight into the impact of colonial systems on resource development in developing countries.

Resource management implications of mountain ecological dynamics

Biologists, ecologists, soil scientists, biogeographers, geologists, hydrologists, geomorphologists and climatologists have made contributions regarding mountain ecological dynamics. Their findings have provided an interdisciplinary treatment by helping to identify the biophysical components and to analyse the functional linkages in mountain ecosystems. The analysis and subsequent findings have important implications for resource management. In this section, temperate and tropical mountain ecosystems are compared.

A general impression from the literature is that unlike in lowlands, the stability of mountain ecosystems is vulnerable to even slight disturbances. Effects of altitude, slope angle and aspect, climatic variability and location of most mountains within zones of high seismic risk all converge to predispose mountain ecosystems to sudden and sometimes catastrophic reactions to changes which otherwise are safer in lowlands. It is largely because of this vulnerability and because of rugged topography, thin and poor soils, cool and variable climates, isolation and inaccessibility that mountainous environments should be considered 'sensitive', 'harsh' or 'economically marginal'. Otherwise, several other lowland ecosystems (karst, coastal zones, semi-arid and deserts) possess less resource development potential but the relative stability of their biophysical conditions permits reliable resource exploitation, albeit in minimal supply. Thus individual limiting factors as well as their general sensitivity make mountainous environments economically marginal.

In the broader context of resource management, the situation is worsened if the mountain ecosystem is isolated and inaccessible as the human community therein becomes further marginalized due to their limited power in the decision-making process. These generalizations can be illustrated further by considering the details of mountain ecodynamics.

Morphology and mountain ecodynamics

Both morphology and climatic conditions play a leading role in shaping the relationships amongst mountain ecosystem components and elements. Ultimately, the characteristics of mountain morphology and climate distinguish mountainous environments from other terrestrial environments. Mountain ecosystems are much more dominated by effects of altitude, relief, and slope aspect as these factors influence the characteristics of climate, soils, and flora and fauna.

In the context of resource management, altitude is a measure of the degree of air rarefaction and of gravitational energy. Air rarefaction results from the vertical decrease of air pressure with increasing elevation. The decrease in air pressure reduces the oxygen and water vapour content of the air, thus setting a potential limitation on moisture supply and expansion of human settlement upslope. Under low levels of oxygen, normal functioning of human physiology is possible only if the density of red blood corpuscles is increased above the normal level. Furthermore, in rarified air, insolation is intense and the heat is pricking thus causing discomfort whenever there is direct solar radiation on to the human body.

The other effect of altitude is on gravitational energy distribution. Acting through high relief, altitude provides a source of energy which accelerates the rate of denudation and makes mountain ecosystems high energy systems whose slopes become most vulnerable to disturbance. Hewitt (1972) noted that the vigour of geomorphic processes depends most directly on relief and distribution of slope angles. Peak heights, their distribution and slope angles are directly associated with infiltration and erosion rates (Cooke and Doornkamp, 1974; Caine, 1974; Dingwall, 1972; Rapp and Stormquist, 1976). Peak heights and slope angles have also been associated with floral and faunal distribution on mountain slopes (Troll, 1972). These studies attribute the complex differentiation between biological communities on mountain slopes to the topographic features. The steepest slopes and mountain peaks are often sparsely vegetated with stunted trees and grass. It is important to note that the relative significance of morphological features varies among mountain regions. For instance in glaciated mountains sharp contrasts exist in morphological features as wide u-shaped valleys, ridges, cirques, and aretes form common scenery. In these mountains, bare rock surfaces are common on the higher and more steep slopes while in the lower and less steep slopes, glacial deposition and weathering produce a relatively thick sediment overburden. Where glaciation has occurred to a limited extent such as in many tropical mountains, topographic features are relatively limited and less varied. For instance, the valleys in the Ruwenzori (Uganda), Kilimanjaro (Tanzania) and Mount Kenya (Kenya) and other tropical mountains tend to be confined and narrow. Topographic features of tropical mountains therefore are often dominated by contrasts between narrow valleys and mountain plateaux, between steep cliffs or slopes and gentle slopes. Because of such topographic restrictions and poorly developed flood plains, even large mountain ranges such as the Ruwenzoris have not attracted much intramontane valley settlements.

Relief and slope angles underly the causes and concentration of rapid mass movements on certain slopes. Rapid mass movements are prevalent in deeply weathered slopes of 20° to 40° (Gardner, 1970; Rapp and Stormquist, 1976; Selby, 1976). Of particular significance to resource use is the effect of slope on rates of erosion:

> Water velocity is about doubled when the slope (expressed as a percentage) is quadrupled. Doubling the velocity of water increases its erosive or cutting capacity four times and increases the size of particle it can roll or push along 84 times. (Rutter, 1968: 2)

L. G. Leopold et al (1964:359) also noted that slope erosion reaches a maximum at 40° and decreases to zero as steepness approaches 90°. Topographic effects of steep cliffs and presence of gorges provide hostile and costly conditions for construction of transport routes, agricultural extension, human settlement and other resource use practices. In the Elgon mountains (Uganda), the least steep slopes are reserved for cultivation while grazing and forestry occur on the more precipitous slopes (Omara-Ojungu, 1978). In the other mountain regions of south-west Uganda, parts of the Andes and the Himalayas as well as many steep areas of the Kenya and Drakensberg Highlands, slopes are modified by terracing in order to support cultivation and soil moisture conservation.

Slope length is another variable often associated with erosion. The rate of erosion is said to increase with length of slope because greater volume of water accumulates on long slopes, thereby increasing velocity (L. G. Leopold et al, 1964; Cooke and Doornkamp, 1974). It seems, however, that several factors combine to induce erosion and slope length may not play a significant role in some cases. Hence, Rutter (1968) pointed out that rainfall intensity, soil properties, vegetation cover and slope steepness may change with slope length thus diminishing any effect the added length may have.

The other variables in slope morphology which are significant for resource management are aspect and topographic shading. In the northern hemisphere, south-facing slopes intercept more solar energy per unit area. The reverse is the case in the southern hemisphere. There is, however, some doubt as to whether differential energy distribution due to slope aspect exists on slopes in equatorial regions where overhead sun is normal. In equatorial regions, slope aspect exerts influence especially on moisture bearing winds

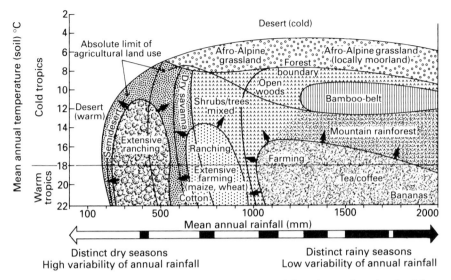

Fig. 5.1 Ecological diversity and land use potential and practices in the Mount Kenya region
Source Winiger (1986)

(rain shadow effects). As discussed below, in Mount Kenya the southern and eastern slopes are wetter than the northern and western slopes. Through differential energy and moisture distribution, slope aspect and topographic shading affect flora and fauna distribution, microclimate, soil development, geomorphic processes and ultimately the dependent resource use practices (Figure 5.1). For instance, Scargill (1975: 10) found in the European Alps that greater resource use concentration is in the south-facing slopes and that during emigration 'slopes facing north have been deserted over larger tracts'.

The dynamics of mountain climate

Climatic conditions in the mountainous environments are a product of great contrasts in the complex interaction of altitude and slope exposure with prevailing sources of heat and moisture. It is generally accepted that climatic change with altitude in mountainous regions is similar to the horizontal climatic change from equator towards the poles. Hitherto this viewpoint provided a traditional conceptual framework for the study of mountain climates (Miller, 1961).

To conceptualize mountain climate as simple replicas of horizontal or latitudinal bioclimatic changes raises the danger of simplifying and ignoring the complex, variable and unique climatic conditions caused by variations in intramontane features. For instance, the characteristic feature of insolation in the polar zone is the long summer day of oblique sunshine through thick atmosphere while the feature of insolation in alpine climate is the intensity of sunshine through a thin or rarefied and often clear atmosphere. In describing mountain climate, distinctions have to be drawn between macro, meso and micro-scale features in order to introduce the vertical changes that dominate mountain climatic characteristics.

Mountain climates are characterized by extremes of spatial and temporal variability of heat and moisture (Hewitt, 1972). At a macro-scale, climatic characteristics of mountains are determined primarily by

1 latitude
2 coastal or continental location
3 location in relation to tracks of the transient major air masses.

Latitude determines particularly the solar radiation (length of day). Higher latitudes are cooler with larger annual variation in solar radiation than lower latitudes. For instance, the Rocky Mountains of south-western Alberta, Canada, exhibit variations in daylight hours from eight hours in late December to more than sixteen hours in late June (Kananaskis Pilot Study, 1974). In Alberta, such variations together with Alberta's continental location contribute strongly to the cold winters, much warmer summers and to the short transition period characteristic of the region (Longley, 1972). The Rocky Mountains in Alberta lie in close proximity to the source of Arctic air

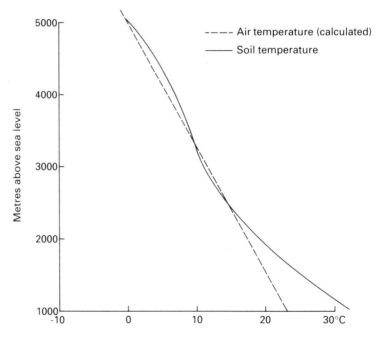

Fig. 5.2 Air and soil temperatures on Mount Kenya in relation to elevation
    Source after Winiger (1981)

masses and the region therefore experiences outbreaks of cold, transient high pressure cells from the north, especially between November and March. During spring and summer, the region comes under the influence of the eastward-moving extratropical cyclones and in late spring precipitation in south-western Alberta reaches its maximum.

At a macro-scale, regional differences in climatic conditions are important considerations in mountainous environments. It is generally accepted that both temperate and tropical mountains are characterized by a relatively regular decrease in temperature with increasing elevation (Figure 5.2). However, important differences occur when annual temperature conditions are considered. For instance, tropical mountains tend to have isothermal climate with little, if any, marked differences in temperature between summer and winter or between wet and dry seasons of any one year. As a result, plant growth and resource development in the tropics can be continuous throughout the year and at various elevation levels up to the snowline (5,000m near the equator).

In contrast, temperate mountains show marked seasonality in temperatures (differences between the summers and winters). The result is rapid deterioration in conditions for resource use from season to season and from one altitude level to another. For instance, Monheim (1974) found that in the European Alps the growing period decreases by six or seven days for every 100m increase in elevation. Frost therefore becomes of significant concern to resource users as frost occurrence limits the length of growing season for cultivators and livestock farmers.

Precipitation conditions are more difficult to generalize. Both tropical and temperate mountains are thought to be characterized by an increase in precipitation with increasing altitude (Figure 5.3). Tropical mountains receive much of their precipitation in the form of rain. In the tropics there is an alternation of dry and wet season, the latter involves heavy rainfall and sometimes short-lived thunderstorms. The dry season, because of its associated heat, reduces vegetation cover and causes soil tension cracks and promotes bush or forest fires. Because the effects of the dry season precede the rainy season, soils either become pulverized or cracked and severe erosion and landsliding become potentially widespread problems on tropical slopes. Thus in the tropics, seasonality in precipitation becomes a critical factor in slope stability considerations.

The morpho-climatic conditions outlined above produce spatial variations in resource use across mountain regions (Figure 5.1). In temperate zones, most of the population lives in the mountain forelands and generally in relatively lower slopes (Monheim, 1974). In tropical mountains, resource use is possible even in higher elevations of inner mountains because of better climatic conditions. Monheim (1974) found that population density was highest between 2,500m and 3,000m in the Peruvian Andes. In Ethiopia and other parts of the Andes, dense settlements are found even where extensive mountain plateaux rise above the tree line. In the Andes, the lower slopes of

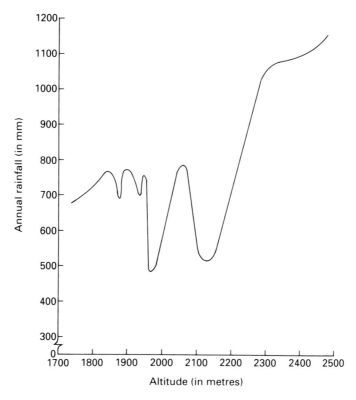

Fig. 5.3 Relationship between precipitation and elevation in the Mount Kenya region
Source Data from Mount Kenya weather stations (1969–81)

the forelands are covered by dense tropical forest which are often disease ridden and only sparsely settled.

On a relatively small scale (meso or micro), sometimes the effects of local factors can be greater than those of latitude, relative continentality and transient air masses. In this case, spatial and temporal variations in heat and moisture arise from differences in altitude, especially as it exerts a vertical effect on air pressure.

As indicated earlier, air pressure decreases with altitude. However, the decrease in air pressure per se is of less significance to resource use than the fact that the phenomenon of mountain climate is a direct function of air rarefaction. The vertical decrease in air pressure reduces absolute humidity and both Hewitt (1972) and Miller (1961) state that more than half of the earth's water vapour exists below 2,500m above sea level. Both of them attribute the droughty conditions above 2,200m to this vertical decrease in humidity. As pressure decreases with altitude, the air becomes increasingly ineffective in absorbing the sun's radiation and in holding water vapour. Insolation is thus intensified above 2,200m. Low humidity in high elevations plus high wind velocity may support rapid spreads of fires once they are started.

Because of orographic effects, precipitation is generally known to increase with altitude. It seems, however, that this is possible only up to the upper limit of high pressure in many mountain regions. Hewitt (1972) and Miller (1961) noted that above 2,200m precipitation begins to decrease with altitude.

Of particular importance to resource users is the effectiveness of that precipitation. Temperature and winds affect rates of evaporation and evapo-transpiration which in turn affect soil moisture balance. Average wind velocity increases with altitude and so does evaporation potential (Miller, 1961; Hewitt, 1972). All these combine to produce more humid conditions in the lower slopes than in higher altitudes (Winiger, 1986).

The macro and meso scale (spatial and temporal) climatic variability is further complicated by micro-scale effects of aspect, local topographic variations, cloud cover, vegetation density, small water bodies, soil effects on radiation, turbulence of valley winds, temperature and moisture. Micro climatic characteristics are often not analysed because of inadequate data. In mountainous environments, micro-scale factors have such effective influences that significant differences in climatic conditions occur within small areas. As a result, a linear relationship between altitude and climatic variables may exist only when mean rather than absolute values are considered. It is therefore inappropriate to expect precipitation to increase or temperature to decrease always with increasing elevations (Figure 5.3). For instance, topo-graphic shading at lower elevations may cause more chilling temperatures than temperatures at higher or even similar elevations elsewhere. The passage of cloud cover cuts out sunshine and produces sudden chilling temperatures and as the clouds open to sunshine intense insolation results in pricking heat within minutes.

Climatic condition is one of the most important biophysical components which set limits on the type and intensity of resource use. In steep slopes, moisture from precipitation and snowmelt together with available soil sedi-ment provide for erosion by overland flow and rapid mass wasting. In deeply weathered slopes in different climates, both high intensity rains of short duration and prolonged low intensity rains cause rapid mass movements (Rapp and Stormquist, 1976; Selby, 1976; Blong and Dunkerley, 1976). Such mass movements can be readily accelerated by human use of resources (Sharpe, 1960; Eckholm, 1975; Cooke and Doornkamp, 1974).

Frost is another feature of mountain climate when temperatures remain at or below 0°C. High altitude depressions in valley floors and locations protected from winds are particularly susceptible to frosts. Frosts affect resource use as length of growing season is reduced. When heavy snow accumulation occurs, some resource practices (e.g. livestock grazing) are simply brought to a halt. Snow effects are most pronounced when avalanches occur. Because snow avalanche tends to recur on the same site year after year, it keeps vegetation in such areas in a permanently immature state.

Soils in mountainous environments

Mountain soils are distributed largely according to topography, climate and vegetation zones. Because of gravitational pull, oversteep slopes have little or no soil except at their base where alluvial fans or cones may develop. Such slopes with thin soils, or with freshly weathered debris and new moraines, have poor resource potential and vegetation development is limited to lichens, mosses and tussock grasses especially in higher elevations. On moderate slopes, thicker soils are more common towards the base than on the slope crests where mass wasting and erosion affect soil accumulation. Higher elevations tend to have thin soils due to the fact that biochemical changes by soil organisms are most sensitive to temperature as well as moisture (Brady, 1974). Therefore, areas of low moisture, low temperatures and subsequently poor vegetation will have thin soils. In reverse, this statement implies that soil forming processes are more active at lower than higher elevations. In the higher and less vegetated slopes, frost shattering, rockfalls and colluvium development are more active while in lower slopes landslides, slumps and erosion assume greater significance because of deeper soils (Omara-Ojungu, 1980). This is a significant observation because it is in the lower slopes, such as the foothills of most tropical mountains, where resource use and human settlement are often concentrated.

Because of high relief and moisture due to orographic effects, soil erosion is a fundamental concern amongst mountain communities. In general, practices such as cultivation, grazing, logging, and road construction increase the dangers of erosion and mass wasting on mountain slopes (Eckholm, 1975; Kollmannsperger, 1977).

Effects of forest removal are well documented. Bishop and Stevens (1964), Swanston and Dyrness (1973) and Eckholm (1975) have all attributed the increasing incidence of soil erosion and landslides to forest removal. However, careful analysis seems to indicate that forest removal plays only an indirect role in inducing rapid mass movements. For instance, Blong and Dunkerley (1976) found that landslides in the Razorback area of Australia predate clearing of forests. Similar findings had earlier been made by O'Loughlin (1972), Csallany et al (1972) and Meeham et al (1969).

Forest removal reduces infiltration capacity which subsequently increases run-off and subaerial erosion. This assertion is supported by Selby (1976) who found that in the South Auckland District, New Zealand, infiltration rates into forest soils are three to four times as great as those into grassland soils. The consequences of decreased infiltration and increased run-off must lead to lower soil saturation rates and soil stability on slopes. There is also a possible decrease in overburden pressure due to lower biomass resulting from conversion from forest to grass. The logical consequences of these events

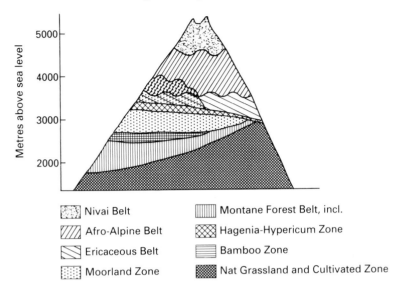

Fig. 5.4   Vegetation belts and zones
             Sources Lind and Morrison (1974); Trapnell et al (1976)

must increase slope stability after forest removal. Since forest removal per se is often not accompanied by landslides, it is logical to contend that effects of root decay on infiltration and soil anchorage are either inadequate for stimulating slides or are counteracted by combined effects of lower overburden pressure and sometimes rapid weed and grass regeneration following sudden exposure of soils to solar heat. Root decay, in any case, is a slow process.

The argument that forest removal accelerates mass movements holds only when other practices such as anthropogenic slope overburden and excavations for building and road construction complement the effects of channels left by decaying roots, reduced soil anchorage and possible increases in infiltration rates where soil tension cracks develop after forest removal.

Biota patterns in mountains

In mountainous environments, patterns of vegetation in each mosaic are determined primarily by moisture, temperature and soil conditions. Consequently, mountain vegetation zones change according to altitude and topography. Vegetation zones tend to form horizontal belts which are occasionally interrupted by interfingering due to river valleys and linear topographic (ridges) alignments (Figure 5.4). Other factors which complicate community arrangements include slope aspect, slope angle, location in respect to paths of storm and moisture-bearing winds, distance from the sea and overall size of a mountain range. These factors cause significant changes in community types within small areas and make floral patterns in mountains significantly complex and different from those in lowlands (Figure 5.1). Towards the base of mountains it is possible for hybridization to occur between lowland and alpine communities. Studies of species composition on the Elgon mountains in Uganda indicate higher species diversity in the lower slopes and foothill than on higher slopes and in surrounding lowland (Omara-Ojungu, 1978).

In the Mount Kenya region, however, drier conditions contribute to poor vegetation development in the lower slopes. Between 1,976m and 2,736m above sea level, average rainfall is about 1,154mm except in the eastern slopes where up to 2,308mm of rain is received. The lower slopes especially in the north-west are dominated by the coarse Manyatta grass (*Eleusine Jaegeri*), the Kikuyu grass (*Pennisetum Clandestinum*) and wire grass (*Pennisetum Schimperi*). Forest development is more significant on the wetter eastern slopes. Above (2,700m) but below (3,600m), the bamboo and forest communities become dominant. As indicated in Figures 5.1 and 5.4, actual altitudinal limits of these zones vary according to slope aspects and in relation to the effects of moisture-bearing winds.

Faunal patterns show a close relationship with vegetation zones and therefore with topographic variations. In general, animal size tends to decline with increasing elevation. The Afro-Alpine sections of the Elgon, the Aberdares and Mount Kenya are inhabited by rodents, tree and rock hyraxes, alpine lizards, rats and some duickers. Birds are relatively more numerous in the alpine zone (black ducks, owls, eagles, sunbirds, etc. abound). Below the alpine zone through the bamboo zone to lower elevations duickers, warthogs, rhinoceroses, buffaloes and elephants roam the mountain slopes as well as the surrounding lowlands.

Implications for resource management

The analysis of ecological dynamics has indicated that mountain ecosystems are characterized by *complexity, variability* and *vulnerability* in their component relationships. Such ecosystem states have important implications for resource management and they distinguish mountains from other terrestrial ecosystems.

For instance, most of the problems of resource development arise because mountainous environments exhibit extreme variability in morphology, climate and ecological conditions. Topographic variability makes accessibility and isolation a prime consideration amongst mountain communities. Yet morpho-climatic conditions are such that diversity of lifeforms, habitats and ecological zones change within short distances. One effect of this is to leave mountain ecosystems with more diverse resource potential than a similar areal unit in lowlands (Figure 5.1).

Diversity of land use opportunities in its turn generates other problems such as

1 high prospects for resource use conflicts due to the juxtaposition of incompatible resources (Figure 5.1)
2 proliferation of resource development agencies and their subsequent competition for jurisdictional powers
3 the need for co-ordination of different interest groups (forestry, wildlife, livestock, agriculture) so that overlap and duplication of functions are minimized.

Variability in biophysical conditions creates generally harsh conditions for resource use and raises management costs above average rates in lowlands. In many mountainous regions, extreme fluctuations in weather have been associated with relatively high frequencies of valley floods, landslides and slumps, severe soil erosion, snow storms, forest fires and snow avalanches. Furthermore, the horizontal alignment of ecological zones corresponds with resource use patterns and contrasts significantly with the vertical flow of materials during erosion, landslide and snow avalanches. Such material flow may transverse different land use systems and aggravate conflicts between upslope and downslope users, hence reinforcing the need for effective co-ordination of resource development in mountains.

The relative vulnerability of mountain ecosystems is further worsened if the slope geology is composed of young and weak thrust-faulted surface bedrock, as is the case for many major mountain ranges of the world. Such slopes will have high risk from seismic damage and tremor-triggered landslides. The thrust-faulted slope will also be most vulnerable to effects of such relatively high-impact activities as dam construction, underground mining, highway construction and quarrying and underground construction for urban storage and transportation systems. On such slopes, land-use zoning is needed in order to differentiate between high and low risk areas.

Because of complexity, variability and vulnerability of mountain ecosystems, careful management has to be adopted. In general, resource management must be guided by a sensitive (responsive) and restorative approach. Careful selection of place and time is required for allocation of resources. The nature of mountain ecosystems requires many small management units (even to the level of first-order stream basins) in order to monitor efficiently trends and effects of resource development. However, such a large number of management units may not only raise personnel costs but also entrench the problem of co-ordinating diverse interest groups. It is also possible that too many levels of management may lead to overmanagement or management overkill.

Resource development and management in mountainous environments

Mountainous environments of the tropics have experienced resource use for many centuries. According to McIntyre (1973), the Inca civilization in the

Andes is known to have existed earlier than the fifteenth century. Most of the tropical and sub-tropical mountain slopes have been under human use for over 300 years (Peattie, 1936; Ogot, 1968). However, relative to lowlands, resource development started late in mountainous environments of the tropics. There is a general consensus that human expansion into mountains was a response to social stress within the traditional settlement areas in lowlands.

During the pre-industrial (pre-colonial) period, mountains were perceived as difficult and relatively uninhabitable because of

1 cold climates and extensive snow cover at higher altitudes
2 steep slopes, rugged topography and thin and poor soils
3 isolation and inaccessibility
4 high altitude, air rarefaction and decreasing oxygen content of air
5 devastating landslides, floods, earthquakes and severe natural erosion
6 traditional anti-mountain myths and tales.

Such perception was reinforced by poor technological development and inability to explore the truth about mountains and their resource potential.

However, as social pressure in lowlands accumulated, mountains began to be valued because of

1 abundance of defensible locations
2 effective refuge
3 opportunities for agriculture, pastoralism, timber and minerals.

In Nigeria, the East African Highlands, Papua New Guinea, the Philippines and Mexican hills, inter-ethnic warfare pushed weaker tribes from lowlands into upslope refuges (Moss, 1963; Ogot, 1968; Waddell, 1972). It is also possible that human expansion into the Atlas mountains of Algeria, the Pre-European Kenya Highlands and the Ulluguru mountains of Tanzania was due to droughty conditions in the neighbouring lowlands.

These early mountain settlements were created largely through the process of internal colonization. During the pre-industrial period, isolation and inaccessibility were the principal influences on the lives of mountain people. Because of inaccessibility, many mountain communities became relatively more self-reliant and less dependent on external trade. A money economy was weak. Resource activities were labour intensive with major practices being subsistence agriculture, pastoralism and logging.

With the advance of industrialization and importation of technology from Western Europe into the developing countries, mountain resources became increasingly valuable for commercial purposes. Deterrent factors of isolation and inaccessibility had to be tackled. In the Andes, Nepal, Mount Kenya and the Bundibugyo area of the Ruwenzori mountains in Uganda, communication routes were opened to facilitate migration into and out of the mountain regions. The routes, together with the institutionalized system of maintaining law and order (courts and police patrols), brought about increased interaction between lowland and mountain communities. The industrial (colonial) period therefore witnessed greater expansion of commercial farming, logging, livestock keeping, mining, hydroelectric power development, conservation of water and forests and some recreation and wilderness preservation.

Developments during the pre-colonial and colonial periods led to the establishment of numerous resource practices in some of the settled tropical mountain regions. Improvements in medical facilities lowered human mortality rates and population pressure mounted, especially in the Andes, Nepal, Kenya Highlands, Kilimanjaro foothills, and the Elgon mountains. In recent times, an environmental crisis has arisen in some of these densely settled mountain slopes. The crisis is characterized by

1 increasing incidence of severe erosion, devastating landslides and flood hazards
2 high population pressure, land shortage and fragmentation
3 increased awareness amongst mountain communities of their limited political power and general 'backwardness'
4 inadequate social services
5 outward migration and increasing proportion of elderly people in the mountain population structure
6 relatively marginal economic performance and land-use conflicts.

The relative impact of those problems varies from one mountain region to another. There are indeed mountain regions (the Ruwenzori, Mount Kenya and the Highlands of Papua New Guinea) where such a crisis is not yet evident and opportunity still exists for further resource development. But in Nepal, Peru, Bolivia and to a lesser extent the Elgon and Bufumbiro mountains of Uganda, resource exploitation has exceeded the carrying capacity of the land. For instance, Eckholm (1975: 769) summarized environmental deterioration in some tropical and subtropical mountains thus:

On the basis of already available knowledge, it is no exaggeration to suggest that many mountain regions could pass a point of no return within the next two or three decades.

In an extreme case, Turnbull (1972) described the way that environmental stress, leading to severe food shortage and malnutrition, has dehumanized the IK tribe of Southern Sudan, causing total loss of even maternal feeling for the young.

The rather gloomy picture depicted by Eckholm and Turnbull and in some mountain regions of developing countries has arisen because of widespread application of a *laissez-faire* approach to resource management. In many settled slopes of tropical mountains, traditional systems of resource development have persisted without much government intervention or regulation. Many of these systems are simple with little inbuilt measures for resource conservation and low capacity for large-scale production to meet increasing resource demands. This is made worse by the fact that the relationships among biophysical components (which affect slope stability and resource potential) are poorly understood by many mountain communities. With the exception of general policies for forest, soils and wildlife conservation, governments in developing countries have not formulated policies exclusively for mountain ecosystem exploitation. Occasional concern for watershed preservation prompts creation of forest reserves in higher elevations while the lower slopes continue to be developed with little or no government intervention.

In the next section of this chapter, an attempt is made to discuss some of the features and problems of resource development in selected mountain regions of Asia and Kenya. Positive aspects of resource development in these areas could be shared or form a base for rectifying resource development problems elsewhere. Because of poor information, only the salient features of resource development in the mountain regions of Asia are discussed.

Resource development and management in the mountain regions of Asia

In relation to mountain regions of Africa and other developing countries, some mountain regions of Asia have incorporated the Western system of resource management into their traditional systems of resource development. In the western Himalayan region, Nepal, Uttar Pradesh (India) and South East Asia attempts have been made to manage mountain resources with additional use of foreign technology, ideas and expertise.

An examination of various development programmes in mountain regions of Asia shows the application of two basic approaches. The first approach involves projects perceived for and confined to local areas. Such projects are relatively limited in scope and areal coverage. The second approach consists of multipurpose projects whose scope and areal coverage are broad enough to reinforce overall regional development. The first approach is illustrated by describing the Mandi Project while the Mekong Valley Project will substantiate the nature of the second approach.

The Mandi Project

Mandi is a hill state in India in the western Himalayas. The project was established in the early 1960s as an agronomic and animal husbandry scheme with the following objectives:

1 to improve existing subsistence agriculture
2 to change the peasant economy from subsistence to cash crop
3 to rationalize agricultural production to suit ecological zones between 600m and 2,800m elevations.

A German team of 'specialists', an Indian team and funds controlled by the state Development Commissioner were employed. Methods adopted to achieve the above objectives included:

1 activation of agricultural extension service
2 introduction of improved technology
3 provision and improvement of infrastructure and services for agriculture
4 provision of fertilizer, animal drought equipment, soil conservation and dairying.

The Mandi Project was managed within the context of the state's overall development plan, with infrastructure development for roads, rural electricity, transport, education and health. The overall management of the project emphasized participation of local representatives with high-level management control left to the German team.

Between 1961 and 1972, sharp rises in the consumption of fertilizer, increased cereal production and improved agricultural implements were notable consequences of the Mandi Project. However, during this period the population of the project district rose from 384,000 in 1961 to 515,000 in 1971. As a result of an increased population, per capita consumption increased only marginally from 0.21 tonnes to 0.24 tonnes over the decade, despite the doubling of rice and wheat production (UNEP, 1982a). Instances of landslides and slumps became more frequent as settlement density increased near badly constructed major roads. But a cash crop economy gained increasing acceptance amongst the community.

The Mekong Valley Project

The Mekong River has one of the largest basins in the world. The river rises from the eastern slopes of the Himalaya mountains and traverses some of the poorest areas in developing countries. The economy is characterized by low agricultural productivity, low income per capita and rural poverty. The riparian countries of the lower Mekong (Thailand, Laos and Cambodia), where the project is located, have a high annual population growth rate of 2 per cent. The population in these countries is expected to grow from about 120 million to 160 million by the year 2000. Presently the population is predominantly rural with about 80 per cent of the labour force engaged in agriculture, forestry, fisheries and small game hunting (World Resources Institute, 1988).

The Mekong Valley Project is the most extensive upland project in Asia. It is international in concept and scope and its administration and objectives are duplicates of the Tennessee Valley Authority (TVA). The Mekong Valley Project is multipurpose and covers electricity, irrigation, agriculture, flood control, drainage, navigation improvement, and watershed management in various states in the Mekong River basin.

Much of the development is concentrated in the downstream portion of the Mekong River areas (UNEP, 1982a). Even in these areas scientific management is still lacking to adequately regulate waterflow, reduce sediment load and ensure environmental protection. The enormous scale of the project has made it difficult to provide adequate staff, organization and funds. In addition the general war atmosphere of East Asia hinders professional and governmental efforts in developmental programmes.

In evaluating the various projects in mountain regions of Asia, the FAO noted some common features in the regions where the projects were established.

1 universal lack of data on precipitation, run-off, sedimentation, hydrology, land capability and land-use patterns
2 widespread subsistence agriculture with low peasant incomes
3 high population pressures and increasing deforestation and soil erosion
4 poor accessibility and bad road construction in the past leading to severely eroded hillsides
5 no vocational education on agriculture, animal husbandry, soil conservation and watershed management.

For the projects themselves, the following appear to be the major limitations:

1 resource allocation and management not necessarily based on land capability or prior knowledge of local community needs
2 strong emphasis on economic considerations without ecological considerations or concerns for management institutions to ensure appropriate management
3 lack of an ongoing research to monitor environmental consequences of the projects
4 The Mekong and many other projects have too many organizational levels with insufficient communication with the local people and little co-ordination amongst the various sub-levels.
5 The Mekong Valley Project is too large and multi-state a venture to be properly managed with the limited finance and management capabilities of the South Asia region
6 The ongoing military conflicts make co-operation and co-ordination almost impossible.

The projects in these mountain regions exhibit some of the common concerns about development projects in developing countries. In most cases economic considerations overwhelm other aspects as emphasis is laid on economic growth and in social services development. The Mandi and Mekong Valley Projects both lack management programmes backed by adequate research, knowledge of land-use potentials, well-organized administrative institutions, and adequate planning. Above all, the two projects illustrate the danger of importing technology and applying it without adequate respect to local situations, including the nature of the institutions.

Ecological relationships and resource development in Mount Kenya

Mount Kenya is a mass of tertiary volcanics with a diameter of about 80 km. It rises from an elevation of 1,500m a.s.l. (above sea level) in the surrounding plains to over 5,000m a.s.l. It is situated directly on the equator, 150 km north of Nairobi and within one of the most densely settled regions in Africa.

Climate

Like other mountain regions, the climate of Mount Kenya is dominated by effects of altitude, slope aspect, location on the equator and in relation to trade winds (south-east and north-east trades), and the relative position of the inter-tropical convergence zone.

Temperatures generally show little seasonal variation, usually less than 3°C (Griffith, 1972). However, there are marked variations in diurnal temperatures arising from the passage of clouds and changes from day to night. Night temperatures of below 5°C are common (personal observation, 1989). Spatial variations in temperatures are due to altitude, slope aspect and exposure.

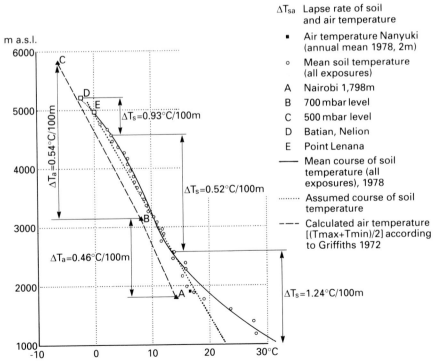

Fig. 5.5 Relationship between free atmosphere, calculated air temperature and soil temperatures in Mount Kenya altitudinal profile
Source Winiger (1986)

109

Several authors have demonstrated temperature variability by studying subsoil temperatures. Winiger (1986) noted that within a depth of 70 cm, there are small seasonal variations in soil temperatures but large spatial variations due to altitude (Figure 5.5). According to him, lapse rates change with elevation. At the footzones there is a much more rapid decrease of soil temperatures at a lapse rate of 1.5°C/100m. In the middle altitude zones (Afro-Montane and Afro-Alpine belts), the lapse rate is about 0.5°C/100m. Towards the mountain peak, the lapse rate is 1.0°C/100m. Such temperature variability is due to effects of vegetation cover, radiation, air temperatures, topography, soil type and soil moisture. The southern and eastern slopes of Mount Kenya are cooler than the western and northern slopes.

Rainfall on Mount Kenya is also affected by altitude and slope aspect.

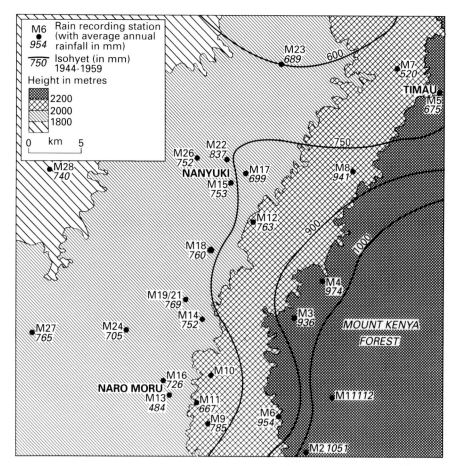

Fig. 5.6 Spatial relationship between rainfall and altitude in Mount Kenya region
Source Records from fifteen weather stations in north-west zones of Mount Kenya

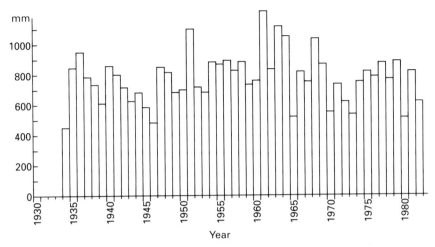

Fig. 5.7   Temporal variability in rainfall on Mount Kenya (1934–82)
Source Rainfall records of weather stations in Mount Kenya region

According to Thompson (1966), Coe (1967), Winiger (1986), and my personal observations in March, April and June 1989, the southern and eastern slopes of Mount Kenya receive much higher rainfall (averaging 2,300 mm) than the north and western slopes (averaging 1,200 mm). The southeast trade winds are responsible for the higher rainfall in the windward south and east-facing slopes. Winiger (1986) further noted spatial variations in the zone of maximum rainfall where in the eastern slopes maximum rainfall occurs in the foothills but the zone rises to 2,500m in the south and 3,000m in the west. Above 3,000m, rainfall begins to decrease with increasing elevation. This finding supports the earlier assertion by Hewitt (1972) that above 2,200m a.s.l., mountain precipitation begins to decrease with increasing altitude.

Figures 5.3, 5.6 and 5.7 show spatial and temporal variability in rainfall. The fifteen weather stations from which data for figures 5.3 and 5.6 were obtained are all located in the semi-arid north-west foothills of Mount Kenya. These two figures show significant variations in annual rainfall within small distances while figure 5.7 shows yearly variability within the forty-nine-year period (1934–82). These variabilities, as mentioned earlier, exert significant influences on ecological and resource development conditions (Figure 5.1).

Ecological zonations in Mount Kenya

Ecological conditions in Mount Kenya are characterized by complexity, variability and vulnerability. In the more marginal areas in the drier foothills to the north and west, there are extensive grasslands with acacia and sclerophyllous bush while the higher and cold elevations in the moorland are

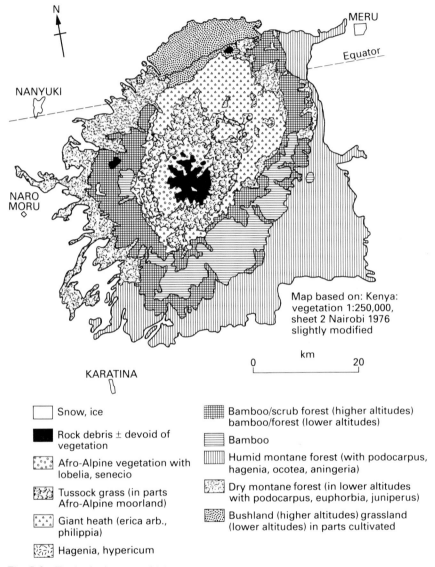

Map based on: Kenya:
vegetation 1:250,000,
sheet 2 Nairobi 1976
slightly modified

km

0   20

☐ Snow, ice

■ Rock debris ± devoid of
vegetation

Afro-Alpine vegetation with
lobelia, senecio

Tussock grass (in parts
Afro-Alpine moorland)

Giant heath (erica arb.,
philippia)

Hagenia, hypericum

Bamboo/scrub forest (higher altitudes)
bamboo/forest (lower altitudes)

Bamboo

Humid montane forest (with podocarpus,
hagenia, ocotea, aningeria)

Dry montane forest (in lower altitudes
with podocarpus, euphorbia, juniperus)

Bushland (higher altitudes) grassland
(lower altitudes) in parts cultivated

Fig. 5.8 Ecological zones of Mount Kenya
Source Winiger (1986)

covered with tussock grass. As indicated in Figures 5.4 and 5.8, the middle
and lower slopes have zonations of Ericaceous, Hagenia-Hypericum,
bamboo, Podocarpus and euphorbia species. Climate, topography and slope
aspect are the main factors which cause complexity in ecological zonations.
As a result, ecological zones and the resulting resource use practices vary
within short distances (Figure 5.1). From Figure 5.1, differences in land use

practices between the north and west and south and east-facing slopes are discernible.

Forest management in Mount Kenya

The forest reserves on Mount Kenya are subject to regulations that govern all the other forest reserves of the country (3 per cent of Kenya's land surface). Forest development in Kenya is based on the principle of multiple land use with three major objectives:

1 To offer maximum forest protection to the catchment areas of the country. Much of Kenya is semi-arid and there is a strong demand to guarantee the supply of water through effective watershed management. In the Mount Kenya watershed, protection has been effectively executed. Since 1932, only 2 per cent of the forest area has been excised for agriculture and human settlement (Winiger, 1986).
2 To improve and sustain the productivity of forests as a source of timber and woodfuel. This has involved replacement of indigenous forest species with a plantation forest of softwood species of exotic pine and cypress. In Mount Kenya, by 1976 the plantation forest had covered 15–20 per cent of the western slopes but only 0.1 per cent of the eastern slopes.
3 To conserve areas of particular scenic value and public interest. In Mount Kenya during 1968 areas of tourist attraction were excised from the forest reserve to form part of the National Park in order to preserve the indigenous forest species.

In general, the forest zone lies approximately between 2,000m and 3,300m a.s.l. Much of the forest of Mount Kenya exists above the limit of the agricultural zone at 2,800m a.s.l. The forest zone is composed of species of indigenous trees (natural forest), and exotic species (plantation forest) which gradually grade into the bamboo and Hagenia-Hypericum zone about 2,800m a.s.l.

The forest belt falls under the Mount Kenya Forest Reserve which was established in 1932 and covers an area of 1,800 km² (445,000 acres). Since the establishment of the Forest Reserve and strict government control, there has been little modification of the forest boundary although agricultural pressure is right to the boundary line. The encroachment beyond the forest boundary for settlement and agriculture has been a response to political changes in Kenya, especially after independence in 1963.

In the early 1950s, white settlers demanded more land for residential and agricultural settlement. Some fifteen excisions were gazetted in 1950–51 in the western and north-western margins of the Forest Reserve. Other significant changes in the forest boundary took place after independence in 1963. During the struggle for independence, the indigenous Kenyans were promised some land as a reward for participation in and the success of the Mau Mau war of independence. Between 1965 and 1969, parts of the south-western forests were converted to settlement schemes. Up to 30,000 landless families were settled on smallholder farms. In some of these settlement schemes, the government encouraged the growing of tea on a small scale by the African farmers. On the whole, only 1 per cent of the forest reserve has been excised since independence.

Within the forest reserve, there were two categories of forest: Protective and Productive. *Protective forests* are situated in areas vital for watershed and soil conservation. This includes forest on higher and steep slopes and along river courses. Protective forests are entirely composed of indigenous species and exploitation for timber is prohibited.

Productive forest occurs in areas set aside for timber production. In such areas the management policy is to replace indigenous forest species with plantations of exotic cypress and pine. Productive forest on Mount Kenya is managed on the basis of three interdependent stages:

1 exploitation stage
2 cultivation stage
3 re-afforestation stage

Exploitation stage

The forest department designates and maps an area for exploitation. Licences which specify the extent and duration of exploitation are issued to exploiters for timber, charcoal and firewood. The forest officers at the local forest department stations supervise the operation of licensees. Clear-cut logging is the accepted method of timber harvest.

Cultivation stage

After exploiting the forest products by licensees (sawmillers, individuals, etc.), the clear-cut area is then subdivided into small plots and allocated to the landless forest department employees. A maximum of 6 hectares is allocated to an employee. The forest land is then cultivated under the following regulations:

1 Cultivation should last for up to two years.
2 No perennial crops or animals or permanent structures (houses, fences) are allowed.
3 The cultivated area must be properly cleared of bush and shrub without using much burning.
4 Growing of maize and potatoes is recommended.
5 The temporary landowners are allowed to sell their produce to generate personal income.
6 As employees of the Forest Station, the temporary squatters are required to re-afforest the area after a two-year period.

Re-afforestation stage

The forest department stations raise seedlings of exotic species (dominated by *Cypresses Lusitanica*) and the temporary squatters plant them. Some crops are allowed to be grown in the early re-afforestation period in order to check weed growth. After one year, neither cultivation nor livestock grazing is allowed in the re-afforested area.

Implications of the forest management policy

By the 1960s, large areas of indigenous forests were replaced by exotic softwoods (Figure 5.9). Several problems have resulted, however, from the Mount Kenya forest management policy:

1 Rapid rise in demand for licences as population pressure builds up in the surrounding lowlands.
2 It has become increasingly difficult over the years to remove temporary squatters. In some cases the squatters gradually invite their family members and lay claim (backed by political connections) over the forest land, thus affecting the re-afforestation stage.
3 In some cases the forest stations may not have adequate labour to clear indigenous forests and undertake re-afforestation.
4 Land pressure from surrounding lowlands promotes political pleas to lease

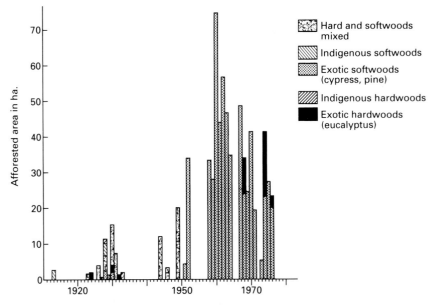

Fig. 5.9 Trends in indigenous and exotic forests on Mount Kenya
Source Winiger (1986)

out the forest land in order to ease pressure in the overcrowded areas.

5 It is feared that the monoculture plantations may become more vulnerable to pests and diseases. In any case, pine and cypress species are not as resistant to termites as indigenous species of cedar (*Juniperus procera*). There is also the problem of increasing soil acidity in cypress plantations (McLean, 1971).

6 There is observed conflict between exotic tree plantations and wildlife and livestock. The exotic species are more easily damaged by elephants, buffaloes and warthogs. In addition, there is poor growth of grass understory, thus rendering the plantations as poor grazing areas for wildlife and domestic livestock.

On the whole, however, the forest resources of Mount Kenya are well managed. This is due to a rather strict centralist approach employed by the Forest Department. However, rising population pressure in the surrounding lowland together with political pressure pose significant threats to the continuation of the centralist approach.

Agricultural land management on Mount Kenya

Before the beginning of the twentieth century, the Mount Kenya region was occupied by the indigenous tribes of Kenya (the Embu, Meru and the Kikuyu tribes). These pre-colonial communities practised small-scale subsistence agriculture and livestock husbandry in the lower eastern and southern slopes below 1,700m a.s.l. During the colonial period the Mount Kenya foothills to the north and west became occupied by European settler farmers and was therefore part of the Kenya 'White Highlands'. The European farmers operated large-scale, market-oriented farming systems. They established large-scale ranches for cattle and sheep and maize and wheat plantations, thus displacing the pastoralist Masai from their grazing lands in the lower foothills and the surrounding plains. Several large farms and ranches of up to 50 km² were owned by the European farmers. As a result, a sharp contrast emerged between the European farming systems in north and western slopes and the smallholder farms of the indigenous Kenyans in the south and east.

Through the introduction of taxes, the colonial administration gradually introduced a monetary economy amongst the indigenous communities. Cash crop growing and employment were sought and population mobility increased. In addition, better medical facilities and improvements in living conditions led to increasing population pressure in the tribal settlement areas. When soil erosion set in, the colonial administration launched compulsory construction of terraces to prevent soil erosion. Because of strict government controls, there was widespread adoption of conservation measures by communities in the south and eastern slopes. Presently slope terracing, mulching and agro-forestry are common measures adopted in the Meru and Embu areas of Mount Kenya. As a result, there is little evidence of environmental deterioration, although population density on these slopes is one of the highest in Africa. The eastern and southern slopes presently support intensive agriculture with coffee, tea, bananas, potatoes, beans and peas being the dominant crops. Hardly any land is left uncultivated, a situation which has forced many farmers to adopt 'zero-grazing' techniques to sustain livestock production. Agro-forestry is widespread with species of Grevilla, remnants of Meru oak, guava and fruit trees (mango, oranges, pawpaw) mixed with crops so that the whole landscape retains a green forest appearance.

Because of the high population density and land use intensity and the threat on natural forests in higher slopes, the government has created the 'Nyayo Tea Zone' to mark the limit of settlement explansion upslope. The 'Nyayo Tea Zone' is a presidential directive which allocates for tea plantation, a strip of land (100 metres wide) at the margins of forest reserves. The narrow band of tea plantation checks any upslope human encroachment into the forest reserves for illegal exploitation of the forest resources. The tea zone also limits movements of wild game to destroy crops in the lower slopes.

In the northern and western slopes, resource development trends took a different direction. On becoming independent of the British colonial rule, the Kenya government instituted several resettlement programmes in various parts of the country. Many of the large European farms, which were a major supplier of grains to international markets, were subdivided and allocated to indigenous Kenyans. The white farmers themselves were compensated with funds from the British Government as part of an agreement within the package for Kenya's independence. The transfer of landownership led to several other new landholders:

1 Some farms were purchased by private individuals or private firms who either continued with large-scale farming or leased the farm to small-scale farmers.
2 Other farms were purchased by government. The government farms either sustained the large-scale, market-oriented system or the farm became a settlement scheme and the plots were handed over to landless and unemployed people as an appeasement.

The Wangu Embori farm illustrates the trends that followed Kenya's independence. The Wangu Embori farm is located in the north-western foothills of Mount Kenya. After independence the white farm of 30,875 hectares was sold by the Kenya government to 11,000 indigenous shareholders. The shareholders obtained a bank loan to meet part of the cost of purchasing the farm. The loan was later paid fully by selling 8,645 hectares (28 per cent) of the farm to other individuals. The rest of the farm together with its management system was retained for the production of wheat, barley, oats, beef, dairy and bacon. During my personal visit to the farm in 1989 it was still managed on modern farming systems (using tractors, combined harvesters, fertilizers, and artificial insemination techniques). Personnel included a general manager (a university graduate), assistant general manager, two assistant managers, and supervisors, with a total employment strength of 312. During the long rains between February and April of 1989, the following production was recorded on the farm.

Farm product	Land area
Wheat and barley	14,326 hectares
Oats for silage	395 hectares
Beef	200 Galloway animals
Sheep	11,871 Corriedale sheep
Pigs	418 large white pigs
Dairy cattle	520 including 42 milk calves

The average yields in the farm are relatively high. For wheat and barley, the average yield is 42 bags of 90 kg per hectare while the average dairy herd produces 15.8 kg/day of milk. These figures are twice as high as yields in the neighbouring small holder farms that were subdivided and managed under traditional farming systems. In the smallholder farms evidence of sheet and gulley erosion is common and farmers complain of low yields, water shortage, poor pricing and lack of farm implements (personal communication, 1989).

The post-independence trends led to significant effects in resource development in the northern and western slopes:

1 Large influx of population from hitherto overcrowded areas especially of the wetter parts of Kenya took place.
2 Subdivision of large-scale farms and agricultural intensification in relatively semi-arid and marginal lands. Most families were allocated fewer than 10 hectares of land per household.
3 Problems of coping with and adjusting farming techniques developed for wetter areas and new crop patterns to the new environment.
4 Severe threats of aridity, soil erosion, deforestation, declining water quality, declining agricultural productivity, timber and fuelwood shortage.

Despite those problems, the Kenya government remains quite alert to the problem of resource development in marginal environments. A research team, the Laikipia Research Programme, is currently studying the ecological and socio-economic basis of resource development in the north-western region of Mount Kenya. In addition, the government in 1989 created a ministry exclusively responsible for arid, semi-arid and wastelands of Kenya. Furthermore, Mount Kenya as a whole is well documented by various research specialists. There is therefore reasonable cause for optimism about the future state of Mount Kenya's environment. However, the northern and western slopes seem to be poised for rapid environmental deterioration if the ongoing management programmes do not succeed.

Summary

Throughout this chapter, attempts have been made to demonstrate that mountainous environments can be harsh, sensitive and economically marginal. As a result, mountainous environments pose unique challenges which require careful and prompt response. The experiences of mountain communities throughout the tropics portray a rather gloomy picture and therefore deserve an important position in the field of resource management. More than a half of the countries in the Third World have mountains with high density human settlements. In other cases, mountains offer the only important alternative for human expansion from the already crowded lowlands. Thus environmental deterioration in mountains has significant effects on human communities in both the lowlands and the mountains themselves.

Because of inadequate attention from governments, many mountain regions are threatened with irreversible environmental deterioration. Poor understanding of mountain ecological dynamics has exacerbated environmental crisis in many mountains. Due to this awareness, this chapter has provided a detailed account of ecological dynamics in tropical mountains. Many of the ecological relationships discussed in the chapter have been documented elsewhere in earlier publications but often not in the context of resource management. This chapter offers insight into ecological implications of resource development problems in mountainous environments.

In general, previous publications on mountain environments have tended to be crisis-oriented. In this chapter positive experiences from Asia and Mount Kenya are cited to allay fears based on negative or sceptical appraisal of resource potential in mountainous environments. No doubt sustained resource development requires strict controls on levels of resource exploitation and persistent monitoring of trends in resource quality. In addition, knowledge and experiences of various mountains communities, have to be shared in order to supplement local resource management strategies. In the chapter it has also been stressed that for effective resource management, economic and technical goals need to be backed by social inputs.

CHAPTER 6

The management of marine and coastal resources

Introduction

Oceans and seas have played a significant role in the life of people for millenniums. Initially, open and vast bodies of water obstructed communication. As navigation facilities were improved, oceans became a medium of world exploration, trade, military activities and international interactions. Like land, oceans began to be partitioned and today property rights over them are increasingly consolidated as various laws of the sea emerge. These trends reflect increasing awareness of the value and resource potential of marine ecosystems.

Marine and coastal ecosystems provide a major source of food as 6 per cent of the world's protein and 18 per cent of the animal protein are derived from them (FAO, 1977). Marine foods are therefore important supplements of terrestrial and freshwater food supplies. In addition, these ecosystems are a potential source of living space, raw materials and energy besides playing a vital role in controlling the world's climate, the composition of the atmosphere and the functioning of major mineral cycles. These roles make marine ecosystems a dynamic and an integral part of the life support system which can no longer be viewed merely as an inert source of raw materials, foods and other commodities.

In developing countries, marine and coastal resources only slowly attracted concern, especially in the 1980s. In the past, fishing and other resource practices were undertaken on a small scale by a few members of the coastal communities. Today, coastal and marine resources occupy a significant position in the national economies. For example, Saetersdal (1979) noted that two-thirds of the world's fishing nations belong in the developing countries, although they account for only one-third of the total world catch. In addition, resource utilization is increasingly being diversified as, in Africa crabs, shrimps, lobsters, etc. begin to become popular dishes. These trends, together with the displacement of small-scale fishermen by heavily capitalized export-oriented large-scale fishing operations, present issues worthy of careful analysis.

This chapter describes the ecological dynamics of marine and coastal ecosystems and relates them to resource development potential, issues and strategies in the East African coastland. Technical details are provided in order to indicate the implications of ecological input in resource management as discussed in Chapter 2.

The ecological dynamics of marine and coastal ecosystems

Although oceans have been given various names (Atlantic, Indian, Pacific), all of them are connected to form a continuous body of water. Any barriers within and between oceans are therefore due to differences in temperature, salinity, depth and local variations in light intensity. Oceans become increasingly deeper away from the continental shelf, with life forms more concentrated near the continental shelf. Currents, waves, tides and trade winds ensure continuous circulation in oceans thereby aiding the horizontal and vertical transfer of nutrients and matter throughout the entire ecosystem.

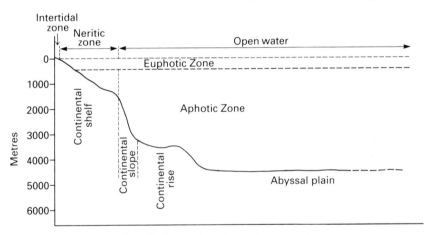

Fig. 6.1 Horizontal and vertical zonations in marine ecosystems

Oceans have a relatively narrow *autotrophic* zone (Figure 6.1), rendering much of the ocean biologically infertile because of low concentrations of dissolved nutrients. However, salt concentrations (Odum, 1971, rates it at 35 parts per thousand) are much higher than in freshwater ecosystems (lakes, rivers, ponds). Due to lateral tectonism, ocean floors are constantly spreading thereby exposing new and young geologic structures to marine life forms.

Structure and processes in marine ecosystems

The ecological diversity of marine ecosystems is not often obvious at a first glance. But marine ecosystems vary from the rich coastal zone to the relatively impoverished biological semi-desert of the open water zone. The ecosystem can therefore be divided into two primary subsystems:

1 the oceanic subsystem stretching from the continental shelf to the open water
2 the coastal and estuarine subsystem which is ecotonal between oceanic subsystems and terrestrial and freshwater ecosystems.

Life-form diversity in a marine ecosystem decreases horizontally away from the coastal zone and vertically with increasing depth. Figure 6.1 displays the horizontal and vertical zonation in marine ecosystems. Horizontally, marine ecosystems stretch from the INTERTIDAL zone to the NERITIC and then the OPEN WATER zones. The intertidal zone (or the littoral zone) lies between high and low tides, forming the coastal and estuarine subsystem. The neritic zone is the shallow water section existing near the shore and on the continental shelf and opening into the vast expanse of the open water zone. Both the neritic and open water form the oceanic subsystem which is basically an underwater habitat. Nutrients and other matter from terrestrial and fresh water ecosystems enter oceanic subsystems through the intertidal zone before being dispersed and transported by currents, tides, waves and winds toward the centre of the open water zone. Thus nutrients and matter concentrations decrease with distance away from the intertidal zone.

On a vertical analysis, the oceanic subsystems are subdivided into the upper and thin EUPHOTIC zone and the lower APHOTIC zone. Below the aphotic zone but over the continental slope and rise is the BATHYAL zone which may be geologically and geomorphologically active with canyons, ridges and trenches and features of subterranean (underwater) erosion. The bathyal zone descends into the region of ocean deeps or the ABYSSAL region forming a plain which may be 2,000m to 5,000m below the ocean surface. The Euphotic zone is an illuminated autotrophic stratum which is shallower in coastal and turbid water (about 30 metres) but deepening to 200 metres in clear water. Because of light penetration, the Euphotic zone is a zone of high biological productivity and most of the life forms in the rest of the zones depend on the Euphotic zone for their sustenance.

In the East African region, the continental shelf is generally narrow, averaging between 15 and 25 km in width (Figure 6.2). The shelf area is largest in Madagascar (135,000 km^2) and Mozambique (120,000 km^2) and smallest in the Comoros Island (900 km^2). From the continental shelf, the ocean bed of East Africa drops sharply to 2,000m then to a general depth of 4,000m, except where the plunge is interrupted by submerged platforms associated with major islands.

Structure and processes in coastal and estuarine subsystems

The second subsystem of the marine biomes is the coastal and estuarine

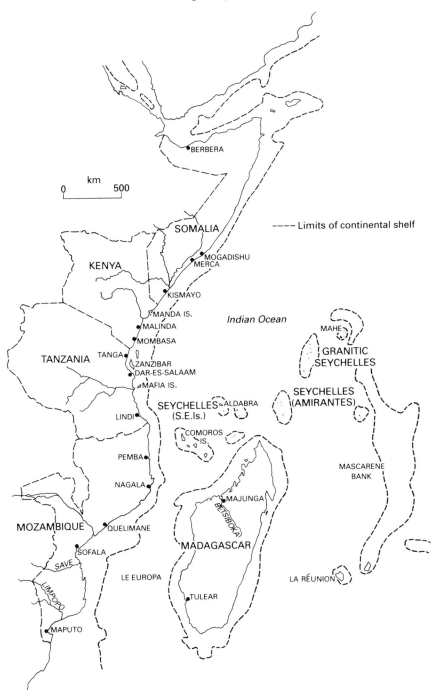

Fig. 6.2 The East African coastal region
Source UNEP (1982b)

environment. These are transitional areas existing within the intertidal zone and between terrestrial (land based) and the open sea (water dominant) ecosystems. Although by inference coastal and estuarine subsystems are ecotonal, there are certain permanent features and endemic communities which make the subsystem a unique zone. In the literature, coastal and estuarine subsystems are referred to as soft bottom habitats, thus distinguishing them from the water based habitats of the open sea, and the 'hard'-land based habitats of terrestrial ecosystems.

There are two types of soft bottom habitats:

1 open soft bottom habitats
2 enclosed soft bottom habitats.

Open soft bottom habitats

These are habitats where water circulation is not restricted. The biotopes are in direct contact with waves, currents, and offshore winds without hindrance. Examples of these habitats include bays, beaches with wide expanses of sand, silt, mud or hillocks. The habitat has niches for shrimps and there are numerous goby holes. Where there is fine sand, a veneer of micro algae may exist and in its turn, the algae may support dense populations of molluscs. Landwards of the beach sands, or intruding through the beach towards the sea, is often dense growth of seagrasses.

In relative terms, the open soft bottom habitat is ecologically poor with low species diversity. However, it provides habitats for turtles, dugongs, crabs and other small burrowing animals. Often the open soft bottom habitat has substrata and other conditions which do not favour the development of coral reefs. In East Africa, open soft bottom habitats consist of extensive sandy flats exposed to strong waves. For example, the granitic islands of Seychelles have extensive length of shoreline without mangrove forest or coral reefs. Seagrass meadows dominate much of the open shoreline of East Africa.

Enclosed soft bottom habitats

Because of geomorphological (submergence, emergence, coastal erosion and deposition) and biological (coral formations) evolution of tropical coasts, enclosed soft bottom habitats are semi-sheltered and water circulation is restricted. There are restricted contacts (unlike in open soft bottom) with currents and waves. The enclosure has relatively calm water which promotes the deposition of fine sediments to form the substratum.

Due to occasional surges of land (run-off and fresh water flushing) and open sea (winds and currents) processes, the enclosed habitats tend to exhibit a higher fluctuation and range of temperatures, salinities and oxygen levels than occurs in the open soft bottom habitats. The enclosed soft bottom habitat includes mudflats, sandflats, coastal lagoons, estuaries, lagoons associated with coral reefs, and mangrove forests. These habitats occur mainly in areas where rainfall is high, slopes are gentle and where low-lying plains are adjacent to the sea. They are therefore well developed in the coast of South East Asia, East African coastlands, and parts of West African and the American coastlands.

Because of the flush of fresh water and the steadiness with which land based nutrients settle down, the enclosed habitat is richer in species and has more diverse biotopes than the open soft bottom habitats. The discussions below on mangroves will illustrate this position.

Mangrove swamps

Mangrove forests are one of the most extensive features of the intertidal zone in tropical and subtropical marine coasts (Table 6.1). They are com-

Table 6.1 Distribution of the mangroves in Kenya coasts

Locality	District	Area (hectare)
Kiunga	Lamu	3 987
Lamu	Lamu	30 475
Kapini (Witu)	Tana River	1 595
Mto Tana (Witu)	Tana River	250
Mto Kilifi (Formosa-Bay)	Kilifi (1 515) Tana River (820)	2 119
Mto Fundisa (Formosa-Bay)	Kilifi	330
Ngomeni	Kilifi	1 673
Mida Creek (Malindi)	Kilifi	1 600
Takaungu (Malindi)	Kilifi	30
Kilifi Creek	Kilifi	360
Mtwapa Creek	Kilifi (410), Mombasa (115)	525
Tudor Creek	Mombasa	1 465
Port Reitz	Mombasa (380) Kwale (1195)	1 575
Maftaha Bay	Kwale	615
Ras Mwachema	Kwale	5
Funzi Bay	Kwale	2 715
Vanga	Kwale	4 625
Distribution by districts	Lamu District	33 500
	Tana River District	2 665
	Kilifi District	6 060
	Mombasa District	1 960
	Kwale District	8 795
Total		52 980

Source after Doute et al (1981)

posed of *halophytic* plants which cover the enclosed soft bottom habitats located between mean sea level and extreme high water level. They occur both in coastal and estuarine subsystems. Mangroves are fragile and sensitive to frost and cold. As a result, they occur approximately between 32°N and 38°S. The forests, however, are much more developed in the east than the west coast of continents. For example, mangrove formations in the coastal areas of East Africa and South East Asia have between twenty and twenty-five species while those on the west coast of Africa, Australia and the Americas have only between five and fifteen species (Rao, 1985). Because of their location, mangrove swamps are a resource unique to coastal areas in developing countries.

Mangrove forests are composed of species which evolved mainly from five tree genera:

1 Avicennia
2 Rhizophora
3 Bruguiera
4 Sonneratia
5 Ceriops.

From these genera, up to sixty species of mangrove plants have evolved and organized themselves into assemblages controlled by the degree of salinity and flooding. For instance, in humid regions, *Avicennia alba* and *Avicennia marina* grow preferentially in more saline conditions towards the sea while *Avicennia lanata* and *Avicennia officinalis* grow in less saline conditions towards the mainland. Similarly, *Rhizophora Mucronata* can grow well in more saline conditions than *Rhizophora Apiculata* which prefers less saline conditions.

The salinity requirements and ecological succession of mangroves imply that slight environmental disruption will easily affect the composition of the mangrove forest formation. In South East Asia, the successional series of mangrove begin with the growth of sonneratia as pioneer species. Sonneratia produces abundant aerial roots (pneumatophores) as they grow towards the sea. Other species of Avicennia also produce aerial roots and in the coast of East Africa, Avicennia species with aerial roots are also pioneer species. The aerial roots help to absorb and supply oxygen to the rest of the plant. The roots will also trap and control the movement of silt, thus initiating the process of land building. As silt is trapped and the coastal land becomes more firm, the actual ground level slowly rises with silt increment. At a point, the habitat will become more favourable to Rhizophora species. Rhizophora will invade the habitat and produce stilt roots which anchor the tree and fix the coastal land. As the ground level rises further, the duration of inundation becomes increasingly shorter. The habitat then becomes more favourable to Bruguiera which are less tolerant of long periods of flooding. Therefore changes in salinity and flood water level will easily disrupt the gradient of mangrove community development.

Several studies have been undertaken to determine the ecological successional stage of mangrove communities. Some studies associate mangrove with pioneer or early seral succession stage (Rao, 1985). However, Dawes (1981) pointed out that mangroves are a steady state community which is in part changing the environmental conditions within it and in part under the control of external environmental factors. Indeed in East and West African coasts there are relatively stable communities whose lifespan may be longer than that of an old mangrove plant species.

In addition, mangrove species are well adjusted to environmental hostility of poor oxygen supply and high salinity in soils and surrounding waters. The presence of salt in water limits water uptake by the plant because salinity exerts an *osmotic* force thus inducing the withdrawal of the less saline solution from plant cells.

To overcome the limitations of poor oxygen supply and water stress, mangrove species have evolved the following mechanisms for survival:

1 They possess modified roots or pneumatophores which absorb oxygen directly and pass it to the buried parts of roots.
2 They possess thick, succulent leaves which store water and enable the plant to withstand water stress.
3 Through the transpiration process, excess salt is released as *epidermal* or *laminal* secretions. Because mangroves grow in tropical and subtropical climates, salt secretions are easily washed away by rainfall or evaporated into the humid atmosphere.
4 The seeds sprout while still on the tree; the seedlings will then drop off and float in water until they establish themselves in mud in shallow water.

These adaptive characteristics do not reflect pure ecotonal features but indicate that mangrove ecosytems are to a large extent fully fledged ecological communities.

As they establish themselves, mangrove species will influence their environment by playing such ecological roles as:

1 aiding soil formation by trapping sediments and detritus from adjacent upland areas
2 filtering run-off and removing organic matter derived from terrestrial ecosystems
3 stabilizing coastal land and by resisting wave action reducing coastal erosion
4 producing detritus which supports off-shore productivity
5 serving as a habitat for many species of fish, invertebrates, epifauna, birds and other higher animals (monkeys).

Once established, the growth and distribution of mangrove communities will depend on a number of environmental factors such as climate, oceanographic and edaphic conditions, to mention but a few.

Mangrove plants thrive in warm, tropical temperatures which do not fall below 20°C in any month and seasonal temperature range should not exceed 5°C (Dawes, 1981). As mentioned earlier, mangroves do not tolerate frost – the most northern sites they occupy are the tip of the Red Sea in the Gulf of Aqaba (30°N) and in southern Japan (32°N). The most southern site is at 38°S in Australia and Chatham Island, east of New Zealand at 44°S (Walter, 1977). However, various mangrove species will show different temperature requirements. The most frost-resistant species is *Avicennia Marina* found as far north as southern Japan. On the whole, mangrove species diversity tends to decrease with distance away from the equator and as latitude increases the area occupied by mangrove community tends to decrease.

The distribution of mangroves is also affected by wave action. Violent waves prevent building of new land and the young seedlings from establishing themselves because they are frequently uprooted. Thus mangroves tend to develop on shores which are either well sheltered from strong waves, covered with coral reefs or on shores which run parallel to the direction of the major prevailing winds. In most tropical islands, the widest belt of mangrove is on the leeward side and the narrowest on the windward side.

Edaphic factors also affect the growth and distribution of mangroves. Mangrove soils are alluvial because they are formed by river sediments deposited in calm waters where coarser loads of sand and gravel are deposited earlier than silt and clay. The soils have a high salt and water content, low oxygen, abundant hydrogen sulphide (H_2S) and are rich in ferrous sulphides. Mangrove soil types affect the distribution and composition of mangrove communities. For example, *Rhizophora Stylosa* in East Africa will occur more often in sandy substrate while *Rhizophora Mucronata* dominates muddy areas. In parts of Malaysia, *Avicennia alba* is associated more with firmer, more sandy soils and *Sonneratia alba* with softer mud (Rao, 1985). However, the most significant edaphic influence is soil salinity. In humid climates, salt is leached from the soil and the landward side becomes less saline than the seaward side. Salt resistant species such as Avicennia are therefore established towards the sea and the less resistant species towards the land. In arid climates, evaporation of soil water leads to higher salinity on the landward side causing the most salt resistant Avicennia to occur on the landward side.

The combined influences of terrestrial, freshwater and marine conditions create unique and diverse biotopes for fauna in coastal and estuarine subsystems. The faunal community is typically composed of species which are endemic to estuarine, freshwater and marine environments. Because of that ecological transition, this subzone is much richer with higher species diversity than either the open sea or the fresh water. In the mangrove forest of East Africa, the faunal community includes

1 fish (e.g. mudskippers, mullets, seabass, serranids)
2 crustaceans (e.g. barnacles, prawns, crabs, shrimps, snails)
3 amphibians and reptiles (frogs, crocodiles, water monitors and pit vipers)
4 birds and mammals (sea eagles, kingfisher, stocks, flamingos, herons, monkeys, wildpig, otters).

Resource development in the coastal and marine ecosystems of the East African region

The East African coastal region is located on the western frontiers of the Indian Ocean. The region includes the countries of Somalia, Kenya, Tanzania, and Mozambique and the islands of Madagascar, the Comoros, Mauritius, Seychelles and La Réunion. It covers a total land area of 3,540,169 km² (Figure 6.2).

In East Africa, the coastal region has a relatively narrow continental shelf, averaging between 15 and 25 km in width. The narrowest section is located between Pemba and Mozambique but at the Bight of Sofala the continental shelf reaches its largest width of 145 km. In comparison to coastal regions of South East Asia and Latin America, the East African coastline is biologically less productive because of the restricted size of its continental shelf.

In a broad sense, the region's shoreline is geographically similar, featuring alternating regimes of sandy beaches and rocky outcrops, fringing coral reefs and coral atolls, large estuarine areas with deltas and mangrove swamp formations. From the shoreline, the landscape grades into a relatively narrow coastal plain which generally lies about 100 metres above sea level and is of variable width (from several to tens of km). In some parts, the coastal plain is almost negligible. For example, on the granitic islands of Seychelles, the volcanic islands of Mascarenes and the Comoros and the entire eastern coast of Madagascar, the coastal plain is almost absent.

From the continental shelf, the sea-bed of the East African coast drops abruptly to reach a depth of 2,000m below sea level. The descent continues and levels off at an average depth of 4,000m except where submerged platforms of islands interrupt the plunge.

The resource potential of the East African coast therefore varies from the coastal plain, the intertidal zone, the nerritic and the open and deep sea zones (oceanic zone).

Resource development in the coastal plain of East Africa

The narrow coastal belt is fringed on the landward side by the relatively drier but elevated savannah plateau which is occasionally broken into by hills and mountainous country. Because of extreme temperatures, unfavourable rainfall variability and poor soils, the coastal plains of East Africa are generally of low or marginal agricultural productivity. However, in parts of Kenya and southern Somalia and in some riverine floodplains, higher agricultural productivity has been recorded. Except in Mozambique, the coastal plain of the East African region supports no more than 10 per cent of the national population even when a major urban centre such as Dar-es-Salaam or Mombasa is located on the coast (UNEP, 1982b).

By 1981, the total population of the East African coast was about 62 million with an average annual growth rate of 3.0 per cent. About 75 per cent of the population depends on agriculture and the people are either cultivators, pastoralists or mixed farmers. The remaining 25 per cent, especially those who live along the coasts and main rivers, practise artisanal fishing. Much of these activities are mainly subsistence in nature and involve the use of simple tools and techniques.

Along the Kenyan coast, agriculture provides crops for local consumption as well as for export. Important food crops include cassava, maize, cowpeas with rice being grown in irrigated areas, marshes and floodplains. Bananas, mangoes, pawpaws and pineapples are also grown for domestic consumption and export. Major export crops include cashew nuts, coconuts, sisal, coffee and cotton.

The island of Madagascar exhibits significant differences in its coastal resource potential. The north-east section is a mountainous region with little habitable area near the coast and cultivation of tropical crops is possible only in valleys. The south-west section of Madagascar is well watered and supports both large herds of cattle and subsistence farming of paddy rice and manioc. The hot and humid east coast is the most productive area of Madagascar where such valuable tropical crops as coffee, vanilla, cloves and sugar cane are grown for cash, especially in international markets.

Resource development in the soft bottom habitats of East Africa

The seashore zone of East Africa consists of estuaries, mangrove swamps, coral reefs, sandy beaches, seagrasses and rocky coasts and cliffs. Because of increasing population, coastal urbanization and general affluence, the seashore zone has become an important area for resource development.

The coastal wetlands and associated mangroves support a number of lucrative economic activities. Mangrove swamps are used for cultivation of food crops especially rice and tropical fruits, and as a source of fuelwood, tannin and construction timber and as a dumping ground for domestic and industrial wastes. Mangrove swamps and estuaries are also important habitats for local fish, prawns, shrimps, crabs, lobsters and oysters. For example, the Rufiji delta provides more than 50 per cent of the prawn catch in Tanzania (UNEP, 1985). There are also unconfirmed verbal reports that mangroves are used in Madagascar (just as in South East Asia) for medicinal purposes. Other soft bottom habitats also serve as feeding and breeding grounds for a variety of such locally important fish as *Johnius Spp.*, *Liza Macrolepis*, *Hilsa Kellee*, *Polydactylus Spp.*, *Pomadasys hasta* and *Panaeid Shrimps*.

Because of affluence, shrimps and prawns are becoming popular dishes even among inland communities of Africa. The central and southern Mozambique coasts, western and north-western coasts of Madagascar, Mafia Channel and the Rufiji delta of Tanzanian coast are the most important shrimp fishing grounds in the East African coastal region.

The seagrass section also provides a habitat for coral-associated free swimmers such as gobies, blennies, mullets, barracuda, snappers, siganids, turtles and dugongs. In addition, there is also large exploitation of seagrass areas for lobsters, crabs and shrimps. In Madagascar, Comoros, Mauritius and the Seychelles, large amounts of sea shells are also collected from the seagrass area for curio markets. Other resources are indirectly linked to seagrass communities. In Kenya, particularly near Lamu town, the brown algae (*Cystoseira, Turbinaria* and *Sargassu*), the green algae (*Ulva*) and the red algae (*Hypnea*) are part of the seagrass community and they are harvested and used as baits. There is also increasing use of the leaves of seagrass (*Enhalus acoroides*) for weaving mats and the rhizomes for food in the Kenyan coast.

The other significant and, in this case, spectacular aspect of the East African coast is coral reefs. Especially in Kenya, coral reefs run parallel to the coastline keeping a distance of between 0.5 km and 2 km from the shoreline. Coral reefs are produced by minute coral-building polyps and calcareous algae. A true coral reef is therefore a fusion of a coral-algal growth consisting of the polyps, associated symbiotic plants and algae, molluscs, worms and resident and transient fish.

The reefs thrive and develop in relatively shallow and clear (sediment free) water with a temperature range of 20° to 28°C. Corals are more specific in their environmental requirements than mangrove species. The reef-building organisms occur more commonly in tropical waters that are not deeper than 70 metres and where salinity is about 35 ppt.

Besides their contribution to the scenic beauty of the East African coasts, corals also protect the coastline against waves and storms, prevent coastal erosion and help in the formation of sandy beaches and sheltered harbours. Coral reefs are also a valuable source of food. Especially in Madagascar and Mauritius, women and children collect several species of molluscs, spiny lobsters (*Panulirus*), green mud crabs (*Scylla serrata*) and echinoids (*Tripneustes gratilla*) for local consumption while holothurians (*holothuria Scabra*) are exported to Asian countries (UNEP, 1985). In addition, coral rocks and coral sands are used as a building material and for the production of lime. Most of the stone walls and residential buildings in Malindi, Mombasa and Kwale (Kenya) are constructed from coral rocks (personal observation, 1989).

Finally, the shoreline of East Africa has become a major centre for both local and foreign tourism. In Kenya and Tanzania, there are extensive developments of the beaches and other coastal areas. Recreation facilities include hotels of international standards, marine parks and conservation areas, historical monuments, local traditional art and crafts. These recreation activities are supplemented by rapid urbanization, industrialization and infrastructural development especially in Mombasa (Kenya).

Most of the recreation facilities including hotels are developed on rocky and cliffed shores which occur throughout the entire length of the East African coast. In Tanzania the cliffed shores are also extracted and used for lime production while in the Seychelles and Mauritius guano for fertilizers and seabird eggs are collected from the rocky shores for commercial purposes (Salm, 1978).

Fishing in the oceanic subsystems

The oceanic subsystem can be further divided into the open sea and the deep sea sections. The open sea is an area extending from the high tide zone and descending to a depth of 2,000 metres. The deep sea occurs at depth, exceeding 2,000 metres.

The open sea is characterized by a variety of macro and micro habitats which support equally diverse communities of sedentary, bottom feeders and free swimmers. Where channels and canyons exist, deep sea fauna find easy access to this zone. The zone is biologically active and supports a large volume of strong swimming fish such as tuna, sardines, sail fish, bill fishes and mammals such as the dolphins. Because of poor fishing facilities in East Africa, the stocks of these fish are mainly exploited by foreign fishermen from Japan, Korea, Taiwan and some European countries.

Large volumes of fish catch in East Africa are obtained in waters nearer to the shoreline. Although fishing facilities are being improved in Kenya, Mauritius, Madagascar and Somali, much of the fishing is still artisanal. In 1979 only 10 per cent of the 2,050 artisanal fishing boats present at the Kenyan coast were mechanized and as result virtually all fishing occurred within the twelve-mile limit of territorial waters (Anon, 1982). Little has changed since then and gillnets, beach-seines and bottom lines are extensively used in the artisanal fishing. In Tanzania, 80–90 per cent of marine production comes from artisanal fisheries (UNEP, 1985). Simple gear such as hooks and lines and cast nets from non-motorized canoes are used. However, sardine fisheries have been developed and fishermen from Dar-es-Salaam and Tanga are beginning to explore increasingly distant waters. Because of poor technology, the deep sea section, although relatively rich in fish, remains unexploited by fishermen of the region. In the Comoros, however, a significant deep sea catch is for the 'living fossils', the coelacanth which is used mainly for scientific studies and not for food.

Resource management issues and strategies in the East African coast

The coastlands of East Africa are characterized by a coalescence of effects of inland resource practices and those from the marine coastal zone. High population densities and poor techniques of resource development amongst inland communities create significant impact on coastal resources. The situation is worsened by rapid expansion of coastal construction works, of oil exploration, dredging for minerals, and rapid expansion of urban settlements. As a result a number of resource management issues have emerged. They include

1 impact of human activities on coastal and marine ecosystems, especially the specific effects of construction work
2 ways of developing resources in sensitive areas such as mangrove swamps, coral reefs and floodlands and effects of marine storms
3 regulation of resource development activities so that growth is sustained without irreversible impairment of coastal and marine ecosystems.

Within the East African coast, specific resource management problems have emerged in association with the stated issues. Today, problems exist with

1 continuous sedimentation
2 environmental pollution
3 direct destruction of coastal habitats
4 urbanization and influx of tourists.

Continuous sedimentation

Coastal sedimentation has become a glaring problem throughout the shores of the East African coast. Silt-laden river waters, muddy beaches, and expansion of river deltas, mangrove forests and swampy ecosystems and destruction of coral reef formations are some of the outstanding effects and evidence of excessive coastal sedimentation. The major rivers such as Juba Guiba (Somalia), Tana, Galana (Kenya), Rufiji, Ruvuma (Tanzania) and Zambezi (Mozambique) all traverse densely populated agricultural regions before entering the Indian Ocean. From these inland areas, large loads of sediment are generated because of poor farming techniques, deforestation, overgrazing and undue pulverization of the soil. Vast quantities of silt are deposited in deltas, estuaries, beaches, the continental shelf and the sea bottom. It is estimated that the total volume of continental material reaching the Indian Ocean from East African watersheds amounts to 4.8×10^{14} cubic metres.

Sediment discharge through Stiegler's Gorge on the Rufiji River alone is estimated at about 5 million cubic metres per year (Finn, 1983; UN/UNESCO/UNEP, 1982). Similar high rates of sediment discharge were estimated on the Sabaki River (Kenya). According to engineers of the Kenya Water development department, sediment discharge on the Sabaki River (at 3 million cubic metres per year) has destroyed the prospects of harnessing electricity from the power station on the Sabaki River.

Throughout East Africa, shifting cultivation is widespread. As indicated in Chapter 4, shifting cultivation involves burning down the original vegetation in order to bring new areas into cultivation. This practice has brought cultivation and human settlement into ever marginal areas. In Kenya where the population growth rate is at 4 per cent, cultivation has encroached into areas of marginal rainfall, dry season pastures, slopes greater than 15° and river margins (personal observation, 1988–9). Although soil conservation measures (terracing, strip cropping, mulching) are increasingly being adopted in some parts of Kenya (e.g. Machakos District), most farming practices remain traditional without adequate care to sustain soil productivity. As in other upland areas of East Africa, inadequate application of soil conservation measures by Kenyan farmers has resulted in severe erosion of the uplands and sedimentation at the coast.

Direct deforestation has also had its toll in causing soil erosion and sedimentation. Deforestation in East Africa is either due to organized commercial forest harvesting or random felling of trees by peasants for domestic fuelwood. Organized forestry is usually licensed and controlled through the national departments of forestry, but the harvest for domestic fuelwood is basically *laissez-faire*, poorly recorded and involves greater volumes of wood than in organized forestry. This exerts enormous stress on soils, especially those in marginal environments. An example is the shale areas of the Kenyan coast where gully erosion and piping are common processes of soil loss (personal observation, 1989).

The other problem of soil erosion arises from the villagization programmes. In Tanzania, Mozambique and to a lesser extent Madagascar, rural populations have been moved considerable distances and concentrated in previously undeveloped areas. Although a strong political ideological overtone (socialism) underlined the shift of people into villages, the stated pragmatic purpose was to ease the development of social infrastructure (water, schools, hospitals, roads) in nucleated rather than in the formerly dispersed settlements. This concentration of population into village centres has resulted in sudden ecological stress due to overcultivation, overgrazing and intensification of agriculture in restricted areas. Vegetation within the vicinity of the villages has been overexploited. Because technical assistance, soil-conservation measures and appropriate resource allocation strategies have not been effectively integrated into the villagization policies, the villages have become point sources for erosion and large sediment yields to local run-off and rivers.

Livestock grazing also contributes significantly to high sediment supply to the coastal waters. Much of the upland watersheds of East Africa are semi-arid but extensively grazed by large numbers of animals, especially cattle. According to a FAO report of 1978, Kenya had 9.8 million, Tanzania 15.2 million, Somalia 4.0 million, Madagascar 9.0 million and Mozambique 1.3 million cattle. Such large numbers, especially if congregated, have caused overgrazing, pulverization of soils and erosion particularly near river banks, irrigation works and watering ponds and dams.

As a result, the deltas of the Rufiji, Tana and of almost all the major rivers are rapidly expanding. Similar siltation effects have occurred in lagoons, creeks, bays, beaches and sea bottom throughout the coastal stretch of East Africa. The most notable effect of sedimentation is the encroachment of mangrove swamps into hitherto clear water and the subsequent destruction of coral reefs.

Beside sediment transported from inland areas, other coastal activities result in large sediment output to marine ecosystems. Coastal activities such as mining, construction work associated with port and urban expansion, and dredging contribute significant quantities of sediments to the coastal waters of East Africa.

Excessive sedimentation exerts a series of other damaging effects on specific coastal and marine resources. Throughout the coast of East Africa, especially in Kenya, Tanzania, and Mauritius, sedimentation has led to the following:

1 Declining attraction of beaches and coastal landscapes as muddy conditions prevail and coral frontiers break up.
2 Reduction in fishery potential as lagoons, reefs and coastal waters become choked and muddy.
3 Direct killing of fish, prawns and other marine organisms. Some mangrove species and other green plants are also killed when sediments block pneumatophores or settle on leaves and stems, thus impairing photosynthesis especially in seagrass and algal communities.
4 Rise in local sea level and extensive coastal erosion when wave energy strikes without being abated by coral reef formation.
5 Sediment accumulation affects the natural courses of rivers, extending floodplains and flood damages and reducing hydroelectric and irrigation potential.

Similar problems due to sedimentation have been noted in the coastal areas of South East Asia and the Caribbean. In South East Asia, inshore waters continue to receive mounting quantities of silt which result from inland erosion. Some sediments are derived from sea-based activities such as tin dredging where tailings are deposited directly into the sea. Cruickshank (1979) noted that off the south-west coast of Thailand and north-east of Sumatra, 16 major dredgers and up to 3,000 small illegal vessels are operating in coastal waters at depths of less than 50m. Such dredging generates enormous quantities of sediments. In general, excessive sedimentation in the coastal waters of South East Asia and the Caribbean is due to effects of poor agricultural practices and deforestation (UNEP, 1985; UNEP, 1982b).

Environmental pollution

Within the last two decades, the coastal zone of East Africa has witnessed a significant amount of growth in the various sectors of its economy. Several urban centres along the coast are rapidly expanding in population, levels of urbanization, in the use of hydrocarbon and agro-chemical products and in their extractive and processing industries. This expansion, coupled with increasing use of fertilizers, pesticides and other chemicals to promote livestock and agricultural production in the upland hinterlands, has raised the level and potential of environmental pollution in the coastal ecosystem of East Africa. The major sources of environmental pollution include

1 oil pollution
2 industrial pollution
3 pollution from domestic sources
4 pollution from agro-chemical sources

Oil pollution

In East Africa the problem of oil pollution is increasingly becoming entrenched because the West Indian Ocean serves as a major route for supertankers carrying crude oil from the Middle East to Europe, the Americas and Africa. Ever since the oil crisis of the early 1970s, the volume of marine traffic has significantly increased in the Indian Ocean (Figure 6.4). The relatively calm waters off the East African coast, the absence of effective surveillance systems and the proximity of the region to the Middle East ports have caused oil tankers to deballast and clean their tanks within the zonal waters of East Africa. As a result, increasing quantities of oil and other petroleum products drift to litter the shoreline and beaches in the region. In Kenya, Tanzania, the Comoros and Mauritius, tarballs have become a frequent and offensive beach feature.

Oil pollution is especially evident at ports and harbours of Mombasa, Dar-es-Salaam and Beira because of routine discharges and occasional spills from visiting vessels and from local refineries. Such spills, even from local tanker traffic, can severely affect water quality and marine life. Spills in Mombasa, Dar-es-Salaam and Motala (Mozambique) have destroyed large areas of mangrove forest (UNEP, 1982b; personal observation in Mombasa, 1989).

Another source of oil pollution is from exploration of oil and natural gas. Almost all the countries of the region are actively engaged in exploration along the continental shelf, coastal banks and plains (Figure 6.3). Tanzania and Mozambique have already discovered natural gas deposits and new oil fields. Successful exploration will lead to an increase in the number of oil refineries, local oil traffic and occasional oil spills during production and transport of oil. These explorations also involve discharge of drilling fluids (muddy stuff), cuttings and formation waters which can affect benthic life.

The problem of oil pollution in East Africa is likely to grow worse unless administrative responsibilities are taken against oil pollution. Only Kenya has a national contingency plan which indicates details of measures against oil spills. Significant quantities of oil spills can smother marine life forms, become entrained in sediments thus poisoning benthic life and life in reefs, lagoons, intertidal areas as well as lower the tourist value of beaches and coastal landscapes.

Industrial pollution

The industrial sector in every country of the East African region is relatively small and it concentrates mainly on processing primary agricultural and

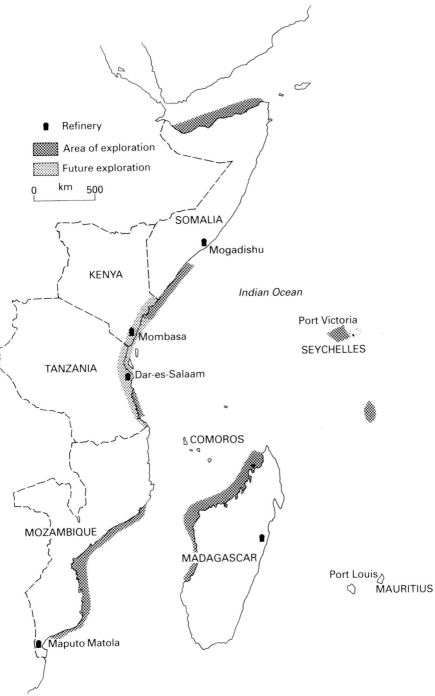

Fig. 6.3   Oil exploration and refineries
Source UNEP (1982b)

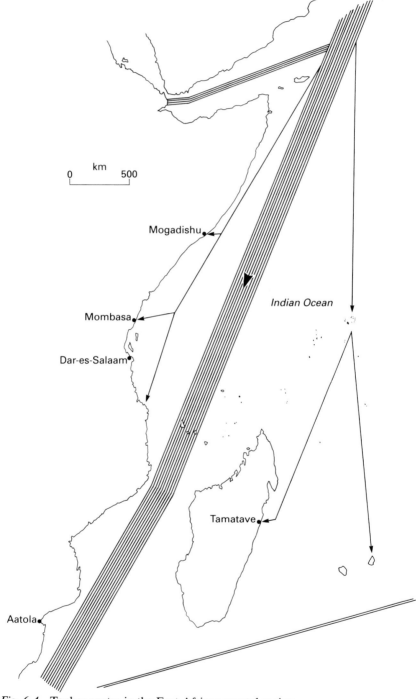

Fig. 6.4   Tanker routes in the East African coastal region
Source UNEP (1982b)

livestock products. There is little spatial disparity in the types of industries, although meat and leather processing dominate industrial scenes in Somalia and Madagascar. In the rest of the coastal states, agriculture and silvicultural commodities provide a base for industrial development. Industrial activity therefore includes cashew nut and copra processing, vegetable oil extraction, coffee bean roasting and grinding, sugar and molasses refining, brewing, rice milling, sisal processing, paper and pulp production and soap production. Most of these industries are concentrated in the major coastal cities of Mogadishu, Mombasa, Dar-es-Salaam, Maputo, Beira, Toamasina, Port Louis and Victoria.

These industries contribute large quantities of aquatic discharges which comprise suspended solids, chemicals and heavy metals, sludges and other dissolved substances. Because of concentration on agro-industries, large amounts of organic wastes are produced which contribute significantly to total biological oxygen demand (BOD). As a result, features of water eutrophication (algal growth) are beginning to appear in sheltered bays and lagoons, especially those near large urban centres. These pollutants will definitely cause toxic effects, lower biological productivities and increase turbidity of waters in rivers, bays, wetlands, and coral reef formations once the natural threshold is exceeded.

Pollution from domestic and agro-chemical sources

Although actual growth in other sectors of the economy of East Africa is relatively slow, human population numbers are increasing at an alarming rate. As indicated earlier in this chapter, the coastal strip of East Africa supports about 10 per cent of the total national populations. The average population and urbanization growth rates in the coastal region are at 3.0 per cent and 7.6 per cent respectively. Because of much higher rates of growth, several unplanned settlements have sprung up to compound problems within even the planned urban centres.

The most obvious problem relates to inadequate collection and treatment systems of both sewered and non-sewered domestic wastes. Only the major coastal cities have piped sewerage systems but almost all of them have inadequate capacities for collection of non-sewered garbage (Table 6.2).

However, Mauritius and Seychelles have substantive sewerage services. Two-thirds of the coastal urban population in the region discharge their wastes directly to the sea and waste treatment is limited only to removal of coarse suspended materials (UNEP, 1982b).

Domestic waste disposal contributes enormously to pollution by organic substances, nitrogenous compounds, phosphates and other inorganic salts. Improper excreta disposal leads to danger of bacteriological infections which has resulted in frequent outbreaks of cholera in fishing villages along the coast. Foul smell is becoming a menace in the vicinity of discharge points and particularly during conditions of calm winds. These trends pose significant

Table 6.2 Estimated discharge of domestic sewage from major cities on the coasts (estimated 20 kl/capita/year)

Country and cities	Population 1980 (estimated)	Length of coastline (km)	Population sewered	%	BOD_5 (biological oxygen demand) (ton/yr)	BOD km coastline (ton/yr)
Kenya	15,300,000	500				
Mombasa	440,000		88,000	20	2,760	3.52
Malindi	14,000					
Lamu	6,000					
Regional/total	460,000		88,000	19	1,760	3.52
Tanzania	17,540,000	800				
Dar-es-Salaam	760,000		112,500	15	2,250	2.81
Tanga	100,000		10,000	10	200	0.25
Lindi	30,000					
Regional/total	890,000		122,500	14	2,450	3.06
Mozambique	10,200,000	2,500				
Maputo	770,000		77,000	10	1,540	0.62
Beira	220,000		55,000	25	1,100	0.44
Quelimane	100,000		10,000	10	200	0.08
Nampula	100,000		10,000	10	200	0.08
Pemba	30,000		3,000	10	60	0.02
Regional/total	1,220,000		155,000	13	3,100	1.24
Comoros	400,000	350				
Moroni	16,000					
(G. Comores)						
Moheli	4,500					
Anjouan	10,000					
Regional/total	30,500					
Madagascar	8,500,000	4,000				
Tamatave	60,000		9,000	15	180	0.05
Majunga	70,000					
Tulear	40,000					
Diego-Suarez	45,000		4,500	10	90	0.02
Regional/total	215,000		13,500	6	270	0.07
Mauritius	936,000	200				
Port Louis	250,000		150,000	60	3,000	15.00
Plaines Wilhems/ Curepipe	57,000		40,000	70	800	4.00
Beau-Bassin/ Rose-Hill	72,000		50,000	70	1,000	5.00
Phoenix	36,000		25,000	70	500	2.50
Regional/total	415,000		265,000	64	5,300	26.50

Table 6.2 (*Cont.*)

Country and cities	Population 1980 (estimated)	Length of coastline (km)	Population sewered	%	BOD$_s$ (biological oxygen demand) (ton/yr)	BOD km coastline (ton/yr)
Seychelles	65,000	600				
Victoria	25,000		6,250	25	125	0.21
Regional/total	25,000		6,250	25	125	0.21
Somalia	3,850,000	3,000				
Mogadishu	400,000					
Marca	55,000					
Kismayo	60,000					
Berbara	50,000					
Regional/total	565,000					
Grand total	3,820,000		650,250	17	13,005	

Source UNEP (1982b)
Note No data available for La Réunion

eutrophication dangers to resources of estuaries, lagoons, beaches and coral reefs in the region.

There is little information about the level of agro-chemical pollution throughout the East African region. It is true, however, that the use of organochlorine, nitrogenous and phosphate compounds is on the increase in homes and cultivated fields. Through surface run-off and rivers these chemicals reach the coastal waters, thus compounding the effects of mineral salts and other pollutants from domestic sources. Both domestic and agro-chemical pollution stimulate eutrophication in estuaries, lagoons and waters near the shoreline. In Mombasa several lagoons and estuaries can no longer support life forms (personal observation, 1989).

Direct destruction of coastal habitats

In addition to effects of sedimentation and environmental pollution, habitat destruction is another problem which compounds resource base deterioration in the coastal ecosystems of East Africa. Direct habitat destruction is due to several causes which include poor fishing methods, land reclamation, mining and dredging activities, construction works and oil prospecting.

One of the most important habitats in the coast of East Africa is the coral reef. It supports a diversity of fish species besides enhancing the landscape beauty of the coast. The coral reefs are threatened with permanent destruction because of continuous and widespread use of explosives (dynamite) to kill and stun fish. Because of dynamiting, poisoning and trampling by both industrial and artisanal fishermen, coral reefs around Dar-es-Salaam have been so badly damaged that fishermen are moving northward and southward from the city in order to dynamite fresh coral habitats. Together with crude methods of harvesting coral species for curio markets, the direct extraction of coral for the production of building limestone and poor trawling methods have significantly destroyed fish habitats and lowered the beauty of the coastal landscape. Trawling has particularly affected seagrass communities through uprooting and choking leaves and stems with suspended materials.

The other destructive effects arise from the construction of ports and harbours (e.g. Port Victoria), cement industries, oil prospecting, mangrove swamp reclamation for expansion of coastal towns and siting of industries, hotels and access roads. These developments have involved large-scale destruction of mangrove forests, dredging of sand from sea-bed, and mining of beach sands. Besides mangroves, the seagrass, beaches and lagoons have been transformed into mudflats especially around high growth towns such as Mombasa, Victoria and Dar-es-Salaam. Unlike in the Comoros and Seychelles, beach sand mining in Mauritius has not resulted in much habitat destruction because, by law, the pits are replanted after sand extraction.

As a result of those activities, there has been a gradual but constant decline in the resource base of the East African coast. Ray (1968) estimated and Bryceson (1978) confirmed that the reefs in Dar-es-Salaam would be completely destroyed within a decade. Today this danger has gripped coral reefs in the entire East African coast. The disappearance of reefs and beaches has led to severe coastal erosion. At Anjouan (Comoros), coastal erosion has reached a degree where it affects coastal roads (Finn, 1983). Mangrove swamps are equally threatened both by effects of reclamation and rising demands for charcoal, fuelwood, construction timber and cultivation land. All these, unless averted, will cause a shrinkage in the coastal resource base as even prawns, lobsters, shrimps and other fish will continue to lose their habitats.

Urbanization and influx of tourists

The coast of East Africa has several urban centres (Figure 6.2). Some of these centres were established hundreds of years ago (Malindi, Dar-es-Salaam) while many sprang up more recently. Some urban centres such as Mogadishu, Dar-es-Salaam and Maputo serve as national capitals and display such general urban problems as discussed in Chapter 7. Others, such as Mombasa, are not capital cities but have surpassed other national capitals in levels of growth in population and municipal services. But all these coastal urban centres were established to exploit the special circumstances of maritime resources and commerce, industrial and mining prospects, and tourism and recreation.

Resource management problems in these urban centres vary according to the level of growth and resource endowment of each nation. The smaller urban centres such as Malindi, Lamu, Tanga, Beira, etc. face three major problems:

1 Lack of a physical plan which sets aside areas for residential, industrial and infrastructural developments.
2 General lack or inadequate provision of municipal services such as sewerage system, water supply, markets, slaughter houses, etc.
3 Poor housing and sanitary conditions – unplanned semi-permanent structures for residential houses and pit latrines are common and they are a potential health hazard.

The effect of these problems is reduced by the fact that these small towns are witnessing relatively slow rates of population growth. However, Malindi (Kenya) needs to be singled out from this category. During the 1980s, Malindi witnessed a significant growth in tourist visitors. This led to development of some new accommodation facilities and arts and craft industry which in turn improved prospects for employment. The small town is therefore rapidly expanding in population. This expansion has overtaxed the capacity of the local government authorities and the private sector to upgrade existing utilities and provide adequate housing and public services. For a long time, Malindi residents have used pit latrines and a proper sewerage system is only now being constructed.

The major urban centres and capital cities have large populations, and high rates of population and industrial growth. They are therefore important employment centres, a condition which has pulled large numbers of rural people into the urban centres. As a result, problems exist in two main areas:

1 Planning, expansion and upgrading of municipal utilities and services to keep pace with population growth and the need to preserve urban amenities and eliminate unsanitary conditions.
2 Controlling the proliferation of unplanned squatter settlements and associated unsanitary conditions and regulating trends in development of housing, industry and mining.

All these large urban centres receive a growing number of tourists. Mombasa leads in tourist population and amenities. But growth based on tourism creates other problems. Seasonal fluctuations in tourists overload public facilities during peak periods leading to overpricing of every amenity and service. Yet existing municipal facilities in most of the large coastal cities are inadequate even for its permanent residents. In some cities, centralized sewerage and treatment systems have yet to be developed for the entire city population. By 1982 only 17 per cent of Mombasa's population (then estimated at 500,000) had access to piped sewage and treatment systems while elsewhere septic tanks and soak pits were used. Although in recent years enormous improvement has taken place in sewage disposal and treatment in most of the large coastal cities, the dangers of water pollution, coastal eutrophication and unsanitary conditions have not been eliminated.

Resource management strategy

Contrary to the more popular view, resource conservation is increasingly being accepted in developing countries as an unavoidable complement of growth and development. Especially in the 1980s many countries have formulated and ratified several resource management acts and regulations. Within the East African region, government ministries, departments and institutions have been established to tackle environmental and resource problems. However, two problems seem to undermine the authenticity of the efforts of developing countries. These problems leave the false impression that developing countries deliberately pay only lip-service to resource conservation.

1 Throughout developing countries, there is a pressing need to support and expand facilities for education, health and other social services. This is a most legitimate priority but it often takes the scarce capital and manpower from sectors such as resource conservation whose benefits come slowly and less conspicuously.
2 Generally there is a poor knowledge about the functioning of marine and coastal ecosystems. Little is known about the interactions and interdependencies between sea and land, the vulnerability of estuaries and coastal subsystems, and the impact of human practices on some critical habitats.

Because of these problems, progress with conservation measures has been slow and has never kept pace with environmental deterioration. In almost every country in the region, conservation legislation takes considerable time to be passed, ratified and implemented while destructive resource practices continue at an ever increasing magnitude. According to the UNEP regional seas reports and studies of 1984, the following remarks are pertinent regarding the problems and resource management needs of the coastal region of East Africa:

1 There are generally no specific national policies and no clear institutional responsibility for the conservation of marine and littoral habitats and species. Environment ministries deal generally but not specifically with them.
2 There are only a few trained personnel capable of planning and implementing conservation programmes in the marine and coastal environments.
3 Conservation related to tourism development has received greatest priority, whereas the safeguarding of subsistence and commercial fisheries is hardly considered.
4 Until now there has not been the mechanism to manage jointly marine resources shared among two or more states in the region.

Although government ministries and institutions for environmental protection have been established, it is only in a few instances where legislation deals specifically with marine and coastal resources. Often the concern of

Table 6.3 Conventions ratified by states of the East Africa region

Convention	Country	Ratification date
International convention for the prevention of pollution of the sea by oil, London	Kenya La Réunion Madagascar	1975 1972 —
International regulation for preventing collisions at sea, London	La Réunion Madagascar	1981 —
International convention for the prevention of pollution from ships, London	Kenya La Réunion Tanzania	1975 1981 —
Convention on the high sea, Geneva	Kenya Madagascar Mauritius	1969 — —
Convention on the continental shelf, Geneva	Kenya La Réunion Madagascar Mauritius	1969 1965 — —
Convention on the prevention of marine pollution by dumping wastes and other matters, London	Kenya La Réunion Seychelles	1972 1979 —
African Convention on the conservation of nature and natural resources, Algiers	Kenya Madagascar Seychelles Tanzania	1969 1978 1978 1974
Convention on international trade in endangered species of wild flora and fauna, Washington	Kenya La Réunion Mauritius Seychelles Madagascar Tanzania	1979 1978 1977 1977 1977 1980
United Nations Convention on the law of the sea, Kingston	Kenya Seychelles Mauritius Somalia Tanzania	1982 1982 1982 Signatory only Signatory only
The Indian Ocean Commission – comprises of Seychelles, Comoros, Madagascar and Mauritius to foster co-operation within the region		1982
UNESCO Man and Biosphere Programme to establish biosphere reserves, Kenya has established marine parks in Kiunga and Malindi-Watamu	Kenya Tanzania	

Source UNEP (1985)

Table 6.4 Protected areas in the East Africa region

	Somalia		Kenya		Tanzania		Mozambique		Madagascar		France (La Réunion)		Mauritius		Comoros		Seychelles	
	No	Area (ha)	No	Area (ha)	No	Area (ha)	No	Area (ha)	No	Area (ha)	No	Area (ha)	No	Area (ha)	No	Area (ha)	No	Area (ha)
Existing marine protected areas																		
Category I	0		0		0		0		5[a]	?	0		0		0		1	35,000
Category II	0		2	3,901	0		1	8,000	0		0		0		0		4	3,031
Category IV	0		0		0		1	?	0		0		0		0		0	
Category VI	0		2	46,309	0		0		0		4	3,000	6	8,400	0		11[b]	?
Category VIII	0		0		0		0		0		0		0		1	?	0	
Category IX	0		2	79,600	0		0		0		0		0		0		0	
Totals	0		6	129,810	0		2	8,000+	5	?	4	3,000	6	8,400	1	?	16	38,000+
Proposed marine protected areas																		
Category I	0		0		0		0		0		0		3	841.2	1[c]	5	4	100+
Category II	0		2	35,000+	0		3	?	0		0		0		0		2	?
Category IV	0		0		0		0		0		0		14[d]	?	0		1	34.4
Category VI	0		0		5	?	1	?	0		0		0		4	?	0	
Category VIII	0		0		0		0		0		0		2[e]	?			1	?
Totals	0		2	35,000+	5	?	4	?	0		0		19	841.2+	5	5+	8	134+
Existing coastal protected areas																		
Category I	0		0		0		0		1	740	0		0		0		2	98
Category II	0		2	221,669	0		0		0		0		0		0		0	
Category IV	0		1	4,331	0		1	?	1	520	0		8	594	0		1	8.3
Category VI	0		0		0		4	240,000	0		0		0		0		1	25.2
Category VIII	0		0		0		0		0		0		0		0		1	3,045
Totals	0		3	226,030	0		5	240,000	2	1,260	0		8	594	0		5	3,176.5

Table 6.4 (Cont.)

	Somalia		Kenya		Tanzania		Mozambique		Madagascar		France (La Réunion)		Mauritius		Comoros		Seychelles	
	No	Area (ha)	No	Area (ha)	No	Area (ha)	No	Area (ha)	No	Area (ha)	No	Area (ha)	No	Area (ha)	No	Area (ha)	No	Area (ha)
Proposed coastal protected areas																		
Category I	0		0		0		0		0		0		0		0		3	?
Category II	0		0		0		2	?	0		0		0		0		1	?
Category IV	0		0		0		0		0		0		3	?	0		0	
Category VIII	0		0		0		0		0		0		0		0		2	469.6
Unclassified	0		0		0		0		0		2	?	0		0		0	
Totals	0		0		0		2	?	0		2	?	3	?	0		6	469.6+

Notes Category I = Strict Nature Reserve   a Reproduction of green and hawkbill turtles
    Category II = National Park   b Nesting seabirds, turtles and mollusc protection
    Category IV = Managed National Reserve   c Coral reef research
    Category VI = Resource Reserve   d Nesting seabirds, turtles, coral reefs
    Category VIII = Multiple Use Reserve   e Buffer zones for HR's
    Category IX = Biosphere Reserve
Source UNEP (1985)

these institutions is with wildlife conservation, soil erosion control and forest conservation in upland regions. Table 6.3 lists conventions that would assist in conserving marine resources, and the date and countries which ratified the conventions. With the exception of Kenya and La Réunion, the other countries of the region are not a party to most of the conventions. It is also clear that those countries became signatories of these conventions only recently. Even after ratifying, only a few of these countries have actually implemented any national legislation arising from accession to these conventions.

According to UNEP (1985) reports, the few legislative provisions in the countries of East Africa deal with protection of marine environments by preventing oil pollution and regulation of shipping activities in territorial waters. There are also other laws and regulations relating to the operation of ports but their implementation rests with port authorities. In Kenya, legislation such as the Water Act and the Fish Industry Act has provisions against a variety of pollutants. However, effective implementation of these acts requires adequate and prompt surveillance of the sea traffic. The countries of the region do not have and cannot often afford the necessary surveillance facilities.

A number of countries of the region have provisions within Fisheries Acts for general guidelines governing over-exploitation of marine resources (e.g. Seychelles Fisheries Act, 1942; Mauritius Fisheries Act, 1980). In both Mauritius and Seychelles, there are specific acts governing the removal of sand and gravel from the sea while in almost every country in the region dynamite fishing on coral reefs has been outlawed. However, due to inadequate surveillance, these acts and regulations have not been fully implemented nor enforced.

One positive development has occurred in the region. According to an earlier survey by UNEP (1983), several countries of the region, especially Mauritius and Seychelles, have made considerable effort in the creation of

Table 6.5 Threatened marine species of the East Africa region

Species	Som	Ken	Tan	Moz	Mad	Fra (Réu)	Mau	Com	Sey
MAMMALS									
Dugong									
Dugong dugon	V	V	V	V			Ex		Ex
Humpback whale									
Megaptera novaeangliae				E					
Blue whale									
Balaenoptera musculus			E	E	E				
BIRDS									
Madagascar fish eagle									
Haliacetus vociferoides					E				

Table 6.5 (Cont.)

Species	Som	Ken	Tan	Moz	Mad	Fra (Réu)	Mau	Com	Sey
REPTILES									
Green turtle									
Chelonia mydas	E	E	E	E	E	E	E	E	E
Hawksbill turtle									
Eretmochelys imbricata	E	E	E	E	E	E	E	E	E
Olive Ridley turtle									
Lepidochelys olivacea			E	E	E				
Loggerhead turtle									
Caretta caretta		V	V	V	V				
Leatherback turtle									
Denmochelys coriacea				E					E
MOLLUSCS									
Triton's trumpet									
Charonia tritonis		R	R	R	R	R	R	R	R
Commercial trochus									
Trochus niloticus					CT				
Green snail									
Turbo marmoratno	?	CT	CT	CT	CT		CT	CT	CT
Fluted giant clam									
Tridacna squamosa	?	I	I	I	?	I	I	?	I
Small giant clam									
Tridacna maxima	?	K	K	K	?	K	K	?	K
Horse's hoof clam									
Hippopus hippopus							?		
Pearl oyster									
Pinctada spp.	CT	CT	CT	CT	CT		CT	CT	CT
CRUSTACEANS									
Coconut crab									
Birgnolatro			R		?		R/Ex	R	R/Ex
Spiny lobsters									
Panulirus spp.	CT	CT	CT	CT	CT	CT	CT	CT	CT
CNIDARIANS									
Black coral									
Antipathes dichoioma	?	?	?	?	?		CT	?	CT
Whip coral									
Cirrhipathes spp.	?	?	?	?	?	CT	CT	?	CT

Source UNEP (1985)

Notes Ex = Extinct, E = Endangered, V = Vulnerable, R = Rare,
I = Indeterminate, K = Insufficiently known, CT = Commercially
threatened, x = Status not assigned, ? = occurrence suspected but not
confirmed, areas with no symbols require further investigation.

protected areas (Table 6.4). The table uses management categories of protected areas defined by IUCN (1982). Kenya, Seychelles, Mauritius and Mozambique have more protected areas than the rest of the countries in the region. Protected areas have to be expanded in view of the large numbers of endangered and vulnerable species (Table 6.5).

There is a pressing need at a national level to undertake research in order to

1 protect critical habitats and support systems of harvested species so that resource exploitation is sustainable
2 protect endemic and endangered species and their habitats as a national heritage
3 protect critical habitats of shared species to safeguard regional heritage and reduce regional conflict
4 integrate land-use management in the uplands with development and ecosystem conditions of the coastlands and the sea.

The rationale for such national action rests in the fact that marine and coastal ecosystems are characterized by *linkage, exploitability* and *invisibility* (UNEP, 1985). These characteristics, as indicated below, reflect on the unique characteristics of marine and coastal ecosystems and call for an institutionalized focus on resources therein.

Streams and surface run-off link activities far inland and those closer to the shores with oceans and coastal subsystems as do winds, currents and animal migration. These agents transport sediments, pollutants, nutrients, eggs, larvae, seeds and seedlings, and micro-organisms across ecological zones and regions. This form of linkage calls for well-integrated management and regional co-operation in order to sustain the quality of coastal and marine resources. The earlier discussion on problems of sedimentation, pollution and direct destruction of coastal resources brought to attention the need for integrated management through sub-regional (intra-national) and regional co-operation.

The other rationale is that marine and coastal ecosystems have valuable exploitable resources. Some of these resources have only recently gained value and markets amongst the communities of East Africa. These resources have contributed enormously in diversification of the resource base of the region in addition to their role in dietary balancing. However, some specific marine species have been overexploited and others endangered as are the economies based on them. Because of the harvest value of marine and coastal resources, it becomes relatively easy to justify costs of conservation programmes and to mobilize public interest in conservation.

Furthermore, much of the sea, unlike land or even the national boundary, is hidden from human view. As a result, observers are not often reminded of the effects exerted upon marine ecosystems and we continue to dump unlimited quantities of garbage and exploit resources as if they were inexhaustible.

There is therefore need for continuous research and education into the unique characteristics of marine and coastal resources. These resources combine territorial and regional interest and control. Funding research or management strategies on a joint venture basis, involving the countries of the region, should be feasible.

CHAPTER 7

The management of urban resources in developing countries

Urbanization in developing countries has become one of the most important phenomena transforming the nature of the human–environment relationships. A study of urban resource management introduces issues associated with land allocation, human settlement, industrialization and general development planning in a non-rural setting. In particular, such problems as poor housing, infrastructure, transportation, social services, employment opportunities and environmental quality deterioration are more intensified in urban centres than in rural areas of developing countries. Furthermore, a reciprocal relationship exists between rural and urban centres because the majority of resource development decisions for any part of a developing country originate in urban centres. As a result, an urban centre in a developing country is not just another region but a mirror of the nation which reflects both its achievements and failures.

This chapter examines some key resource development issues and problems which arise because of the reciprocal association of urban to rural areas. Because of poor data, only the key issues of land, housing and industrialization are discussed to illustrate some specific resource development problems (e.g. housing for the poor, urban land allocation, inadequate legislation, private gains vs. public good, environmental pollution) which dominate urban resource management studies but could not be adequately treated in earlier chapters.

The land issue in urban areas

The purpose of this section is to discuss the intricacies of land-related issues. The discussion emphasizes the potentially explosive but persistent conflict between the rich and the poor in developing countries, and a common dilemma in resource management where often a choice has to be made between equally legitimate alternatives. For instance, in the development of urban resources, governments in developing countries are often placed in a dilemma of choosing between lucrative enterprises and social justice and equity. The discussion here is supplementary to Chapter 3 because it throws additional light on the process by which the poor become increasingly marginalized, especially when economic considerations become paramount during the development of resources. The other underlying rationale for this section is to introduce land as a key subject, some aspects of which are often taken for granted within the field of resource management.

In both rural and urban areas of developing countries the issues of land availability at affordable price and land supply are of critical concern, especially among the low income groups. In rural agriculture, the poor are increasingly losing access to productive land. A growing proportion of the rural labour is becoming landless as population pressure turns millions of farms into small non-economic units. According to a Habitat (United Nations Centre for Human Settlement, 1984a) report, 14 per cent of rural families in Bangladesh are landless while 23 per cent have only homesteads without any attached agricultural land.

Inadequate access to productive land is one of the most critical barriers to rural development. The World Conference on Agrarian Reform and Rural Development, held in Rome in July 1979, blamed political, social and economic factors for the inequalities in land supply and recommended the following remedies:

1 reorganization of the land tenure system
2 acquisition and reclamation of new land
3 initiation of land distribution to tenant-farmers
4 preparation and maintenance of land records
5 improvement in security of tenant farmers
6 regulation of changes in customary land tenure systems
7 consolidation of fragmented landholdings
8 increase in community control of land by encouraging group farming
9 promotion of settlement of unoccupied public lands.

Rural landlessness and subsequent poverty, and shrinking economic and employment opportunities, have led to a large influx of migrants into urban centres. The receiving urban centres have not been able formally to accommodate the influx. As a result, a growing number of the urban poor have no legal access to land, housing and public utilities. This section of the chapter will focus on the urban poor because they are the most critically affected.

In urban areas of developing countries competition amongst land users, high land prices, poor systems of land allocation, commodification of land, and the absence of legitimate residential status are problems which have obscured the chances of the poor from obtaining even minimal plots of land within proximity of employment centres. Yet urban land reform is one of the most neglected issues in developing countries. Because land has become a market commodity (land commodification), there is blatant land monopolization where the rich and large investors seek quick speculative gains in urban fringe land. As a result, land becomes overpriced, leading to exclusion of the poor majority from legally obtaining land. Land speculation and commodification have pushed many poor urban households out of formal systems into ill-suited swamplands, railway margins, unsuitable hillsides and flood-prone valleys. Such lands are of low commercial potential but are relatively safe from eviction. Because of their illegal status in such marginal lands, the poor receive little support from public authorities for infrastructure such as access roads, water, sewerage systems, schools, health centres, housing credit, etc. The uncertainty of tenure discourages the poor from investing in improving the family house, further entrenching substandard livelihoods.

Urban landlessness in developing countries arises from the nature of socio-economic systems rather than from absolute scarcity of land. Within the boundaries of many municipalities in developing countries, there often are large areas of unutilized land. For instance, while in Bombay 3.5 million people live in squatter settlements and substandard accommodations or are homeless, it is estimated by Habitat (United Nations Centre for Human Settlement, 1984a) that Bombay has 20,000 hectares of surplus unutilized land. In the same study, 64 per cent of the area of metropolitan Manila was open space in 1973 while in Bangkok 40 per cent of the urban land is either undeveloped or agricultural. Similar situations exist in Mexico as well as in several African cities.

Many of the problems in urban areas of developing countries arise from the explosive growth in the urban population on the one hand and from inadequate capital resources on the other (Table 7.1). The influx of rural people coupled with the normal urban population growth has caught many urban areas unprepared, leading to the following:

1 Weak institutional controls on developments in general and land development in particular.
2 Low resource bases to fund and provide infrastructure and public services at realistic standards and costs.
3 Undeveloped market for land and housing.
4 Massive infringement of land use laws and regulations as land is informally (unofficially) acquired or subdivided. However, it is through the informal system that urban areas have been able to absorb the millions of rural migrants.

While many governments in developing countries continue to want the return of migrants to rural areas, the urban poor struggle on to establish their roots in urban areas through persistent calls for social justice and equity and demonstration of creative talents and skills ('Jua Kali', in Kenya – Chapter 8). The pressure on the poor has led to mounting tension between public authorities and the illegal squatters as rising land prices continue to make illegally occupied lands 'ripe' for development. The authorities are then placed in the dilemma of choosing between the squatters' demand for secure

Table 7.1 Net rural to urban migration in selected countries, 1950–70

	Number (thousands)		As percentage of urban growth	
	1950–60	*1960–70*	*1950–60*	*1960–70*
Low-income countries				
Nepal	36	241	56.3	81.4
Uganda	123	287	80.9	80.2
Cambodia	123	252	53.5	76.8
Tanzania	153	314	76.9	64.7
Pakistan	2,464	3,524	57.9	56.1
Indonesia	2,476	3,486	53.5	48.6
Kenya	185	189	62.9	48.0
Burma	311	403	40.1	35.6
Sri Lanka		211		33.7
India	3,971	4,630	22.0	18.2
Middle-income countries				
Ivory Coast	265	566	84.4	77.2
Ghana	594	959	68.9	66.6
Korea	3,647	3,540	92.3	63.8
Zambia	193	315	65.9	59.8
Uruguay	392	352	66.9	58.1
Malaysia	729	1,020	63.6	54.2
Tunisia	267	311	59.2	53.7
Algeria	727	952	61.5	51.4
Bolivia	83	99	48.3	46.3
Morocco	695	968	52.9	46.2
Nigeria	1,677	2,759	45.3	45.0
Venezuela	1,263	1,451	55.2	43.4
Chile	811	855	46.8	43.2
Colombia	1,432	1,840	48.6	40.8
Peru	590	708	38.0	40.4
Guatemala	218	305	52.8	39.0
Brazil	6,345	8,360	48.3	37.1
Thailand	371	552	35.8	33.4
Taiwan	673	841	30.1	27.5
El Salvador	41	57	29.5	24.5
Mexico	2,833	3,803	31.0	24.3
Argentina	742	843	28.5	20.6
Paraguay	25	34	15.7	13.6

Source adapted from Meier (1984)

tenure and social justice and the demand from landlords for legal eviction of the squatters in order to allow for lucrative enterprises on the land.

Land allocation in developing countries

As implied in the preceding section, the critical land-use issue in cities of developing countries relates to the quantity and cost of land, its location in relation to place of work and public service, and security of tenure for the poor. Because of land commodification, the bulk of the poor have inadequate land and their households are situated in illegally acquired or subdivided land from which they are most vulnerable to eviction.

In countries which operate on the basis of a market economy (Kenya, Nigeria, India, Mexico, etc.), private land markets are prevalent which allows a few rich individuals to acquire for themselves thousands of hectares. In these countries there is a growing number of large landowners among millions of landless people. As the numbers of the poor enlarge and attract public outcry, a balance must be sought between the rights of the state and that of the private individual. In the cross-fire, the interest of the poor majority can be catered to only when the public rights to acquire, use and develop land have been clearly defined and guaranteed by specific legislation. Often in developing countries such legislation is either absent or ambiguous.

The intricacies of public land acquisition are reflected in the various measures adopted in the public land acquisition policies of many developing countries. The usual policy measures include

1 land allocation on leasehold basis
2 land compensation
3 land-banking
4 land readjustment
5 land ceiling
6 land expropriation and nationalization
7 land value-freezing.

Land allocation on leasehold basis

In many developing countries, all urban lands belong to the state and the individual obtains land for use through grants, leases and licences. Land allocation on a leasehold basis is the most common procedure in urban areas of developing countries. In Uganda, Burma, Zambia, Kenya and Nigeria, urban lands are controlled by the urban authorities (City Commissions and Councils). Applications and associated development plans are submitted to the city authorities. Once approved and payment of ground rent effected, a leasehold running from five to a maximum of ninety-nine years is granted. In Kampala (Uganda), the city council reviews the lease on the second or fifth year and if no development has been initiated, the plot reverts to the pool where it can be allocated to new developers.

While the leasehold method allows the city authorities to have influence over land prices and the nature of development on the plots, the technique offers little solution to the plight of the urban poor. Often corruption amongst city authorities allows the rich to bribe their way and obtain most plots at ever increasing prices. In Kampala, because of poor mapping and registration systems, double allocation of plots often occurs, leading to ownership conflicts and no development on some already leased plots. Thus, unless an efficient and permanent administrative system is established, the costs and difficulties of overseeing the leasehold procedure are likely to outweigh the benefits.

Land compensation

Because of the increasing marginalization and declining power of the urban poor, public intervention is the main avenue through which the poor can acquire land for housing and other developments. Through public intervention, authorities can acquire land at a price related to the owner's or user's original investment in developing that land but not at a price based on market speculation. Several developing countries pay compensation to landowners on the basis of land prices prevailing at a fixed date. In Burma, land needed for public purposes may be acquired for compensation equal to the market value of land in January 1948 or the price which the owner paid prior to January 1948 (United Nations Centre for Human Settlement, 1984a). The method is also applied in a modified form in France and Sweden. In the Philippines, compensation for compulsory acquisition is based on the landowner's 1976 tax declaration. In Hong Kong instead of cash compensation, vendors are given a certificate which entitles them to 0.182 sq. m (2 sq. ft) for every 1.465 sq. m (5 sq. ft) of agricultural land surrendered. The certificate may be resold or exchanged. This system minimizes expenditure on land acquisition for public projects. One major problem with this technique relates to the question of purpose and timing of acquisition and compensation. The definition of public purpose may vary or be vague and controversial, leading to discontent with coming projects.

Land banking

Several developing countries including Ecuador, Chile, India, Singapore and Malaysia have employed land banking techniques to acquire land for developing new urban centres, expansion of existing urban areas, or for rehabilitation of the landless poor. In Delhi (India) during 1961 a land banking programme was implemented and many hectares came under the control of public authority. Such lands are reserved for any public development and as an insurance against future land shortage. The snag with this policy measure is that large capital may be locked up, thus straining public authority budgets. The land itself may not be developed for a long time.

Land readjustment

This is a process where the plots of a group of adjacent land owners are pooled together, and serviced with the necessary roads and infrastructure in accordance with an agreed plan. The owners may sell part of the developed land to meet the cost of infrastructure (as in the Wangu Embori Farm in Kenya – see Chapter 5) and retain the remainder. Besides Kenya, land readjustment is a common practice in Japan and the Republic of Korea where specific laws exist to regulate the procedure. According to the Korean Master Plan for Public Housing Construction and National Land Development (1981–91), as much as 55 per cent of the original land will be removed from landowners. From the acquired land, 30 per cent will be reserved for public uses and the remaining 25 per cent will be for the construction of low-income houses at subsidized land prices. Such an arrangement helps to defray costs of acquiring land and therefore makes more land available to the poor at lower rates.

Land ceiling

This policy measure involves introducing a limit to the amount or value of land that an individual may hold. The method has been applied in Burundi, Bolivia, India, Nigeria and Sri Lanka. The Indian Urban Land (Ceiling and Regulations) Act of 1976 (ULCRA) specifies the maximum land areas that may be owned by an individual, family, firm or association in different cities (e.g. 500 sq. m in Delhi and Bombay: 1,000 sq. m in Hyderabad and Kaupur). All land in excess of this amount becomes public land (United Nations Centre for Human Settlement, 1984b). In Nigeria the ceiling on urban plots is comparatively large and does not limit private holdings of developed land. However, one characteristic of laws in general and land laws in particular in developing countries is the inclusion of exemption clauses. In many cities the local authorities give exemptions to industry, education and religious institutions thus allowing 'key' personalities to manipulate such clauses so that the ceiling is eventually ignored altogether. For instance, in India between 1976 and 1981 only 2.0 per cent of the 'excess' land had been acquired and 42.5 per cent had been exempted from acquisition (United Nations Centre for Human Settlement, 1984b).

Land expropriation and nationalization

In especially non-capitalist countries of Africa, Asia and Latin America, governments exert a direct control over land in order to guarantee public right over land use. In the centrally planned economies of Tanzania, Angola and Mozambique, landownership is a basic right with such strong socio-economic values that it cannot be allocated through the market process. Governments therefore have all the power to acquire land in order to meet emerging public demands.

Public acquisition of land, through such methods, remains an important salvation for the urban poor. With secure land tenure the poor get access to credit facilities, confidence to invest in housing and household improvements, and a legal basis to demand infrastructural provisions (water, roads, health centres, school, etc.). Through public acquisition, urban growth can be guided with a view to achieving equity in resource development. However, effective public intervention in developing countries is frequently undermined by lack of legislation to support public acquisition of land. Where such legislation exists (e.g. India, Nigeria), the administrative structures are so weak and wrought with loopholes that the rich easily manoeuvre to obtain exemptions against established procedures. In most cases governments, hard pressed with numerous other priorities, do not demonstrate firm commitment to resolve the plight of the poor. This together with bureaucracy weakens the pace of implementation, allowing adverse living conditions to persist.

Land value-freezing

In order to overcome speculation, rising land prices and little supply of land for public and low-income programmes, governments may freeze values on sites which have been identified for such programmes. The duration of the freezing varies from country to country. In Turkey, site values are frozen for four years to allow public acquisition and subsequent development of the land by the public authorities.

Summary

Land availability exerts a critical pressure on development in urban areas. For a long time the local authorities have been concerned with the provision and ways of lowering costs of housing and public utilities. Inadequate supply of these items has been seen as the bottleneck to development. But as is indicated in the analysis above, authorities in developing countries have to shift their attention to the supply of land at affordable prices and within the vicinity of the places of work and public services for urban poor. Availability of land becomes an incentive for individual investments in family household and associated utilities. Often the high cost of transport to places of work and public services may undermine any added gains from improved conditions of remote residential projects.

The housing issue in urban areas

Almost all urban centres in developing countries are witnessing a growing shortage of houses and a proliferation of low standard houses. The problems are attributed to several causes:

1 A combined effect of rural to urban population influx and natural population growth causing housing demand to outstrip supply.
2 Slow evolution of infrastructure and institutions which support housing development in urban areas. Because of bureaucracy and inadequate capital, extension of water supply, electricity, sewerage and access roads

takes a long time to reach areas ripe for development. This, together with inadequate housing finance institutions, has inhibited rapid housing development.

3 Unrealistic building standards and building by-laws for low-income housing. In many developing countries very high standards are specified, raising building costs beyond the reach of low-cost housing developers. In addition, many local authorities refuse self-constructed and informal houses because they do not conform to official standards. For instance, Obudho et al (1989:24) noted that 'many settlements in urban areas in Kenya are condemned simply because they do not meet international standards, such as having running water, water-borne sanitation, and being constructed from durable materials'. The durable materials include concrete blocks (stones, bricks) and corrugated iron sheets or tiles. However, earlier researchers (Anderson, 1978; Devyer, 1981) have recognized that houses built from traditional materials (earth blocks, burnt clay bricks, rammed earth mud and timber walls) can last a lifetime. There is therefore a need to exploit or improve some of the traditional technologies and architecture rather than to condemn them altogether.

4 The spiralling price of urban land affects especially the development of low income housing.

5 General national poverty and low purchasing power of urban household. The majority of individuals and urban households do not have the financial resources for investing in housing units. Many housing units within the middle-income housing estates in Nairobi remain unoccupied for long periods after completion of construction (personal observation, 1989).

6 Continuing disintegration of the extended family system. This trend is often overlooked but throughout Africa, Asia and Latin America the communal lifestyle and the associated extended family systems were once widespread among rural and urban communities. The system allowed many blood-related families to congregate in one homestead sharing family land, wealth and household property. In recent times because of education, travelling, urbanization and affluence, many families are preferring a more independent and nucleated livelihood. This has led to pressure for more land, houses and commodities in urban areas while in rural areas household property and farm inputs (ploughs, hoes, oxen, etc.) are no longer as commonly shared amongst families as in the past. It was through such social-interdependence that the extended family system was reinforced and sustained to avert effects of resource scarcity.

These six factors have contributed much to inhibiting housing construction, leading to congestion and declining housing conditions among the urban poor. But underlying the housing problem in developing countries is a common scepticism amongst financiers and economic planners about 'economic wisdom' of investing in housing construction. In traditional economic theory, it is argued that housing is a consumer good and that resources for development should be channelled into investments in producer goods. However, from the viewpoint of resource management, housing development is a means by which resources are organized and mobilized to realize employment, place of work, further capital formation, and improved welfare. Through urban housing development and infrastructure, previously under-utilized land, labour, building materials and savings are brought into production. Many of the self-constructed housing units in slums and squatter settlements represent positive organization and mobilization of human labour hitherto redundant or underutilized in the rural countryside. Therefore, even informal housing construction will make use of some national inputs, thus reducing the gravity of external debt by lowering overall national demand for external inputs. This reasoning does not, however, imply that the substandard conditions in slums and squatter settlements should be left unimproved. The low income groups should be assisted through shelter upgrading programmes, lowering the costs of land, loans and building materials, and by providing technical and legal assistance in accordance with the overall national development goals. The points raised here reinforce the modern position of many developing countries that the housing sector has an important role to play in economic and welfare development (Obudho and Mhlanga, 1987).

Housing policy

Throughout the developing countries, government involvement in housing construction has evolved gradually through various stages. Each stage appears to provide lessons and insights which reinforce and enrich concerns in subsequent stages. Mabogunje et al (1977) and Obudho et al (1989) identified three broad categories of government housing policies in Africa: *laissez-faire, restrictive*, and *supportive*. This categorization is also relevant to several other developing regions.

Laissez-faire policies

In the past, housing was not a sector for important government attention and investment. Housing development prior to the 1960s was the responsibility of private sector employers. Government provided houses to its eligible civil servants (middle income and above) and to all members of the security forces but not to low income groups in urban areas. Prior to the 1960s few private developers in developing countries invested in housing. There was no specific policy which addressed the housing shortage problem. The *laissez-faire* attitude led to early emergence of slums and squatter settlements. For instance, by 1940 slums and squatter settlements began to emerge in Mathare Valley and Kibera in Nairobi, Kenya, as a response to lack of housing units for the surplus labour force (Obudho et al, 1989).

The management of urban resources in developing countries

Restrictive policies

Between the 1960s and 1980 many governments and urban authorities in developing countries disliked the assaulting sight of slums and their juxtaposition to the 'city proper'. As a result, demolition of slums, relocation of low income comunities and the 'back-to-the-land' slogan were used to discourage the proliferation of low income houses. Obudho et al (1989) observed that in Kenya prior to the late 1970s settlements of low income communities were discouraged by denying them such urban services as water, electricity, sewerage and educational and health care facilities or through complete demolition of communities at short notice.

During this period and up to the present time, housing began to emerge as an important sector of government and private capital investment. Both government and private developers throughout the developing countries participated in constructing complete housing units for mainly the middle and high income civil servants. In Singapore, Malaysia and many countries of Africa, high rise apartments (condominiums) and large bungalows were constructed for rental purposes. Building standards were set high to meet international standards. This policy therefore did little to alleviate the housing problems for the poor in the sprawling slums and squatter settlements. In South East Asia and the Pacific, it is estimated that up to 30 per cent of the urban population lives in slums and squatter settlements (United Nations Centre for Human Settlement, 1984a).

Throughout the developing countries, the shortage in housing has been growing over the years. Because of poor finance systems, the housing problem is most acute where housing development depends on the private sector. In Bangladesh where over 90 per cent of urban housing is provided by the private sector, the urban housing needs between 1980 and 2000 are estimated at over 5 million homes. According to United Nations' projections, the housing needs in South East Asia and the Pacific will rise by 33 per cent; from 510 million homes in 1980 to 678 million in 1990. Without considering the existing housing deficits, this estimate means 168 million new housing units had to be produced by 1990. Yet according to United Nations Centre for Human Settlement (1984a), no country in the region, with exception of Singapore and Hong Kong, has achieved the annual construction rate of 10 dwelling units per 1,000 population as urged by the United Nations. The better performers could construct only between 2.5 and 3.5 units per 1,000 population. These developments have created a huge and unmanageable backlog in housing throughout the developing countries.

Supportive policies

In their quest to redress the housing deficits, governments in developing countries have had to broaden their housing programmes. During the 1980s, the major housing policies of many countries consisted of

1 conventional housing schemes of developing complete housing units as described in the preceding paragraphs
2 site and service schemes
3 community upgrading schemes.

Site and service schemes

The World Bank is generally responsible for financing and popularizing the site-and-service housing schemes throughout the developing countries. The first service scheme supported by the World Bank was in 1972 in Likine on the outskirts of Dakar, Senegal. Thereafter it spread to Zambia, Tanzania, Kenya, Zimbabwe, Congo and Asian countries. The scheme provides sites sufficient for a basic housing unit and the required physical infrastructure. In Kenya the government provides land, infrastructure such as electricity, water, sewerage and roads, and allocates the plots of land to the poor for housing construction based on government regulations (Obudho et al, 1989). In Indonesia service sites have other essential items such as shops, community halls and health clinics. The scheme is now widespread in many African countries. Kenya, with schemes in Dandora and Umoja (Nairobi), Chaani and Mikindani (Mombasa) and Nyalenda and Migosi (Kisumu), has played a leading role in Africa in promoting the site-and-service scheme.

The success of the scheme depends on availability of land and prospects for cost recovery so that the scheme can be replicated elsewhere to reduce the housing backlog. As a result, many of these schemes have been developed in the urban fringe because of high costs of land near the city centres. This location in the fringe increases transport costs for the poor as they travel to work and other public utilities (hospitals, etc.). In Kenya the scheme has faced another problem. Middle-class households have tended to outbid the poor for sites since they can complete their houses faster (D. L. Smith and Memou, 1987; Obudho et al, 1989).

Community upgrading schemes

In lieu of slum demolition, many governments in developing countries have decided to upgrade the housing conditions of the urban poor. Slum and squatter settlement upgrading involves legalizing land tenure rights of the poor and improving the existing physical and social infrastructure by providing/improving roads, footpaths, water supply, waste disposal (drainage, ditches, garbage bins), community centres, health and educational facilities. Community upgrading is widespread in such cities as Manila (Philippines), Calcutta (India), Lusaka (Zambia), Managua (Nicaragua), Kingston (Jamaica) and Nairobi (Kenya) to mention but a few (Skinner et al, 1987). According to United Nations Centre for Human Settlement (1984b), these upgrading projects are cost-effective because they ameliorate a situation where residents have experienced a steady deterioration in living conditions, often to levels below those in rural areas. Furthermore, Skinner et al (1987) noted that the upgrading programmes allow the government to become the enabler rather than the provider; it promotes and assists the involvement of others, notably the final users, in housing provision. The final house owners are expected to become involved in building activities, financing and management of housing construction. During such 'self-help' or 'user participation' programmes, the poor improve on and integrate their talents and skills for management and craftmanship in the whole process of urban development. This in turn reinforces their residential credibility and confidence as members of the urban community.

The three major housing strategies are often supplemented by environmental regulations, land-use zoning, building codes and other controls to promote tenure security, welfare and community development.

Summary

While the housing issue continues to exert an intimidating challenge to governments in developing countries, the positive role the housing sector plays in national development is being widely appreciated. Some countries (e.g. Uganda), because of political instability, are still far behind and have not initiated community upgrading programmes. But the attitude of governments to housing in general and low income housing in particular is well summarized in the views of the Kenya government:

> well planned housing and a reasonable standard when combined with essential services affords dignity, a sense of security and proper status in society for the individual. (Kenya, 1966:24)

Housing conditions and strategies vary from country to country and from one city to the other. This variation represents diversity of experience to be shared amongst developing countries so that failures in one place may be avoided by other authorities.

Industrialization and environmental pollution

Industrial process involves the conversion of raw resources into semi-finished and/or finished products. During the conversion, matter and/or energy are released and discharged to the biosphere as wastes or pollutants. Industrial pollutants are those wastes which are not or cannot be recycled but are potentially toxic or carcinogenic in trace quantities. This section examines trends in industrial development and associated environmental pollution in urban areas of developing countries.

Trends in industrial development

Industrial development in most developing countries started during the colonial period. In the 1960s when many countries in Asia and Africa gained political independence, a propelling impetus for industrial development emerged and several reasons were presented to account for relatively large investments in industrial expansion. The reasons include

1 to cause a rise in national and family levels of income
2 to provide consumer goods in order to allow governments to cut down expenses on imports and curb balance of payment problems
3 to expand employment opportunities in order to absorb an ever-expanding labour force
4 to provide benefits which would sponsor the expansion of social services
5 to help achieve a higher standard of living at all levels within a nation.

On these premises, large capital investments were channelled to stimulate industrial growth. In most cases more hope for economic development was seen in industrial expansion than in agriculture. As a result, the two were viewed as alternatives rather than complementary strategies for economic development. Figure 7.1 indicates the share of capital investment for industry, agriculture and services amongst the countries of Western Asia (Middle East) between 1971 and 1985. Western Asia does not have the favourable climate and soil conditions for agriculture as do the humid areas in other countries of Africa, Latin America and the rest of Asia. But the proportion of capital allocated for investments in industrial development is generally

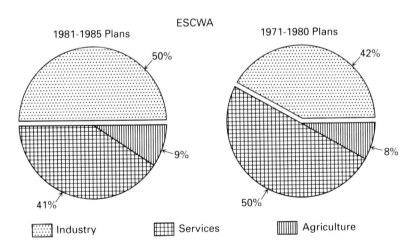

Fig. 7.1 Investment distribution of development plans in ESCWA countries*
    Source UNEP (1987)

* The United Nations Economic and Social Commission for Western Asia (ESCEW) comprises the following members: Bahrain, Egypt, Iraq, Jordan, Kuwait, Oman, Qatar, Saudi Arabia, Syria, the United Arab Emirates, Yemen Arab Republic, People's Democratic Republic of Yemen and the Palestine Liberation Organization.

higher than in agriculture and services as is the case throughout the rest of the developing countries.

Because of a strong emphasis on industrial development, several industries emerged and some of the earlier ones were expanded in Third World countries. In general the rate of industrial growth between 1960 and 1980 (at about 6 per cent) remained higher than the population growth rate (2.5 per cent–3.5 per cent) throughout developing countries.

Table 7.2 presents the nature of growth in GDP and industry in thirty

Table 7.2 Average annual growth rates (%) in Gross Domestic Product (GDP)

	% growth GDP		% growth industry		% growth manufacturing	
	1960–70	*1970–81*	*1960–70*	*1970–81*	*1960–70*	*1970–81*
Bangladesh	3.7	4.2	8.0	9.0	6.6	11.2
Ethiopia	4.4	2.2	7.4	1.8	8.0	2.8
Burma	2.6	4.8	2.8	5.6	3.4	4.6
India	3.4	3.6	5.4	4.4	4.7	5.0
Haiti	0.2	3.4	0.2	7.1	−0.1	7.6
Sri Lanka	4.6	4.3	6.6	4.2	6.3	2.1
Central African Republic	1.9	1.6	5.4	4.0	5.4	−4.3
Pakistan	6.7	4.8	10.0	5.5	9.4	4.4
Senegal	2.5	2.0	4.4	4.1	6.2	2.0
Mauritania	6.7	1.7	14.1	−4.0	9.2	4.6
Indonesia	3.9	7.8	5.2	11.2	3.3	13.9
Bolivia	5.2	4.4	3.0	2.9	5.4	5.3
Honduras	5.3	3.8	5.4	4.9	4.5	4.7
Egypt	4.3	8.1	5.4	7.6	4.8	8.7
El Salvador	5.9	3.1	8.5	3.3	8.8	2.4
Thailand	8.4	7.2	11.9	9.9	11.4	10.3
Philippines	5.1	6.2	6.0	8.4	6.7	6.9
Morocco	4.4	5.2	4.2	5.8	4.2	5.4
Nicaragua	7.3	0.8	10.4	2.1	11.2	2.8
Nigeria	3.1	4.5	14.7	6.0	9.1	12.4
People's Republic of Congo	2.3	5.1	7.4	13.6	7.4	−1.8
Guatemala	5.6	5.5	7.8	7.3	8.2	5.9
Peru	4.9	3.0	5.0	3.4	5.7	2.9
Jamaica	4.4	−1.2	4.8	−3.6	5.7	−2.6
Ivory Coast	8.0	6.2	11.5	9.3	11.6	5.8
Dominican Republic	4.5	6.3	6.0	7.6	5.0	6.1
Colombia	5.1	5.7	6.0	4.7	5.7	5.7
Tunisia	4.7	7.3	8.2	9.3	7.8	11.7
Costa Rica	6.5	5.2	9.4	7.4	10.6	7.1
Turkey	6.0	5.4	9.6	6.1	10.9	5.5
Average	4.72	4.41	7.16	5.63	6.90	4.68

Source World Bank (1983b: 150–1)

developing countries between 1960 and 1981. Because of differences in resources endowment, managerial and capital formation, large disparities can be observed in growth rates amongst developing countries. The period between 1960 and 1970 witnessed much higher rates of mean annual growth in GNP (4.72 per cent), industry (7.16 per cent) and manufacturing (6.9 per cent) than between 1970 and 1981. Haiti recorded the lowest growth rate in GNP (0.2 per cent), industry (0.2 per cent) and manufacturing (-0.1 per cent) while Thailand recorded the highest rates at 8.4 per cent (GNP), 11.9 per cent (industry) and 11.4 per cent (manufacturing). Between 1970 and 1981, 53 per cent of the countries showed a decline in GNP, 67 per cent a decline in industry, and 57 per cent a decline in manufacturing. During this period, mean annual growth rates declined from 4.72 to 4.41 per cent (GNP), 7.16 to 5.63 per cent (industry) and 6.90 to 4.68 per cent in manufacturing. Some countries, of course, performed far worse/better than others. For instance in Haiti the industrial growth rate rose from 0.2 per cent in the 1960s to 7.1 per cent in the 1970s, while in Mauritania industrial growth rate fell from 14.1 per cent (1960s) to -4.0 per cent (1970s). As implied in Chapter 3, the 1970s were trying periods and a test case for many resource development programmes in developing countries.

In Uganda and Tanzania, industrial performance fell much below the growth rates of GNP between 1970 and 1980. For instance in Uganda, the annual growth rate fell from 6 per cent in the 1960s to negative growth rates between 1970 and the 1980s (World Bank, 1983b). Table 7.3 shows trends in the production of key industrial products in Uganda. The decline in Uganda's industrial performance is due to political instability while in Tanzania experimentation with socialist policies led to significant disruption in industrial investments and management. Many industries in Uganda have closed while the rest continue to operate at very low levels of capacity utilization.

The disappointing trend in industrial performance since the 1970s in developing countries can be attributed to several fundamental constraints.

Table 7.3 Industrial production in Uganda

	Units	Peak-year Year	Peak-year Amount	1980 Amount	Ratio of 1980 Peak Production
Spirits (waragi)	'000 litres	1973	910.0	34.0	3.7
Beer	m. litres	1973	45.6	12.0	26.3
Cigarettes	billions	1974	2.0	0.6	30.0
Fabrics	m. sq. metres	1970	49.6	7.5	15.1
Soap	'000 tons	1966	14.9	0.4	2.7
Matches (small)	'000 cartons	1971	64.0	2.8	4.4
Steel ingots	'000 tons	1970	24.8	1.9	7.7
Cement	'000 tons	1971	205.1	4.9	2.4
Paints	m. litres	1974	1.9	0.1	5.3

Source World Bank (1982b)

The relative impact of each constraint on industry varies from country to country. These constraints include:

1 Poor performance in agriculture leading to limited supply of raw materials (e.g. cotton for textiles), entrenched foreign exchange problems for importation of inputs, and reduced effective domestic market for industrial products (Chapters 4 and 8).
2 Over employment and government interference in the management of parastatal industries.
3 Problem of credit worthiness as a result of poor financial management and the impact of yearly devaluations on costs.
4 Excessive government controls and regulations on imports, pricing and taxation policies.
5 Weakness in infrastructure leading to intermittent supply of energy, transport and other required inputs.
6 Spiralling cost of living and low personnel motivation.

Besides lowering performance, these problems also have led to inadequate investment in maintenance and modernization of industries. As a result, composition of industrial products remained little changed, being dominated by production of consumer goods.

Although industrial growth between 1960 and 1981 presents a disturbing picture with evidence of decline after the 1970s, several urban areas in developing countries have developed large and prominent industrial establishments. In Singapore, Hong Kong, Nairobi, Cairo, Lagos, Bombay, New Delhi and Buenos Aires, the industrial sector has become extensive and manufacturing and assembly activities are quickly gaining prominence over processing industries. In general, however, the nature of industrial activities in developing countries is similar to the situation in the Ivory Coast and its capital, Abidjan (Tables 7.4 and 7.5).

Tables 7.4 and 7.5 show that processing and agro-based industries are the most significant industrial activity in the Ivory Coast. The tables show that industrial activities are significantly concentrated in the Abidjan city region which hosts 90.8 per cent of industrial firms and 71.3 per cent of all industrial production units in Ivory Coast. The agglomeration of industrial activities in capital cities is a common pattern throughout the developing countries.

Environmental pollution

For a long time governments in developing countries have argued that environmental pollution is a problem in the developed rather than the developing countries. This argument stemmed from some specific misconceptions:

1 Environmental management has little tangible contribution to make in meeting the pressing need for growth in economy and services – it will only

Table 7.4 Principle industrial establishments in Ivory Coast

Sector of activities	No of firms	No of prod. units	As % of prod. units
Agro-industry and food processing	48	82	28.3
Woodworking: timber production, sawmills, carpentry	30	36	12.4
Paper and board industry: printers, board factories, toilet paper, paper bags	11	11	3.8
Textile industries: cotton ginning plants, spinning, weaving, texturing, printing, dyeing	14	19	6.6
Plastics processing: tubes, thread, moulding bags, miscellaneous PVC, Pet, PP and PU products	15	15	5.2
Paint – varnish – glue	6	6	2.1
Petroleum products and by-products: petrol, gas, oil, fuel oil, bitumen, lubricants	4	4	1.4
Chemical products and by-products: fertilizers, pesticides, electric batteries, latex processing	16	19	6.6
Cosmetics and detergents: soaps, lotions, perfumes, powder and liquid detergents	9	9	3.1
Sundry building materials: cement, ceramics, glazing, floor and wall coverings, decorating, aluminium frames, house paint	23	25	8.6
Mechanical engingeering: wire drawing, nail making, household appliances, metal packaging, tubes, pipes, sheet metal goods, metal furniture, industrial paint, body repair and paint shops	41	41	14.1
Public works, civil engineering and building: (classifiable plant)	10	10	3.4
Public utilities: (classifiable plant)	10	10	3.4
Total	240	290	100

Source Briand (1987)

detract resources and effort, thus slowing down the pace of overall development.

2 Natural resources in most developing countries are relatively abundant. The issue is only how to organize an efficient system of resource exploitation.

3 There is little, if any, link between environmental pollution and economic and social development.

4 Environmental pollution is a product of large-scale manufacturing industries which are more widespread in the developed than in developing countries.

Table 7.5 Principal industrial establishments in Abidjan and surrounding area (20 km: classified by sector of activity – July 1985)

Sector of activities	No of firms	No of prod. units	As % of all prod. units
Agro-industry and food processing	43	36	12.4
Woodworking	24	23	7.9
Paper and board manufacture	11	11	3.8
Textile industries	7	6	2.1
Plastics processing	14	14	4.8
Leather and hides	2	2	0.7
Paint – varnish – glue	6	6	2.1
Petroleum products and by-products	4	4	1.4
Chemical products and by-products	16	14	4.8
Cosmetics and detergents	9	9	3.1
Sundry building materials	23	23	7.9
Mechanical engineering	39	39	13.4
Public works, civil engineering, building (classifiable plant)	11	11	3.8
Public utilities (classifiable plant)	9	9	3.1
	218/240 90.8%	207/290 71.3%	71.3%

Source UNEP (1987)

These misconceptions were rationalized by governments within a background of widespread and persistent poverty, poor knowledge of interlinkages between environmental components, comparative contributions of industrialized nations to environmental pollution, the perceived leadership role of Western-oriented environmental agencies, and poor publicity of pollution incidences and effects within developing countries.

A survey of industrial waste in Abidjan city (Ivory Coast) was undertaken in 1986 and the findings were documented by Briand (1987). According to Briand, Abidjan has only one 'semi-controlled' waste processing centre, located in Akouedo, north-east of Abidjan. It handles both household waste and industrial packaging wastes. Waste conditions vary according to the nature of the industry. The following types of industries and associated waste were documented by Briand (1987), Longhurst and Turner (1987) and Li-Fen Yi and Tian-Min Xie (1987):

Paint and varnish manufacturing

- mixing bath scrapings
- used solvents from oil paint bath cleaning
- paint soiled rags used in cleaning production equipment
- effluent sludge containing fillers and pigments
- raw effluent
- expired chemicals.

Crop sprays – powder and liquid insecticides, fungicides and weed killers

- sand soiled with drippings of used substance
- empty containers holding remains of active substances, solvents, oils
- waste water after cleaning
- expired chemicals including newly banned chemicals.

Surface treatment – short blasting, degreasing, pickling, enamel coating, zinc plating

- soluble oils from mechanical processing
- acids used in pickling bath
- steel and scale metal dusts
- washwater discharge
- sludge.

Crude oil refinery – petrol, kerosene, diesel, oil, bitumen

- sand soiled by hydrocarbon and bitumen
- sludges and floating soils
- spent catalysts and cobalt and platinum based chemicals.

Electric battery manufacturing

- manganese dust
- zinc cup flange trimmings
- crushed, faulty batteries.

Textile industries

- waste water (high temperatures)
- chemicals for dyeing and fabric finishing
- suspended solids
- concentrations of oils, phenols and heavy metals (chromium, zinc and copper).

Pulp and paper industries

- air pollution, CO, NO, NO_2, SO_2
- suspended solids and cadmium, lead, copper, mercury, nickel, zinc, fatty acids, PCBs, cyanides
- air particulates: arsenic, H_2S, Benzene.

Leather tanning industries

• raw trimmings (hair and flesh)
• buffing dust
• effluent containing chromium, sulphides and suspended solids
• offensive odour.

Waste management in Ivory Coast and other developing countries

In Abidjan, as in many cities in developing countries, there are no effective waste management or pollution abatement measures. Briand (1987) observed that waste management in Abidjan involves

1 temporary storage of special and toxic wastes
2 direct discharge of waste into the environment within the vicinity of production sites
3 collection of some wastes (sludge and liquid effluent) into tanks for sedimentation with or without subsequent neutralization
4 disposal in authorized or unauthorized dumps.

Briand further observed that there is no specific legislation for industrial waste in the Ivory Coast but preparations are under way to update existing regulations on classified industries.

The waste situation in Abidjan is similar to what I personally observed in the Kenyan coastal towns of Mombasa and Malindi (Chapter 6). In these towns, wastes are dumped near the shores and in areas where underground aquifers are near the surface. Thus the danger of polluting ocean and local underground waters remains high. Besides the potential threat of industrial waste pollution, another danger of pollution is from domestic wastes. In Kampala, Nairobi, Mombasa, Dar-es-Salaam, Lagos and several other cities in Africa, there is inadequate garbage storage and collection systems. Piles of garbage are a common sight, especially within residential estates. In certain cases as in Masia Estate of Nairobi and Bugolobi Estate of Kampala, there is no site designated for dumping or storing domestic wastes. Residents therefore illegally dump wastes at night in unsuitable neighbourhoods. Such sites breed rats, cockroaches and other parasites, pests and pathogens. The situation is even worse in slum areas where the whole settlement area (e.g. Mathare Valley in Nairobi or Kisenyi in Kampala) becomes permanently engulfed in a shocking stench. Other effects of industrial and domestic waste pollution are discussed in Chapter 6.

Elsewhere in developing countries, successful waste disposal systems serve only a small fraction of the city population. Mabogunje (1974) noted that in Paraguay solid waste collection in the capital city of Asunción covers only 37 per cent of the homes in the city. In Brazil he observed that the burning of garbage was until recently obligatory in apartment houses and all buildings of a certain size had to have an incinerator. In many other developing countries there are standards regulating what individuals can do (e.g. every city house must have a means of refuse disposal) but not what public authorities must do. In a few countries (e.g. Kenya, Argentina, Brazil), it is further specified that refuse chutes should be provided for all buildings exceeding three storeys. In many countries refuse collection using trucks is the responsibility of public authorities (Mabogunje, 1974).

There is an urgent need in almost all developing countries to establish legislation and training programmes which will promote proper waste disposal and management, analysis of chemical content and toxicity of waste products and prospects of waste recycling. Without an urgent move to this end, industry and solid waste will become the leading source of environmental pollution and health hazards before the year 2000 in developing countries.

Summary

This chapter has reviewed the issues and strategies of urban resources management in developing countries. Many of the problems arise from the reciprocal relationship between rural and urban areas wherein urban areas attract rural people but fail to support adequately their survival. The issue of urban land supply and management is particularly important, especially as it complicates the implementation of housing policies for the poor. It is reassuring, however, that step-by-step, poor housing and squalor lifestyles are beginning to receive significant government attention. The problem may not be quickly resolved, however, until specific legislation is formulated to provide a fair basis of action; especially action that is devoid of the corruption tendencies of the wealthy urban people.

In addition this chapter has reviewed industrial development trends in developing countries. By the early 1980s poor industrial performance brought much anxiety and almost loss of hope amongst developing countries. But better industrial performance in the 1960s and early 1970s indicates that with assessment of industrial policies and of general management of other resourced sectors, higher rates of industrial growth may be regained. As developing countries struggle to rehabilitate and restore industries to gainful capacities, pollution problems have crept in. In particular, pollution from solid waste has grown to pose hazards to health and life support capacity of urban systems. The danger of pollution is made worse because many industries in developing countries are relatively small, without the capacity to manage even their own wastes. There is therefore a need to include pollution control in the agenda of government action in almost all developing countries.

CHAPTER 8

Perspectives on the future

In this chapter the salient trends in resource management in developing countries are synthesized and used to establish the critical and common issues and priority areas for future action. Attention is focused on major achievements, their environmental implications, and assessment of prospects to improve the resource management scene in developing countries.

Salient trends

During the United Nations Conference on Human Environment (Stockholm, 5–16 June 1972), it was recognized that environmental problems in developing countries arise because of

1 poverty and inadequate development
2 consequences of the development process in countries where environmental effects were either ignored or given inadequate attention.

As demonstrated in the preceding chapters, those two dimensions are still valid in almost all developing countries.

The launching of the conservation concern, with renewed vigour in 1972, coincided poorly with the development priorities of developing countries. During the 1960s and 1970s developing countries were giving priority to growth in the economy and social services. Attention was concentrated on problems related to location, production, exchange, consumption, marketing and trade, both at national and international levels (Ramesh, 1984; B. Mitchell, 1989). During this period, national resource appraisal was undertaken often using both conventional airborne photography and orbiting satellite techniques. Estimates of resource availability, land capability and associated ecological zones were undertaken in countries such as Brazil, Mexico, Nigeria, Kenya and Malaysia.

In especially Africa and Latin America, agriculture received enormous attention during the 1960s and 1970s. Agricultural modernization was initiated amongst 'progressive farmers' – retired senior civil servants and ex-security officers who had reasonable amounts of capital and awareness of some modern farming techniques. Group farms (collective farming) also were created. The progressive farmers and group farms were assisted to obtain fertilizers, farm machinery, credit facilities, irrigation water and some extension service. These farmers were meant to form a demonstration nucleus from which the outlying peasant farmers would learn and appreciate the benefits of modern agriculture. Attempts also were made to improve the quality of livestock by establishment of ranches, cattle dips, cattle treatment and inspection services. Even in the fishery industries, more boats and fishing gear were made available. As a result, average economic growth rates of 5 per cent (Latin America) and 4–4.5 per cent (Africa) were achieved during the 1960s and 1970s. These developments not only generated greater hope for improvements in living standards but also obscured the pending need for resource conservation.

The preoccupation with growth in the economy and social services forced many governments in developing countries to pay lip-service or to rationalize against calls for resource conservation. For instance, during the formulation of the Stockholm Action Plan, Brazil defended their sovereign rights to treat their tropical forests in whatever way they wished. As a result recommendations on destruction of tropical forests came to be insipid, calling only for more studies, surveys and data collection (Biswas and Biswas, 1982).

Admittedly, the willingness of Third World countries to discuss resource conservation issues in such international forums allowed the matter to remain alive and crystallize in readiness for incorporation into the political agenda of national governments. Indeed there were pressing and justified demands for more schools, health facilities, roads and housing in urban areas. These demands could not be put aside, especially when resource conservation and economic growth were still viewed as incompatible alternatives. During this early period Third World governments, through bilateral arrangements, received invaluable assistance and encouragement from international organizations in their development efforts.

As a consequence of the Stockholm conference, the United Nations' Environment Programme (UNEP) was established in 1972 with its headquarters in Nairobi, Kenya. UNEP was at the outset charged with the responsibility to co-ordinate action proposals internationally for a better understanding and improvement of the quality of the environment (Dworkin, 1974). Since then, UNEP has evolved to become the major source for environmental data, assessment, reporting and sounding-board to national governments on critical issues of resource development. The placing of UNEP headquarters in Kenya, a developing country, helped to stimulate awareness, pressure for actions and promote research on resource conservation in developing countries. The host country, Kenya, has taken commendable steps in wildlife, soil, water and forest resources conservation. A number of countries in South East Asia and Latin America also owe much of their recent conservation programmes to the UNEP impetus. Biswas and Biswas (1982:171) summarized the activities of UNEP and stated that its

> major success has been to make policymakers, especially in developing countries, more aware of the environmental opportunities and constraints. This sensitization of leading political figures and decision makers has been largely instrumental in incorporating environmental considerations in national development strategies.

Several other international organizations have also made commendable contributions. The United Nations' Educational, Scientific and Cultural Organization (UNESCO) through its Man and Biosphere (MAB) programme worked

> to develop the scientific basis of global relationship between man and the environment and thus increase man's ability to manage efficiently the natural resources of the biosphere and to predict the consequences of today's action on tomorrow's world. (Dworkin, 1974:347)

Biosphere reserves in developing countries covering highlands, coastal areas, wetlands and arid and semi-arid zones have been gazetted for management on a prescribed-use basis. National Committees and research projects also have been created to help establish acceptable harmony between ecological dynamics and socio-economic demands in these ecosystems (Chapters 5 and 6).

The United Nations' Food and Agriculture Organization (FAO) has been active in dealing with problems of soil conservation, mechanization of agriculture, irrigation, locust control, fisheries, forestry and nutrition and rural development. Because of the FAO, research on ways of improving productivity of different farming systems in the tropics has gained prominence and aided the success of the 'Green Revolution'. Through the Green Revolution (Chapter 4), new varieties of high-yielding crops such as rice and wheat were introduced in several developing countries (e.g. India) in conjunction with more use of chemical fertilizers, pesticides and irrigation (Arnon, 1981).

Other international organizations have incorporated a regional perspective for resource management. In Africa, the World Health Organization (WHO) helped to co-ordinate research on major African diseases, especially malaria with sub-regional schemes in northern Nigeria, Cameroon and northern Tanzania. In Latin America, the efforts of the United Nations Development Programme (UNDP) have also been far-reaching. The UNDP established projects concerned with control of Pesticide Residues (Argentina), Air Pollution Control (São Paulo, Brazil), Environmental Sanitation (El Salvador and Brazil), Environmental Improvement (Mexico) and a regional project for Wildlands for Environmental Conservation. In addition UNDP, operating through its regional offices in Africa and Asia, has been involved in river basin management, development of natural resource information systems, formulation and evaluation of development projects (e.g. the Kagera River

Basin Organization, the Mekong Valley Authority).

The participation of international organizations not only helped to reinforce economic growth efforts of the Third World but also consolidated awareness, in an institutionalized manner, of the pending issues of resource management.

From the late 1970s to early 1980s the pace of growth achieved in the earlier period could not be sustained. As indicated in Chapters 3 and 7, several countries registered negative growth rate or halted growth in the 1980s. Many developing countries began to experience effects of increasing poverty, population pressure, deforestation, soil erosion, water shortage, unemployment, declining agricultural productivity, shrinking resource base, unmanageable foreign debts and general diminishing returns from development investments. These trends led to widespread anxiety and complex responses: civil strife, political instability, unprecedented rural–urban migration, refuge problems, brain drain into 'areas of greener pastures', often a huge backlog of unpaid salaries of civil servants, low motivation within offices and farms, ineffective planning and poor policy implementation. Amongst many governments, a bitter realism emerged that neither education nor political ideology could effectively counteract the increasing level of poverty and declining productivity amidst explosive growths of population.

The effects and magnitude of these problems brought to focus a strong need for a new and appropriate strategy for resource development and management. Governments began to establish ministries or institutions to deal with environment and natural resources. In Kenya the Ministry of Environment and Natural Resources (reinforced by the personal participation of President Daniel Arap Moi) promoted reafforestation through annual nationwide tree planting exercises, soil conservation techniques, water supply projects, Nyayo Tea zones, agro-forestry, zero grazing, irrigation and dry farming techniques, and wildlife conservation (Chapter 5). As indicated in Chapter 6, some legislation regarding resource conservation emerged and was ratified by governments in developing countries.

In other developing countries the need for resource conservation also began to receive attention at the high echelon of government. According to Biswas and Biswas (1982:169–70), the following statements testify to the changing attitudes amongst Third World governments:

1 In Costa Rica in 1978, President Rodrigo Carazo Odio stated that:

Costa Rica is approaching the point of no return with regard to the management of its renewable natural resources . . . Travelling through the interior of the country, especially in the dry season, it is possible to contemplate how vast areas have been completely cut over and burned and suffering the effects of the cancer of Erosion. The most lamentable part of this picture is the obvious instability and poverty of the rural communists, the reduction in the potential for productivity of the soil, and the loss of options for uses having greater economic and social benefits.

2 The 1980–5 development plan of Nepal states:

> Problems like population pressure, limited cultivable land, and destruction of natural resources will adversely tell on the whole development process itself.

3 India's Five-year Plan (1980–5) had as one of its objectives the following:

> Bringing about harmony between the short and long term goals of development by promoting the protection and improvement of ecological and environmental assets.

Although the above statements do not confirm actual implementation of resource conservation strategies, there is no doubt that by 1980 there was a change of attitudes of governments to the relationship between resource conservation and development.

In 1980 the International Union for the Conservation of Natural Resources (IUCN) had published the World Conservation Strategy. In the strategy the core message of IUCN was that sustained regional economic development and ecological integrity were complementary. This new insight helped to demonstrate the compatibility between economic growth and resource conservation. The IUCN document was circulated to governments and elaborated upon by several researchers (Kayastha, 1982; L. R. Brown and Shaw, 1982; McCormick, 1986). In 1987, the Brundtland report (World Commission on Environment and Development, 1987) defined conservation as the management of human use of the biosphere so that it may yield the greatest sustainable benefit to current generations while maintaining its potential to meet the needs of the future generations.

The critical issues

The fundamental issue of resource management in developing countries is to eradicate *poverty* through *increased growth* and *sustainable development*. This has been the message throughout this book. It is the new direction to which developing countries must shift their efforts. But it is a direction with formidable, intimidating and soul-searching challenges for it calls for patience, broader social responsibility, sometimes staggering strategies (alternating government forcefulness), co-existence with nature through a grasp and appreciation of planetary interlinkages and interdependence, mutual sacrifice and goodwill for all rather than for the few, changes in attitudes and lifestyles and promotion of rights of the individual to self-determination for a better life. The new direction requires careful integration of ecological, economic, social and technological concerns.

On the surface the new direction appears over-ambitious and untenable especially for countries where the level of poverty leaves no time and effort except for actions that can instantly 'deliver the goods' for survival. But this is a direction dictated by our own past folly and mismanagement. In a number of cases (e.g. the hole in the ozone layer, desert invasion, threat of nuclear disaster) we can no longer afford to ponder and make mistakes. The shift to the new direction is imperative and mandatory and the prospects for its success are high. During the 1960s Africa, Asia and Latin America achieved economic growth rates (>4 per cent) which were higher than both current growth rates in economy (<2 per cent) and in population (3.0–3.5 per cent). This is a precedent against which prospects for the new direction can be evaluated and justified. In addition, the potential of scientific knowledge is strong enough to unravel resource development issues which are sometimes less complex than the requirements for the journey to the moon.

But the real fear, ironically, is whether different human communities and organizations will be willing to change and make the required adjustments in time. Christian experience has shown that the threat of human extinction is often not a sufficient guarantee for reform. There is often a strong sense of social relativity in which the individual's fear for death is aggravated more by the reality that others are not dying rather than by the fact of one's own imminent death. As a result, the threat of human extinction often sounded by resource specialists may not necessarily release the ultimate panic for real action in conserving natural resources. This reservation calls for a mixture of caution, flexibility, hindsight and vision in dispensing strategies for eradicating poverty through increased growth and sustainable development. There is better prospect in elevating the level of individual's interest, capacity and preparedness to problem-solving as a way of life than to stun the individual (into action?) by the threat of universal extinction.

Yet universal extinction is no myth. Effects of poverty, extinction of genetic material, nuclear wastes, pollution, soil erosion, the hole in the ozone layer, and desertification all lead to progressive deterioration in the life-support capacity of ecosystems. But fear of universal extinction per se may not land the conservation message home. In traditional societies of developing countries, conservation was effected to sustain availability, value and future use of a particular resource unit. Genotypes of poultry, livestock, crops, and shade-providing trees were conserved and passed from one generation to another purely because of their peculiar value and/or performance. Today people are often more aware of the value of wildlife conservation than about the peculiar value of a monkey, a lion or a hardwood tree species in the national park. Desertification is more feared than the depletion of specific plant species which are valued for fuelwood, timber, building poles, and fodder. Highlighting the threats posed to specific species whose values are known is more convincing and cost-effective in conserving against desertification. For specific action, it is more effective to communicate conservation messages more at the level of household needs for a particular genetic resource unit than at a larger community level with a holistic ecosystem viewpoint.

In discussing a comprehensive approach to resource management, B.

Mitchell (1989:305) observed that the

> idea of an holistic approach is intuitively appealing to many and certainly is reinforced by the ecological research theme . . . Nevertheless, there often appear to be problems in implementing and operationalizing the concept.

He emphasized that the holistic approach frequently is too ambitious for current skills and capabilities and it presents difficulties in moving from planning to action. But at certain levels of operation, the holistic approach can also be useful. It is effective in broadcasting awareness of and rationalizing the conservation strategy at the broader framework of government policies.

Poverty

Poverty presents the fundamental problem and a significant drag on resource management efforts in developing countries. In 1980 there were 340 million people in developing countries who were living in squalor in slums, shanty towns and remote villages. These people lack access to clean water, sanitation, adequate land and calories to prevent serious health risk. In many developing countries the poor rely on tropical agricultural production which is vulnerable to fluctuations in weather and terms of trade.

Escalating poverty forces people to rely directly upon and to exploit ruthlessly environmental resources. National governments are compelled to cut back investments in resource conservation by avoiding introduction of conservation measures into the development planning strategy. To curb the present magnitude of poverty, questions related to diversification of the resource base, controls on population growth and ethics of production, consumption and human relations at international, national and local community levels need to be tackled. According to the World Commission on Environment and Development(1987), diversification of the resource base in ways that will alleviate both poverty and ecological stress is hampered by disadvantageous terms of technology transfer, by protectionism, and by declining financial flows to those countries that most need international finance.

As population pressure mounts, inequality in the distribution of land and assets begins to compromise the ability to raise living standards. In desperation communities begin to encroach on marginal lands (steep slopes, flood-prone valleys, semi-arid areas) to destroy forests, to overexploit resources, and to abandon soil erosion and other conservation measures. All these tend to intensify pressure on ecosystem resilience and undermine human capacity to develop resources in a sustainable manner.

In Chapter 3, several intervention points against poverty were indicated (Figures 3.2 and 3.5). But purely because of national poverty, it would be too costly to tackle the problem by addressing all the indicated intervention

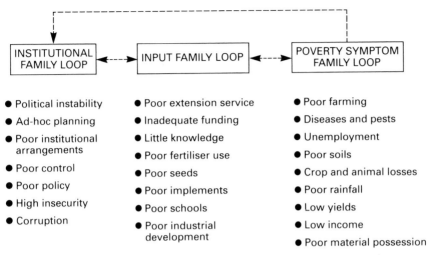

Fig. 8.1   The poverty syndrome family loops

points. It is more cost-effective to select key elements and interactions for timely intervention into the poverty syndrome. To reduce operational problems the causes of poverty can be conceptualized to fall under three major family groups: institutional, input and poverty symptom family loops (Figure 8.1). Each family loop forms a major focus of diagnosis and selective treatment of poverty.

In Figure 8.1 interaction between institutional and input constraints results in several symptoms (indicators) of poverty. Without effective intervention, a vicious cycle can be created in which a community gets trapped in a self-perpetuating spiral of poverty. For instance, crop and animal losses arising from poor policy and poor institutional arrangements may reduce a farmer's capacity to procure farm inputs (seeds, implements, fertilizers), thus reinforcing poverty.

In almost all developing countries, interventions into the poverty syndrome are often symptomatic and concentrated on input constraints. Thus in the 1970s significant attempts were taken to improve the supply of capital, farming implements, and training facilities with the hope of stepping up production and standard of living. By the mid-1980s these attempts appeared futile as poverty became even more widespread and devastating. As demonstrated by the component relationships in Figures 3.5 and 8.1, this failure occurred partly because institutional constraints were left untackled and because of symptomatic treatment on the other hand. The constraints thus continued to neutralize effects of investments at the input and symptom loops. In the proposed new direction, there is need to pay greater attention to institutional constraints as they affect efforts to diversify the resource base, to utilize capital investment, control population growth, increase production, and sustain resource development.

181

Perspectives on the future

Increased growth

In industrialized countries, remarkable standards of living have been achieved through growth in the development of resources and human productivity. In developing countries, better living standards can also be achieved. Productivity must increase to cater first to basic human needs and then to a point where productivity can have a reversing effect on poverty. According to the World Commission on Environment and Development (1987), growth can have an impact on poverty if the rates of increase in GDP and income exceed prevailing national population growth rates. In rationalizing this viewpoint, the Commission observed that population is growing at rates that cannot be sustained by available environmental resources, at rates that are outstripping any reasonable expectations of improvements in housing, health care, food security, or energy supplies. This is made worse by continued decline in yields of crops and other resources. The Commission thus suggested that income growth rates of 6 per cent in Africa, 5.5 per cent in Latin America and 5 per cent in Asia must be achieved in order to counteract the effects of rising population and alleviate poverty.

In particular there must be improvements in the production and supply of food, industrial raw materials, manufactured goods, energy, clean water and household income and material possession. Such improvements will allay the tendency for desperate extraction of resources. Because of the nature of the economies in developing countries, improvements in agricultural productivity are an imperative first step in order to provide a fulcrum on to which growth in other resource sectors can hinge.

As indicated in Chapters 3 and 4, agriculture in developing countries forms a significant corner-stone for overall national growth and development. Agriculture engages much more land and human labour than any other resource sector, it is intrinsically interlinked with other sectors of the economy, there is a long-standing history and experience with agricultural practices amongst all communities in developing countries, and above all, the institutional framework for agricultural development exists in every Third World country. There is therefore a strong foundation for improving agricultural productivity. In discussing the role of agriculture in developing economies Arnon (1981) observed that national economic growth can take place on a wider front if agriculture is promoted to

1 increase food production considerably so as to improve the existing nutrition levels, in quantity and quality, for a rapidly increasing population
2 provide productive employment for a rapidly increasing rural population
3 produce export crops as a source of foreign currency
4 support industrial development by providing raw materials, able-bodied workers, capital and improved rural purchasing power and a market for manufactured goods.

Growth in agricultural productivity is capable of inducing a chain of effects with important implications for the management of other resources. Improvements in food supply, income and rural employment arising from agricultural growth could provide a facelift to the rural countryside. Effective agricultural development will entail upgrading of rural access roads, water supply and conservation, rural infrastructure, and rural commerce to supply farm inputs. In turn these developments will dampen the current survival insecurity amongst rural communities, thus reducing the tendency for rural–urban migration. With improved purchasing power and subsequently enhanced housing and material possession of the rural community, the need to conserve forests, fisheries, soils, water resources and wildlife will be more easily appreciated and adopted. Complementary policies to diversify the resource base, to uplift educational standards, to introduce family planning and population control, modern technology and a sense of community responsibility will become more acceptable as the survival security continues to become more evident and guaranteed.

For agricultural productivity to increase and provide a springboard for effective conservation of other resources, present widespread subsistence agriculture needs to be transformed and modernized. Arnon (1981) stated that growth through agricultural modernization is possible under four conditions:

1 generation of new technology, implying an effective research organization
2 rapid transfer of the new technology to the farmers, requiring an efficient system of education
3 provision of essential incentives and conditions to motivate the farmers to successfully adopt more efficient methods of production
4 devising and implementing an appropriate strategy for promoting the entire process of growth through modernization.

These conditions require changes in the existing systems of technology, training and research, farming conditions and institutional arrangements.

Sustainable development

A main objective of resource development is to satisfy human needs and aspirations for a better life. To meet the essential needs, the full potential of a nation's resources must be realized so that harmony rather than desperation guides the exploitation of resources. To eradicate poverty and associated survival insecurity in developing countries, growth must be sustainable in the long run. According to the World Commission on Environment and Development (1987), sustainable development is development that meets the needs of the present without compromising the ability of future generations to meet their own needs. This viewpoint requires rational exploitation of the productive potential of resources and guaranteeing equitable opportunities for all.

Sustainable development therefore involves more than growth. The Commission (1987:52) asserts that sustainable development 'requires a change in the content of growth, to make it less material- and energy-intensive and more equitable in its impact'. This position implies resource development efficiency in which greater value is derived from increasingly smaller volumes of resources – a situation which is tenable through research and improved technological efficiency.

Sustainable development also requires more effective systems of environmental impact accountability. Comprehensive assessment of 'costs' is required so that beneficiaries compensate the losers. The final costing must include costs of redressing environmental damage. For instance profits from timber extraction must take full account of environmental effects of forest destruction and the cost of reafforestation. Similarly, introduction of large-scale commercial farming may generate revenue rapidly, but may also dispossess many smaller farmers and make the distribution of income and social benefits inequitable and unacceptable. Such imbalances in growth disrupt the required harmony between people and resources. Sustainable development requires a more efficient surveillance system to detect and counteract unnecessary ecological and social impacts of resource development programmes.

Prospects for the future

As has been emphasized, the prospects for resource management in developing countries rest on efforts directed at curbing poverty through increased growth and sustainable development. To achieve this end, developing countries have to adopt and adhere to an integrated approach to resource management.

In resource management, confusion often arises in distinguishing between comprehensive and integrated resource management. In the confusion the words comprehensive and integrated are used interchangeably. According to B. Mitchell (1989), comprehensive management implies a holistic approach which considers all elements and their interactions. In contrast, integrated management suggests considering a selected number of elements and inter-actions. As mentioned earlier there are problems in implementing and operationalizing comprehensive management. In almost all developing countries paucity of data, inadequate capital, poor skills, weak institutions, poor capacity, and inadequate co-ordination and co-operation cause difficult-ies in operationalizing comprehensive managemen.. Integrated approach is therefore recommended for developing countries because it allows different countries to select elements and processes to be tackled on the basis of attendant national resource issues, priorities and capacity. However, inte-grated management should not be mistaken for a sectoral approach. In the integrated approach, interlinkages between resource sectors are recognized. In a sectoral approach, specific resources such as land, water, minerals, forests and wildlife are managed in isolation from each other. As stated in the preceding chapters, most of the contemporary resource use problems have arisen because during resource exploitation, adverse effects of one sector on other resource sectors and processes were often not considered.

Although strategies for resource management will vary from one country to another according to prevailing issues, priorities and means, there are specific resource management problems which are common to and have to be tackled by almost all developing countries. These problems relate to social order, institutional reforms, population, technology, research and training, and international order and co-operation. Efforts to redress these problems will induce a catalysing effect and reinforce prospects for achieving increased growth and sustainable development. If these problems are successfully resolved, other obstacles such as soil erosion, overgrazing, low productivity, overexploitation and encroachment into marginal land will almost simultaneously unfold.

Social order

Apart from widespread poverty, the Third World communities are also known for their persistent adherence to social norms and traditions which are passed from one generation to another. Although traditions and cultural practices give identity and have a number of positive attributes, certain cultural beliefs and practices constitute a formidable barrier to innovation and societal evolution and progress.

Polarized views are expressed about the effect of culture on economic development in developing countries. One school of thought argues that socio-cultural factors have only a marginal role as farmers have, through trial and error, gradually arrived at an optimal solution to the allocation of the limited resources available to them (Schultz, 1964; Mellor, 1969). There is often a state of technological stagnation which is not due to attitudes of the farmers, but to an economic environment over which the farmer has no control (Dandekar, 1969). According to this school of thought, farmers will respond quickly, normally and efficiently to economic incentives in adopting new techniques (Behrman, 1969). In the other school of thought, subsistence agriculture is much more affected by non-economic forces than by pure economic forces. This leads to behaviour that is not within bounds of economic rationality (Balogh, 1966).

In analysing strategies for agricultural modernization, Arnon (1981) provided a less extreme but more acceptable viewpoint. He observed that in developing countries there are two types of communities and groups:

1 Those who do not require much persuasion to adopt new techniques, in which the innovator enjoys respect and prestige.
2 Those in which tradition and established customs are conducive to resistance to change, in spite of all manner of persuasion and inducements. Such communities and groups form the majority and they can refuse to increase their production and income even if opportunities are available.

Based on the works of other researchers, several examples of the second group of communities can be cited:

1 In some areas of China, a taboo against raising and eating of white birds caused the failure of a project to raise white leghorns, a better breed than the indigenous breeds. Similarly, other religious beliefs in these areas, such as respect for scattered burial plots, seriously hamper efforts to consolidate land holdings (Arnon, 1981).

2 Smock (1969) observed that much of the resettlement budget for the Volta Dam in Ghana was allocated for food and drink to pacify the spirits of shrines which had to be relocated. Another drawback to the resettlement scheme came as a result of the belief that women who live in crowded and integrated areas will become barren.

3 Lutfiyya (1966) noted that 'Islam sanctions traditional behaviour and gives it precedence over innovations . . . Innovators are always the objects of shame and ridicule in "Moslem villages". Invariably there is outright rejection of anything new that appears to conflict with tradition.' However, Arnon (1981) later observed that in spite of such beliefs, when favourable conditions occurred for modernization of Arab villages in Israel and the West Bank, the process was never hampered by such traditions.

4 According to Hunter and Jiggins (1978), some hill people of Assam regard it as shameful to sell food because food should be shared freely with those who would otherwise go hungry. Although such a belief is humane and appealing, it promotes resistance to innovations aimed at producing and selling surplus food.

5 Amongst the pastoralists of East Africa (the Masai, the Karamojong and Turkhana), all cattle at one time belonged to them. Any cattle existing outside their communities must have been stolen from them. This has led to repeated cattle stealing and insecurity in districts neighbouring the pastoral districts and difficulty in promoting livestock development (personal communication).

Such beliefs, although slowly being discarded, still exert significant influences in almost every community in developing countries. Reinforced by effects of social orgnaizations such as clans and kinship relationships, class and castes, attitudes to women, and a feeling of pride and dignity about one's culture, the beliefs ultimately determine whether or not resources are properly used to increase and sustain production. A strategy to eradicate poverty through increased growth and sustainable development must address itself to social and cultural factors which condition communities to accepting, rejecting or playing down innovations. There can be no progress without change.

Culture and society must evolve to accommodate new insights and aspirations and to redress negative aspects of cultural practices. The evolution of a culture and the associated changes in community attitudes and practices are neither a weakness nor foreign-induced. Instead, cultural evolution is a necessary and inherent requirement for the sustenance of culture itself. The evolution allows a community to adjust to and build on positive experiences of its travelled, educated and young members and of its local and international friends. Furthermore, cultural evolution allows outstanding features of the community to gain acclaim and become exemplary nationally and internationally thus guaranteeing its continuity into future generations. When a culture is rigid and unalterable, its members may split into opposing and sometimes hostile wings of the versatile *vis-à-vis* the conservative and autocratic groups. Such a split eventually can lead to isolation and the demise of the culture because the number of the travelled, educated and the young members keep on swelling against the dwindling number of the old.

Therefore, in the interest of sustaining cultures, a new social order must be devised to more readily accept and accommodate the required changes in resource development and management strategies. However, M. G. Smith (1966) and Arnon (1981) cautioned that there are limits to the type and volume of innovations that a given culture can accommodate without losing its integrity. The simpler the culture, the narrower are these limits and the less amenable is the culture to change. For agricultural modernization, Arnon optimistically observed that resistance to change need not be exaggerated. Given proper incentives and supporting services and using appropriate extension methods, farmers adopt new practices that provide greater returns at a low level of risk more easily than is generally assumed.

Institutional reforms

This is one of the most important but most neglected aspects of resource management in developing countries. Even in industrialized countries, institutional arrangements need greater attention (O'Riordan, 1971; B. Mitchell, 1989). According to O'Riordan (1971:135),

> there is growing evidence to suggest that the form, structure and operational guidelines by which resource management institutions are formed and evolve clearly affect the implementation of resource policy, both as to the range of choice adopted and the decision attitudes of the personnel involved.

As discussed in Chapter 2, institutional arrangements include the pattern of government and private agencies, their legislative ability to tackle issues and the nature of checks and balances and public accountability. Operational efficiency of institutions therefore depends on established laws, customs, behaviour, responsibility centres and the manner in which they are organized and deployed to tackle a problem in society.

In developing countries institutional constraints provide a bottleneck which is only slowly being recognized. In almost all developing countries institutions for resource management are either inadequate or wrought with cumbersome bureaucracy. Because of this drawback, developing countries cannot effectively implement strategies to increase growth and sustainable development without prior institutional reforms.

Many poor countries, especially those that experience political instability, still retain the pattern of agencies and legislations left by former colonial governments. As a result a number of contemporary resource management problems cannot be dealt with under a specific agency or legislation (Chapters 3, 5, 6 and 7). Often environmental deterioration in oceans and lakes can only be linked to regulations embodied in the Fisheries Act. The Fisheries Act not only is sketchy and inadequate but also is administered by the Ministry of Fisheries and Animal Resources rather than the Ministry of Environment and Natural Resources (Chapter 6). Where legislation is available, implementation is hampered by inadequate communication and poor co-ordination between agencies of various resource sectors. There is need for a thorough review to place governments and other agencies in a position where they can account for, assess or prescribe the means through which resource management strategies can be implemented.

For a long time many government departments in developing countries operated as a closed system: they were compartmentalized and acted independently with a narrow focus of concern. The departments responsible for managing natural resources and protecting the environment (e.g. forestry and wildlife) were always separated from and independent of those concerned with resource extraction and economic development (e.g. agriculture, fisheries, industry). Furthermore, the sectors such as timber industry, mining, manufacturing industries, and road construction whose policies contributed much to environmental damage were not often responsible and were rarely penalized for environmental damage they caused. There was therefore no basis for initiating and effecting environmental impact accountability. By the mid-1980s, however, some governments began to re-examine institutional arrangements and to call for a broader perspective incorporating conservation concerns.

Perhaps the greatest institutional constraint is bureaucracy. The red-tape syndrome has grown into dangerous proportions mainly because of overcentralized authority. In many developing countries there is often an 'inner core' (small section of the Cabinet) which monopolizes power and authority and creates a narrow base for decision making. The authoritarian attitude of the inner core together with widespread corruption creates job insecurity, even amongst parliamentarians, leading to unwillingness to make decisions involving responsibility. As a result issues are not thoroughly discussed even in parliament. This results in hasty and half-baked decisions. In the bureaucracy, government officials adhere rigidly to rules and regulations while encouraging frequent visits and long office-sittings before any action is taken. This behaviour discourages contacts from up-country, thus excluding rural areas from government service. In desperation some of the wealthier visitors break through the bureaucracy by offering bribes. The officials begin to justify taking bribes by quoting cases of corruption at higher levels, irregular payment of salaries, abrupt and unjustified dismissals from office, poor housing, feeding and living standards, and outdated and unworthy pension and gratuity schemes.

Diaz (1974) described the state of bureaucracy in Mexico. He stated that the very roots of backwardness are found in dysfunctional institutional structure which serves agriculture in Mexico. Farmers who wished to acquire credit from Banco Agricola and Banco Ejidal encountered cumbersome and time-consuming procedures for obtaining (and even repaying!) loans; the promised inputs arrived late and they received little technical assistance from banks in their use. As a result, obtaining credit became too costly in terms of time required, and returns to inputs were too low because of late delivery and/or inadequate advice (Arnon 1981).

Arnon (1981) further observed that most of the government officials are, by training and provenance, biased in favour of urban areas. In many cases young, inexperienced and low-paid employees are posted to rural areas, entrenching ineffective operation of rural projects. The effects of all such bureaucracy lead to two fundamental problems:

1 declining respect for government authority and subsequent political instability
2 marginalization and compromise of rural interests and projects aimed at uplifting rural standards of living.

In order to increase productivity and sustain development, institutional reforms have to be effected. The reforms require reviewing institutional arrangements (organizational structures, laws and regulations, staffing, mode of operation, accountability and ethics of public service). Institutional reforms must aim at causing changes which adapt institutions to the new development needs. Specifically there is need to take the following action.

1 Broaden the base for decision-making power by altering the flow of authority through increased grassroots or public participation.
2 Evolve simpler and more precise rules for political and administrative procedures and to institute closer supervision of policy implementation.
3 Review remunerations and standards of living of civil servants. More worthy pension and retirement benefits are also needed to give hope and a sense of security on retirement.
4 Take punitive action against corruption, bribes, extortions and extravagant and unjustified style of living.
5 Review the level of staffing and methods of recruitment to avoid overburdening the budgets without a concomitant work output.
6 Encourage thorough discussion of issues by establishing genuine democratic systems which are free of unfair reprisals and victimization.
7 Reassess the prospects for collective community action such as group farms, co-operative farming, community self-help programmes, and community education to increase the productive capacity of individual family members.

8 Provide internship training to new employees especially those to be posted to rural areas. This will tune the acquired school/university education to practical needs in society.

The need and the remedy for such institutional reforms are well implied in Ruttan's (1977) commendable observation.

The developing world is still trying to cope with the debris of nonviable institutional innovations; with extension services with no capacity to extend knowledge, or little knowledge to extend; co-operatives that serve to channel resources to village elites; price stabilisation policies that have the effect of amplifying commodity fluctuations; and rural development programmes that are incapable of expanding the resources available to rural people.

Population growth

Human numbers and the associated consumption patterns and preferences provide an important factor that influences the relationship between supply and demand of resources. High population growth affects human progress by compromising ability to fight poverty, provide basic needs, education, health care and food security.

Since 1950, developing countries accounted for 85 per cent of the global population increase (World Commission on Environment and Development, 1987). Table 8.1 describes the trends in current and projected population size and growth rates in the world. The table indicates that population growth is now concentrated in Africa, Asia and Latin America. Even between the year 2000 and 2025 population growth rates in Africa will still be high at 2.5 per cent while Latin America and Asia will have declined to 1.4 per cent and 1.0

Table 8.1 Current and projected population size and growth rates*

Region	Population (billion)			Annual growth rate (%)		
	1985	2000	2025	1950 to 1985	1985 to 2000	2000 to 2025
World	4.8	6.1	8.2	1.9	1.6	1.2
Africa	0.56	0.87	1.62	2.6	3.1	2.5
Latin America	0.41	0.55	0.78	2.6	2.0	1.4
Asia	2.82	3.55	4.54	2.1	1.6	1.0
North America	0.26	0.30	0.35	1.3	0.8	0.6
Europe	0.49	0.51	0.52	0.7	0.3	0.1
USSR	0.28	0.31	0.37	1.3	0.8	0.6
Oceania	0.02	0.03	0.04	1.9	1.4	0.9

Source Department of International Economic and Social Affairs (1986)
Note * Medium-variant projections

per cent respectively. This means that for over thirty years Africa will continue to be hard pressed to support rapidly growing human pressure on resources that are shrinking in quantity and quality. Elimination of mass poverty will remain troublesome unless current rates of population growth are checked.

High population growth rates eat up surpluses available for expanding education, health care, roads, agricultural inputs, thus affecting overall economic and social development. In industrialized societies high population densities were coped with through agricultural intensification, production of increasingly higher yields, migration and international trade in food and fuels. As discussed in earlier chapters these options are getting rapidly closed for developing countries. For instance the generally low level of development coupled with ever changing terms of trade already excluded the hope that international trade will improve access to resources. Worse still, dwindling resources mean developing countries have no means to sustain themselves while waiting for populations to stabilize. Because of population pressure people are forced to work under conditions of diminishing returns; farmers work harder on shrinking farms on marginal lands with deteriorating quality of farm inputs and conditions of crop sales. Consequently, household income and material possession cannot be sustained.

In developing countries the population structure is dominated by young people. In 1980, 39 per cent of developing country populations were younger than 15; the figure for industrialized countries was 23 per cent (World Development Report, 1984). The large number of young people in developing countries means large numbers of future parents, so that even if each person produces fewer children, the total number of births will continue to increase (World Commission on Environment and Development, 1987). The large proportion of the young overburdens the development budgets as more schools, food, drugs and jobs have to be supplied to as yet unproductive members of the society.

Because of the effects of population on economic and social development, the World Commission on Environment and Development (1987:95–6) recommended that

Many governments must work on several fronts – to limit population growth, to control the impact of such growth on resources and, with increasing knowledge, enlarge their range and improve their productivity; to realise human potential so that people can better husband and use resources; and to provide people with forms of social security other than large numbers of children . . . Giving people the means to choose the size of their families is not just a method of keeping population in balance with resources; it is a way of assuring – especially for women – the basic human right of self-determination.

But to reduce population growth rates, a multifaceted approach that embraces variables other than population variables must be adopted. Much

191

of the growth in population can be associated with some underlying social and economic conditions of underdevelopment. For instance

1 Poverty leads to high population growth rates because poor families tend to need more children in order to act first as a labour force and later as a means of sustenance for the elderly parents.
2 Women's role in the family, economy and society can affect fertility rates. As women become educated and employed outside the home, as their age at marriage rises, and as they begin to play leadership roles in the community, women begin to avoid needing 'extra' children.
3 Improvements in public health will ensure low infant mortality so that extra children are no longer a necessary insurance against child-death.

There is therefore a need to strengthen the ecological, social, cultural and economic basis of production so that parents are motivated to have smaller families by also making use of family planning programmes, education facilities, technologies and services that will help to reduce family size. It is often alleged that family planning programmes are nearly impossible to implement in developing countries. The success of family planning programmes depends on how they are integrated with other fertility variables such as mother care, nutrition, education, and public health programmes within the area. Most often family planning programmes are operated in isolation of these variables and by 'foreigners' with only nominal contact with local culture and government agencies. A multifaceted approach is desirable because it also helps to tackle such other problems as population distribution, mobility and quality and social services that help to transform the population into becoming assets for society.

Technology, research and training

One of the other widespread problems in developing countries is low productivity due to inability to exploit fully the national resource potential. This is partly due to continued reliance on inefficient technology and inadequate access to more efficient technology.

Technology and research are the main means by which humans can learn to overcome, partly or wholly, the limitations imposed by nature and to make the most effective use of comparative advantages in resource development. Through technology and research, in-depth understanding of natural systems can be gained and exploited to improve the link between people and resources. Under conditions of poor technology, only areas with obvious comparative advantages will be exploited, leading to congestion and rising pressure. Resources that are difficult to exploit, such as in semi-arid, high mountain, wetlands, deeply embedded mineral areas and distant and deep fishing grounds remain out of reach (Chapters 4, 5, 6 and 7), forcing overcrowding of the more accessible resources.

The state and issues of technological development in developing countries have been discussed in detail in Chapter 2 and their resource management implications are dealt with in Chapters 3, 4, 5, 6 and 7. In summary, the current level of productivity in almost all Third World countries is too low to meet the ever rising consumption demands and preferences. This has created difficulties in heeding to calls for resource conservation. Developing countries have henceforth to work individually and together to produce a set of technology with a high benefit-cost ratio; a technology that will enhance and restore the resource base so as to give a promise of higher productivity, increased efficiency and decreased environmental impairment. To achieve this end, developing countries have to spare effort and update traditional technologies, generate alternative technologies, and select and adapt imported technologies.

In Chapters 1 and 2, it was emphasized that traditional technologies in developing countries evolved when circumstances were different from today. Most of the traditional technologies are today too low in productive capacity to meet demands of an ever rising population amidst dwindling resources. The way out is to assess and selectively improve the efficacy of traditional technologies. In a number of developing countries some traditional technologies are being modified. In many African countries new charcoal stoves have been evolved by modifying the original charcoal stoves. The new stove generates more heat per volume of charcoal, uses less charcoal and produces and retains heat for a much longer time than the old stove. In Uganda besides burning timber, charcoal can also now be made by processing coffee husks and other crop residues. Such technological evolution saves resources and allows fuelwood resources to be used on a sustainable basis. A policy to modify traditional technology is relatively easy to implement as the resultant technology will be familiar and more adoptable by the local community. But research is required to determine the direction of technological modification, i.e. which resource sectors should receive what priority, what features are to be maximized and with what social, economic and ecological gains and sacrifices?

In addition, there is need in developing countries to promote local generation of alternative technology from within the local setting. Such alternative technology must be low in capital requirements, simple in the required techniques of management, and must depend on inputs that are locally available, divisible, affordable and easily generated. India almost leads Third World countries in the production of intermediate technologies. India has produced sugar processing plants that can be run within the household of a few families using family plots of sugar cane. In Kenya, a group calling itself 'Jua Kali' (open air, hot sun technologists) has won national acclaim by manufacturing a variety of machines and spare parts for farm equipment, garbage collection, cars and household items.

Jua Kali is a collection of talented but previously unemployed city immigrants. Their contribution has become so important that the Kenya government in 1988 established a ministry exclusively concerned with training, space requirement and promotion of Jua Kali technology. Much of these technologies use scrap metal, promoting the recycling of resources. In addition, the technology is relevant and appropriate because it is developed in response to personal requests or projected demands of known patrons. There is need for an effective research organization with an appropriate research programme to guide the generation of alternative technology and to assess the prospects of technological transfer between developing countries. Local generation of technology not only reduces pressure on limited foreign currency, but also provides employment and place of work and its recycling initiative is resource-saving nationally and internationally.

The other avenue to broaden the technological base of developing countries is to import technology from industrialized countries. There are many resource specialists (McPherson, 1968; B. Mitchell, 1989) who are sceptical of the relative value of technology transfer. This is because many of the Western technologies that were transferred to Third World countries either did not perform as well as they did in their countries of origin or became damaging to the ecology and socio-economy of recipient Third World countries (McPherson, 1968; Ruttan, 1968; Arnon, 1981). The process of technology transfer is not a simple one. The main problem has been that Western technology is not well adapted to the specific ecological, economic and social conditions of those countries to which technology had been imported.

During the implementation of the Green Revolution, technology transfer involving crop varieties and farm equipment took place in Asia, Mexico and the Phillippines. The result was a mixture of failure in one place and success in another. Arnon (1981:186) observed that where the Green Revolution succeeded, the success has been the result of the interaction between the work of the international research centres in which the improved varieties originated, and research work in the individual countries themselves, aimed at adapting agronomic practices to the new varieties under the prevailing environmental conditions.

Wholesale transfer of technology is unrealistic. There is need to review the policy of technology transfer and to deploy local researchers working under local conditions in developing countries to help in the selection and adaptation of imported technology. The local researchers can also help to establish those aspects of technology that are transferable. Ruttan (1968) and Arnon (1981) advised that the other aspect which can be transferred is the capacity to focus scientific efforts on technical problems of economic significance, and the skill that comes from having solved similar problems, even when done in a different environment. Therefore selectivity and adaptability must be the watchwords in the importation of the needed technology.

The need for research and training in the development and management of resources cannot be overemphasized. Research is essential in order to expose the potential, and the limitations of the natural environment *vis-à-vis* resource development goals. In developing countries many basic problems have not yet been adequately studied: tropical soils, their fertility and management problems, the ecology of major pests and diseases, dryland agricultural practices and potential, tropical forestry, pollution control, low cost housing. There are also several research results in universities, national research councils and research institutes which have never been utilized. As a result, research in developing countries often has little or no impact on the development process. Government experimental farms and larger commercial farms are the few areas benefiting from research results.

This situation should not be allowed to continue. Already ineffective decisions leading to mounting problems in rural and urban areas testify to the failure to integrate research into the daily proceedings of government. There is need for greater investment in research, proper formulation of research programmes and prompt application of research results so that growth in economy and acceptable environmental quality are sustained.

For research to be undertaken and its results applied effectively, there is need for formal education and specialized training. Formal education provides useful general knowledge which when combined with practical skills acquired from specialized training, forms the essential foundation for sustainable development. In discussing education for agricultural productivity, Arnon (1981) paraphrased Tang (1961) and outlined the major contributions of general education to increased agricultural productivity. He noted that formal education

1 provides farmers with the basic skills (reading, writing, arithmetic) which facilitate the transmission of technical knowledge, making possible the keeping of farm records and making simple calculations required for deciding on the economic benefits of proposed inputs
2 improves rationality, making it easier to overcome traditional, social or cultural constraints which hinder progress
3 increases inquisitiveness and thereby improves receptivity for new ideas, oppportunities and methods
4 changes values and aspirations, and thereby strengthens the will to economise, and facilitates the adoption of new techniques.

However, formal education in schools and universities does not impart adequate practical skills required for the management of resources. There is still too much book knowledge, theory and urban bias in education in developing countries. There is very little training for extension service in general and for tackling rural community problems in particular. Except for human and veterinary medicine and to some extent forestry, education in other sectors is inadequately designed to give practical skills. Yet on employment many university graduates take up key positions, sometimes as heads of departments or sections in government. There is need for internship training for new employees in order to impart specific skills required for the job at hand. General education and specialized training are also required for the farmers or rural people to expose them to local resource potentials, limitations and safe technologies for resource exploitation. This will require the efforts of extension service officers with the relevant practical skills, adequate knowledge of local cultures, proper public relations and efficient facilities for extension work. Research is itself required to help develop the content of extension service programmes and the nature of community education and specialized training.

International order and co-operation

Because of planetary interlinkages, problems in one part of the world will often affect the rest of the globe. Human practices involving achievements and failures can no longer continue to be compartmentalized within sectors, nations and regions. According to UN projections the world population could stabilize at between 8 billion and 14 billion by the twenty-first century and more than 90 per cent of the increase will occur in the poorest countries (World Commission on Environment and Development, 1987). A significant proportion of the poor country population will roam the world as economic refugees and add to congestion of even cities in industrialized countries. Economic growth in developed countries has often pulled resources from the poor countries, either as raw materials or as a source of labour and market. Growth in technology may improve resource-efficiency worldwide but may also bring forth high risks from pollution and new variety of life forms which may change global evolutionary pathways. These and many other related changes have locked the global economy and ecology together in ways that make mutual goodwill amongst rich and poor nations imperative and mandatory.

Yet up to the present time, international relations, amongst poor nations, rich nations and between poor and rich nations are operationalized basically on the Darwinian principle of survival of the fittest. 'Strings-attached', games, manipulations, taking advantage of weaknesses of others, and egocentric behaviour have prevented foreign aid and charities from effectively fighting poverty and shame in many developing countries. In the height of dangerous irresponsibility some poor nations, in their desperation, have been hoodwinked to accept or ignore the dumping of nuclear wastes within their national boundaries.

A new international order is required in which survival of the fittest is replaced by a sense of fair play for the good of all. Many of the achievements of the present human civilization have a poor ethical basis. For instance it is disproportionate and unethical to do the following:

1 Orbit the moon when millions of poor children lack food, the basic human right.
2 Escalate military defence spending when soil erosion, desertification, diseases and poor housing continue to incapacitate the millions of families for whom military defence is being sought.

3 Manufacture artificial coffee alternatives to outcompete millions of coffee farmers who have little skills and limited options for survival. The poor farmers often occupy areas with natural comparative advantage for coffee farming.

4 Promote agricultural subsidies and surplus production amonst millionaire farmers so that the surplus produce competes for markets with produce from poor countries. Worse still, the surplus production is not channelled to solve food shortages amongst poor families of the world.

International production, consumption and lifestyles need to be harmonized to reflect broader social responsibility and to guarantee the rights of all humans to aspire for a better life. The transfer of capital, technology and benefits must not hurt one for in the long run it will hurt us all.

The resource management problems facing developing countries have to be tackled by developing countries with co-operation and assistance of industrialized countries. All will sacrifice but all can gain (because of planetary interlinkages and interdependencies). A decade of fair play for the good of all should be declared and observed by the international community.

References

Adams, W.M. (1985) 'The downstream impacts of dam construction: a case study from Nigeria'. *Transactions, Institute of British Geographers*, NS **10**: 292–302.

Anderson, K.B. (1978) *African Traditional Architecture: A Study of Housing Settlement Patterns of Rural Kenya*. Oxford, Oxford University Press.

Anon (1982) 'Marine life threatened at Kenya's coast', *Komba* **3**: 31.

Arnon, I. (1981) *Modernization of Agriculture in Developing Countries: Resources, Potentials and Problems*. New York, Wiley.

Aron, R. (1974) 'The industrial society'. In: Cross, N. et al. (eds) *Man-made Futures*. London, Hutchinson.

Baines, G. (1982) 'Traditional conservation practices and environmental management: the international scene'. In: Morauta, L., Pernetta, J. C., and Heaney, W. (eds) *Traditional Conservation in Papua New Guinea: Implications for Today*, Monograph **16**, Institute of Applied Social and Economic Research, Waigani, Papua New Guinea.

Balogh, T. (1966) *The Economics of Poverty*. London, Weidenfeld and Nicolson.

Barch, J.W. (1973) 'Geography and resource management'. *Journal of Environmental Management* **1**: 3–11.

Barrows, H.H. (1923) 'Geography as human ecology'. *Annals of Association of American Geographers* **13**: 1–14.

Behrman, J.R. (1969) 'Supply response and the modernization of peasant agriculture'. In: Wharton, Jr., C.R. (ed.) *Subsistence Agriculture in Economic Development*. Chicago, Aldine.

Bennett, H.H. (1960) 'Soil erosion in Spain'. *Geographical Review* **50** (1): 59–72.

Berry, L. (1981) 'Tanzania: physical and social geography'. In: *Africa South of the Sahara* (1980–81), London, Europa Publications.

Bird, C.D. (1972) 'Botany of the Fan Field trip to the base of Mt Yamnuska'. *Alberta Naturalist* **2** (3): 14.

Bishop, D.M. and Stevens, M.E. (1964) 'Landslides in logged areas in Southeast Alaska'. *U.S. Forest Service Research Paper*, NOR–1.

Biswas, M.R. and Biswas, A.K. (1982) 'Environment and sustained development in the Third World: a review of the past decade'. *Philippine Geographical Journal* **26**: 160–73.

Blong, R.J. and Dunkerley, D.L. (1976) 'Landslides in the Razorback area, New South Wales, Australia'. *Geografiska Annaler* **58A**: 139–47.

Boserup, E. (1965) *The Conditions of Agricultural Growth*. Chicago, Aldine.

Brady, N.C. (1974) *The Nature and Properties of Soils* (8th ed). New York, Macmillan.

Briand, Y. (1987) 'Special industrial wastes in Abidjan – Côte d'Ivoire'. *Industry and Environment* **10** (2): 38–42.

Brooke, C. (1967) 'Food shortages in Tanzania'. *Geographical Review* **57** (3): 333–57.

Brown, D. (1971) *Agricultural Development in India's Districts*. Cambridge, Mass., Harvard University Press.

Brown, L.R. and Shaw, P. (1982) *Six Steps to a Sustainable Society*, Paper 48. Washington, DC, Worldwatch Institute.

Bryceson, I. (1978) 'Tanzanian coral reefs at risk'. *New Scientist* **80**: 115.

Bultena, G.L. and Hendee, J.C. (1972) 'Foresters' views of interest group positions on forest policy. *Journal of Forestry* **70** 337–42.

Burton, I. and Kates, R.W. (1964) 'The perception of natural hazards in resource management'. *Natural Resources Journal* **3** 412–41.

Caine, N. (1974) 'The geomorphic processes in Alpine environment'. In: Ives, J. D. and Barry, R.G. (eds) *Arctic and Alpine Environments*. London, Methuen.

Chambers, R. and Moris, J. (eds) (1973) *Mwea An Irrigated Rice Settlement in Kenya*. Munich, Weltforum Verlag.

Chenery, E.M. (1954) *Minor Elements in Uganda Soils*. Uganda, Department of Agriculture.

Ciriacy-Wantrup, S.V. (1971) 'The economics of environmental policy'. *Land Economics* **47**: 36–45.

Clark, C. (1970) *The Economics of Irrigation* . Oxford, Pergamon.

Clark, R.N. and Stankey, G.H. (1976) 'Analysing public input to resource decisions: criteria, principles and case examples of the codinvolve system'. *Natural Resources Journal* **16**: 213–36.

Clarke, R. (1974) 'Technical dilemmas and social responses'. In: Cross, N. et al. (eds) London, Hutchinson.

Coe, M.J. (1967) *The Ecology of the Alpine Zone of Mount Kenya* The Hague, Dr W. Junk Publishers.

Cole, J. (1978) 'Cultural adaptation and socio-cultural integration in mountain regions'. In: D. Pitt (ed.) *Society and Environment – The Crisis in the Mountains*. New Zealand, Auckland University.

Conklin, H.C. (1963) *The Study of Shifting Cultivation*. Studies and Monographs VI. Washington, DC, Union Panamericana.

Cooke, R.U. and Doornkamp, J.C. (1974) *Geomorphology in Environmental Management: An Introduction*. Oxford, Clarendon Press.

Cowan, I.M. (1968) 'The role of ecology in the National Parks'. In: Nelson, J.G. and Scace, R.C. (eds) *The Canadian National Parks: Today and Tomorrow*. Calgary, University of Calgary.

Craine, L.E. (1969) *Water Management Innovations in England*. Baltimore, Md, Johns Hopkins.

Cross, N., Elliott, D. and Roy, R. (eds) (1974) *Man-made Futures*. London, Hutchinson.

Cruickshank, M.J. (1979) 'Offshore and onshore coastal mining review'. Paper presented at the Workshop on Coastal Area Development in South East Asia and the Pacific, Manila, 3–12 December.

Csallany, S.C. et al. (eds) (1972) *Watersheds in Transition*. Proceedings of a Symposium on Watersheds in Transition' held at Fort Collins, Colorado, 19–22 June.

Dandekar, V.M. (1969) 'Questions of economic analysis and the consequences of population growth' In: Wharton, Jr., C.R. (ed.) *Subsistence Agriculture in Economic Development*, Chicago, Aldine.

References

Dansereau, P. (1957) *Biogeography: An Ecological Perspective*. New York, Ronald Press.

Dansereau, P. (1975) *Harmony and Disorder in the Canadian Environment*. Occasional Paper no. 1, Ottawa, Canadian Environmental Advisory Council, Minister of Supply and Service.

Dasmann, R.F. and Poore, D. (1979) *Ecological Guidelines for Balanced Land Use: Conservation and Development in High Mountains*, Gland, Switzerland, IUCN Publications.

Dawes, C.J. (1981) *Marine Biology*, New York, Wiley.

Day, R.J. (1972) 'Stand structure, succession, and use of Southern Alberta's Rocky Mountain Forest'. *Ecology* **53** (3): 472–8.

Department of International Economic and Social Affairs (1986) *World Population Prospects: Estimates and Projections as Assessed in 1984*. New York, United Nations.

Devyer, S. (1981) *African Traditional Architecture in Historical and Geographical Perspective*. Nairobi, Heinemann.

Diaz, H. (1974) 'An institutional analysis of a rural development project: the case of the Pueblo project in Mexico'. Ph.D. Thesis, University of Wisconsin.

Dingwall, P.R. (1972) 'Erosion by overland flow on an alpine debris slope'. In: Slaymaker, O. and McPherson, J.H. (eds) *Mountain Geomorphology*. Vancouver, Tanatalus Research Ltd.

Dorney, R.S. (1977) 'Environmental assessment: the ecological dimension'. *Journal of the American Waterworks Association* **69**: 182–5.

Doute, R.N., Ochandra, N. and Epp, H. (1981) *A forest inventory of Kenya using Remote Sensing*. Kremu Technical Report Series No. 30, Nairobi, Kenya Rangeland Ecological Monitoring Unit (Kremu).

Duffy, R.G.O. (1971) 'An ecological study of vegetation change in the northern Porcupine Hills, Alberta'. unpublished MSc thesis, University of Calgary, Calgary.

Dworkin, D.M. (1974) *Environment and Development*. Indiana, Scope.

Eckholm, E.P. (1975) 'The deterioration of mountain environments'. *Science* **189**: 764–70.

Eckholm, E.P. (1976) *Losing Ground: Environment Stress and World Food Prospects*. New York, W. W. Norton.

FAO (1957) 'Shifting cultivation'. *Tropical Agriculture* **34** (3).

FAO (1965) *Yearbook*. Rome, Food and Agriculture Organization of the UN.

FAO (1968) *The State of Food and Agriculture*. Rome, Food and Agriculture Organization of the UN.

FAO (1970) *Provisional Indicative World Plan For Agricultural Development*. Rome, Food and Agriculture Organization of the UN.

FAO (1975) *Agricultural Extension and Training*. Rome, Food and Agriculture Organization of the UN.

FAO (1977) *The State of Food and Agriculture 1976*. FAO Agriculture Series no. 4. Rome, FAO.

FAO (1980) *Production Yearbook Tapes*, Rome, Food and Agriculture Organization of the UN.

Fernie, J. and Pitkethly, A.S. (1985) *Resources, Environment and Policy* London, Harper and Row.

Fines, D.K. (1968) 'Landscape evaluation: a research project in East Sussex'. *Regional Studies* **3**: 41–55.

Finn, D. (1980) 'Interagency relationship in marine resource conflict: some lessons from Outer Continental Shelf oil and gas leasing'. *Harvard Environmental Law Review*, 359390.

Finn, D. (1982) 'Soil loss in developing countries and its relationship to marine resources: examples from East Africa'. *Oceans* September: 942–9.

References

Finn, D. (1983) 'Land use and abuse in the East African region'. *Ambio* **12**: 296–301.
Firey, W. (1960) *Man, Mind and Land*. Glencoe, Ill., Free Press.
Garbrecht, G. (1979) 'Increasing of irrigation efficiencies under the conditions of developing countries', P. 3 in *Abstracts: Dialogue on Development. Towards the 21st Century*. Tel-Aviv; Assoc. Engineers and Architects in Israel.
Gardner, J. (1970) 'Geomorphic significance of avalanches in the Lake Louise area, Alberta, Canada', *Arctic and Alpine Research* **2**: 135–44.
GEMS (1984) Uganda Case Study: a sample atlas of environmental resource datasets within grid. *Grid Case Studies Series No. 1* Nairobi, United Nations Environmental Programme (UNEP).
Griffin, K. (1972) *The Green Revolution: An Economic Analysis*. Geneva, Switzerland, UN Research Institute for Social Development.
Griffith, J.F. (1972) *Climates of Africa*, World Survey of Climatology, **10**.
Hamilton, A.C. (1984) *Deforestation in Uganda*. Nairobi, Oxford University Press.
Hart, R.A. De J. (1968) *The Inviolable Hills: The Ecology, Conservation and Regeneration of the British Uplands*. London, Stuart Watkins.
Hewitt, K. (1972) 'The mountain environment and geomorphic processes. In: Slaymaker, O. and McPherson, J.H. (eds) *Mountain Geomorphology* Vancouver, Tanatalus Research Ltd.
Hunter, G. and Jiggins, J. (1978) *Farmer and Community Groups*. Agricultural Administration Unit, Overseas Development Institute, London.
Hyndman, D.C. (1979) 'Wopkaimin subsistence: cultural ecology in the New Guinea Highlands fringe'. Unpublished Ph.D thesis, University of Queensland, Australia.
IUCN (1982) *United Nations List of National Parks and Protected Areas*. Unwin Brothers Ltd.
IUCN/UNEP (1982) 'Conservation of the Coastal and Marine Ecosystems and Living Resources of the East Africa Region. Geneva *UNEP Regional Seas Reports and Studies* no. 11.
Jameson, J.D. (ed.) (1970) *Agriculture in Uganda*, 2nd edn. London, Oxford University Press .
Kalitsi, E.A.K. (1973) 'Volta Lake in relation to the human population and some issues in economics and management'. In: Ackerman, W.C., White, G.F. and Worthington, E.B. (eds) *Man-Made Lakes: Their Problems and Environmental Effects*. Washington, DC, American Geophysical Union.
Kananaskis Pilot Study (1974) *The Mountain Environment and Urban Society*, Calgary, University of Calgary.
Kayastha, S.L. (1982) 'Perspectives on environment and development', *National Geographical Journal of India* **28**: 37–43.
Kaynor, E.R. and Howards. I. (1971) 'Limits on the Institutional frame of reference in water resource decision making'. *Water Resources Bulletin* **7**: 1,117–27.
Kenya, Republic of (1966) *Sessional Paper No. 5, 1966/67*. Nairobi: Government Printers.
Kitchen Cameron, J. (1976) 'Ecology and urban development: the theory and practice of Ecoplanning in Canada'. In: McBoyle, G.R. and Sommerville, E. (eds) *Canada's Natural Environment: Essays in Applied Geography*. Toronto, Methuen.
Kollmannsperger, F. (1977) *Man-Made Landscape Changes in the Himalayas and Change in MicroClimates and biotapes*, German Agency for Technical Cooperation Ltd, West Germany.
Kovda, V.A. (1977) 'Arid land irrigation and soil fertility: problems of salinity, alkalinity, compaction'. In: Worthington, E.B. (ed.) *Arid Land Irrigation in Developing Countries: Environmental Problems and Effects* Oxford, Pergamon Press.
Kuznetz, S. (1959) *Six Lectures on Economic Growth*. Glencoe, Ill., Free Press.
Kuznetz, S. (1964) 'Economic growth on contribution of agriculture: notes on

201

References

management'. In: Eicher, C.K. and Witt, I (eds) *Agriculture in Economic Development*. New York, McGraw-Hill.

Langlands, B.W. (1972) *Population Geography of Bugisu District*. Department of Geography Makerere University, Kampala.

Leiss, W. (1970) 'Utopia and technology: reflections on the conquest of nature. *International Social Science Journal* **22** (4): 576–88.

Leopold, L.B. and Marchand, M.O. (1968) 'On the quantitative inventory of the riverscape'. *Water Resources Research* **4**: 709–17.

Leopold, L.G., Wolman, M.C. and Miller, J.P. (1964). *Fluvial Processes in Geomorphology*. San Francisco, W.H. Freeman.

Li-Fen Yi and Tian-Min Xie (1987) 'A comprehensive treatment of effluents from leather industry'. *Industry and Environment* **10** (2): 17–18.

Lind, E.M. and Morrison, M.E.S. (1974). *East African Vegetation*. London, Longman.

Longhurst, S. and Turner, E. (1987). 'Combined treatment of industrial effluents'. *Industry and Environment* **10** (2) 11–16.

Longley, R.W. (1972) 'The climate of the prairie provinces'. *Climatological Studies* no 13.

Lusigi, W.J. (1978) 'An African approach to national park planning in Kenya'. Paper presented at 2nd International Congress of Ecology, Jerusalem.

Lusigi, W.J. (1989) 'Alternative strategies and approaches for the conservation of African wildlife. Paper presented at Nairobi University Staff Seminar, Nairobi.

Lutfiyya, A.M. (1966) *Baytin, A Jordanian Village: A Study of Social Institutions and the Social Change in a Folk Community*. The Hague, Mouton.

Mabogunje, A.L. (1974) 'Regional and international co-ordination, Africa'. In: Dworkin, D.M. (ed.) *Environment and Development*. Indiana, SCOPE.

Mabogunje, A., Handoy, J.E. and Misra, R.P. (1977) *Shelter Provision in Developing Countries*. New York, Wiley.

McCormick, J. (1986) 'The origins of the World Conservation Strategy'. *Environmental Review* **10**: 177–87.

McHarg, I.L. (1966). 'Ecological determination'. In: Darling, F. and Milton, J. (eds) *Future Environments of North America*, New York, Natural History Press.

McHarg, I.L. (1971) *Design with Nature*, New York, Natural History Press.

McIntyre, L. (1973) 'The Lost Empire of the Incas'. *National Geographic* **144** (6): 729–86.

MacKintosh, E.E. (1974) 'The Hanlon Creek Study: an ecological approach to planning'. *Journal of Soil and Water Conservation* **29** (6): 277–80.

McLean, B. (1971) 'Land-use and ecological problems'. In: Ominde, S.H. (ed.) *Studies in East African Geography and Development*, Berkeley, University of California Press.

McPherson, W.W. (1968) 'Status of tropical agriculture'. In: McPherson, W.W. (ed.) *Economic Development of Tropical Agriculture*. Gainesville, Fla, University of Florida Press.

Major, J. (1951) A functional, factorial approach to Plan Ecology. *Ecology* **32.**

Manshard, W. (1974) 'Tropical systems of agriculture' In: Manshard, W., *Tropical Agriculture*, trans. D.A.M. Naylon; London, Longman.

Marsh, G.P. (1964) *Man and Nature: Or Physical Geography as Modified by Human Action*. New York, Scribner.

Matthews, B.C. (1972) 'Soil erosion: Why the concern?' *Conservation Council of Ontario, Toronto Publications*.

Meeham, W.R., Farr, W.A., Bishop, D.M. and Patric, J.H. (1969) *Some Effects of Clearcutting on Salmon Habitat of two Southeast Alaska Streams*, US Department of Agriculture.

Meier, G.M. (1984) *Leading Issues in Economic Development* 4th edn. Oxford, Oxford University Press.

Mellor, J.W. (1969) 'The subsistence farmer in traditional economics'. In: Wharton, Jr, C.R. (ed.) *Subsistence Agriculture in Economic Development*, Chicago, Aldine.

Miller, A.A. (1961) *Climatology*. London, Methuen.

Millikan, M.F. and Hapgood, D. (1967) *No Easy Harvest*. Boston, Mass. Little Brown.

Mitchell, B. (1979) *Geography and Resource Analysis*, 1st edn. London, Longman.

Mitchell, B. (1989) *Geography and Resource Analysis*, 2nd edn. London, Longman.

Mitchell, B. and Ross, W.M. (1974) 'Problems of evaluation in resource management as illustrated by the British Columbia Salmon Licence Programme'. *GIRMS Papers*, **4**.

Mitchell, B. and Turkheim, R. (1977) 'Environmental impact assessment: principles, practices and Canadian experiences. In: Krueger, R.R. and Mitchell, B (eds) *Managing Canada's Renewable Resources*, Toronto, Methuen.

Mitchell, R.C. and Carson, R.T. (1989) *Using Surveys to Value Public Goods: The Contingent Valuation Method* Washington, DC, Resources for the Future.

Monheim, F. (1974) 'The population and economy of tropical mountain regions, illustrated by the examples of the Bolivian and Peruvian Andes'. In: *Report of the Food and Agriculture Development Centre*, Munich.

Moran, J.M., Morgan, M.D. and Wiersma, J.H. (1986). *Introduction to Environmental Science*. 2nd edn. New York, W. H. Freeman.

Moss, R.P. (1963) 'Soils, slopes and land use in a part of S.W. Nigeria'. *Institute of British Geographers*, **32**: 143–68.

Nash, M. (1973) 'Work, incentives, and rural society and culture in developing nations'. In: *Employment Process in Developing Countries*. Seminar sponsored by the Ford Foundation, Bogota, Colombia.

National Research Council (1982) *Ecological Aspects of Development in the Humid Tropics* Washington, DC, NRC.

Nelson, J.G. and Byrne, A.R. (1966) 'Man as an Instrument of Landscape Change: Fires, Floods and National Parks in the Bow Valley, Alberta'. *Geographical Review* **56** 226–38.

Norman, D.W. (1976) 'Developing mixed cropping systems relevant to the farmers' environment'. Paper presented at the Symposium on Intercropping for Semi-arid Areas, Morogoro, Tanzania.

Norman, D.W. and Hays, H. (1979) 'Developing a suitable technology for small farmers'. *National Development* **21** (3): 67–75.

Obudho, R.A., and Aduwo, G.O. (1989) 'Slum and squatter settlement in urban centres of Kenya: towards a planning strategy'. *Netherlands, Journal of Housing and Environmental Resources* **4**: 17–30.

Obudho, R.A. and Mhlanga, C. (eds) (1987) *Slum and Squatter Settlements in Sub-Saharan Africa: Towards a Planning Strategy*. New York, Praeger.

O'Connor, K. (1978) 'Evolution of a New Zealand high country pastoral community'. In: Pitt, D. *Society and Environment – The Crisis in the Mountains*. New Zealand, University of Auckland.

Odum, E.P. (1969) 'Air-Land-Water . . . an ecological whole'. *Journal of Soil and Water Conservation* **24** (1): 4–7.

Odum, E.P. (1971) *Fundamentals of Ecology*. Toronto, W.B. Saunders.

Ogot, B.A. (1968) *Zamani: A Survey of East African History*. New York, Humanities Press.

Ojala, E.M. (1972) 'International trade in agricultural products'. *Food Resources Institute Studies in Agricultural Economics, Trade and Development*, **11**.

Okigbo, B.N. and Greenland, D.J. (1977) 'Intercropping systems in tropical Africa.

References

In: Papendick, R.J., Sanchez, P.A. and Triplett, G.B. (eds) *Multiple Cropping*. Madison, Wis, American Society of Agronomy.

O'Loughlin, C.L. (1972) 'A preliminary study of landslides in the Coast Mountains of Southwestern British Columbia'. In: Slaymaker, O. and Mcpherson, J.H. (eds) *Mountain Geomorphology*. Vancouver, Tanatalus Research Ltd.

Omara-Ojungu, P.H. (1977) 'The occupancy problems of steep slopes and human adjustments to landslides: the case of Bulucheke sub-county, Uganda'. Unpublished MA research project.

Omara-Ojungu, P.H. (1978) 'The steep slopes of Bulucheke: an evaluation of the resource problems and human adjustments to landslides'. In: Pitt, D. (eds) *Society and Environment: The Crisis in Mountains*. New Zealand, University of Auckland.

Omara-Ojungu, P.H. (1980) 'Resource management in mountainous environments, the case of the East Slopes region, Bow River Basin, Alberta Canada'. Unpublished Ph. D Thesis, University of Waterloo, Canada.

O'Riordan, T. (1971) *Perspectives on Resource Management*. London, Pion.

Pearse, P. (1968) 'A new approach to the evaluation of non-priced recreational resources'. *Land Economics* **44**: 87–99.

Pearse, P.H. (1977) 'Natural resources policies: an economist's critique'. In R.R. Krueger, and Mitchell, B. (eds) *Managing Canada's Renewable Resources*. Toronto, Methuen.

Peattie, R. (1936) *Mountain Geography: Critique and Field Study*. Cambridge, Mass., Harvard University Press.

Pereira, H.C. (1967) 'Effects of tied ridges, terraces and grass lays on a lateritic soil in Kenya'. *Experimental Agriculture* **3** (2): 89–98.

Pernetta, J.C. and Hill, L. (1984) 'The impact of traditional harvesting on endangered species: the New Guinea experience'. *Proceedings of Endangered Species Conference*, Total Environment Centre, Sydney, Australia.

Priddle, G.B. (1971) 'Attitude scaling'. *GIRMS Papers*, **2**.

Ramesh, A. (ed.) (1984) *Resource Geography*. New Delhi. Heritage. Singapore, National University of Singapore.

Rao, A. N. (1985) 'Mangrove ecosystems of Asia and the Pacific'. In: UNDP/ UNESCO Technical Report (RAS/79/002) on *Mangroves of Asia and the Pacific: Status and Management*.

Rapp, A. and Stormquist, L. (1976) 'Slope erosion due to extreme rainfall in the Scandinavian mountains'. *Geografiska Annaler* **58A**: 193–200.

Raup, H. (1964) 'Some problems in ecological theory and their relation to conservation'. *Journal of Ecology* **51**: 19–24.

Ray, C. (1968) 'Marine parks for Tanzania'. *The Conservation Foundation*. Washington, DC.

Republic of Uganda (1982) The provisional results by administration area *Report on the 1980 population census*, Kampala, **1** : 247.

Rosenberg, N. (1974) 'Technology and economic growth'. In: Cross, N., Elitt D. and Roy, R. (eds) *Man-Made Futures*. London: Hutchinson.

Roszak, T. (1974) 'The technocracy'. In: Cross, N., Elitt, D. and Ray, R. (eds) *Man-Made Futures*. London: Hutchinson.

Russwurm, L.H. and Sommerville, E. (1974) *Man's Natural Environment: A Systems Approach* North Scituate, Mass., Duxbury Press.

Ruthenberg, H. (1971) *Farming Systems in the Tropics*. Oxford, Clarendon Press.

Ruttan, V.W. (1968) 'Strategy for increasing rice production in South-East Asia'. In: McPherson, W.W. (ed.) *Economic Development of Tropical Agriculture*. Gainesville, Fla, University of Florida Press.

Ruttan, V.W. (1977) 'Induced innovation and agricultural development'. *Food Policy* **2**: 196–216.

Ruttan, V.W. and Hayami, Y. (1973) *Technology Transfer and Agricultural Development: Staff Paper* 73–1, New York, Agricultural Development Council.

Rutter, N.W. (1968) 'A method for predicting soil erosion in the Rocky Mountain Forest Reserve, Alberta'. *Geological Survey of Canada Paper* **67**.

Saetersdal, G. (1979) 'Nutrition first: fisheries policies'. *Ceres.*

Salm, R. (1978) 'Conservation of marine resources in Seychelles'. *IUCN*, Morges, Switzerland.

Sargent, F.O. (1969) 'A resource economist views a natural area'. *Journal of Soil and Water Conservation* **24** (1): 8–11.

Scargill, D.I. (1975) *Problem Regions of Europe: The Eastern Alps*, Oxford, Oxford University Press.

Schiff, M.R. (1971) 'Some considerations about attitude studies in resource management'. *GIRMS Papers*, Seminar no 2.

Schultz, R.W. (1964) *Transforming Traditional Agriculture*, New Haven, Conn., Yale University Press.

Scudder, T. (1966) 'Man-made lakes and population resettlement in Africa'. In: Lowe-McConnell, R.H. (ed.) *Man-Made Lakes*. London, Academic Press.

Scudder, T. and Colson, E. (1972) 'The Kariba Dam Project: re-settlement and local initiative'. In: Bernard, H.R. and Pelto, P. (eds) *Technology and Social Change*, New York, Macmillan.

Selby, M.J. (1976) 'Slope erosion due to extreme rainfall: a case study from New Zealand'. *Geografiska Annaler* **58A** (3): 131–8.

Sewell, W.R.D. and Bower, B.T. (eds) (1968) *Forecasting the Demands for Water* Ottawa, Queen's Printer.

Sewell, W.R.D. (1973) 'Broadening the approach to evaluation in resources management decision-making'. *Journal of Environmental Management* **1**: 33–60.

Sharpe, C.F.S. (1960) *Landslides and Related Phenomena*. New York, Columbia University Press.

Sheard, J.S. and Blood, D.A. (1973) 'The role of National Parks in Canada and criteria for their management'. *Canadian Field-Naturalist* **87**: 211–24.

Skinner, R.J., Taylor, J.L. and Wegelin, E.A. (1987) *Shelter Upgrading for the Urban Poor: Evaluation of Third World Experience*, Manila, Island Publishing House.

Smith, D.L. and Memou, P.A. (1987) 'Institutional development for delivery of low income housing: an evaluation of the Dandora Community Development Project in Nairobi'. Unpublished report.

Smith, M.G. (1966) 'The communication of new techniques and ideas: some cultural and psychological factors'. In: de Vries, E. (ed.) *Social Research and Rural Life in Central America, Mexico and the Caribbean Region*. Paris, UNESCO.

Smith, R.L. (1974) *Ecology and Field Biology*. New York, Harper and Row.

Smock, D.R. (1969) 'The role of anthropology in a Western Nigerian resettlement project'. In: Brokensha, D. and Pearsall, M. (eds) *The Anthropology of Development in Sub-Sahara Africa*. Lexington, Ky, University of Kentucky Press.

Stanley, N.F. and Alpers, M.P. (1974) *Man-Made Lakes and Human Health*. London, Academic Press.

Stavenhagen, R. (1969) 'A land reform should answer the questions it raises'. *Ceres* **2** (6) 43–7.

Suchman, E.A. (1967) *Evaluative Research: Principles and Practice in Public Service and Social Action Programmes*. New York, Russell Sage Foundation.

Swanston, D.N. and Dryness, C.T. (1973) 'Stability of steep land'. *Journal of Forestry* **71** 5: 264–9.

Tang, A. (1961) 'Research and education in Japanese agricultural development'. Paper presented at *Annual Meeting of the Econometric Society*, Stillwater Oklahoma.

Thompson, B.W. (1966) 'The mean annual rainfall of Mt. Kenya '. *Weather* **21**: 48–9.

References

Trapnell, C.G., Birch, E.R., Brunt, M.A. and Lawton, R.M. (1976) *Kenya-Vegetation Map 1:250,000, Sheet 2*. London, Directorates of Overseas Surveys.

Troll, C. (1972) *Geology of the High-Mountain Regions of Eurasia*. Wiesbaden, Franz Steiner.

Turnbull, C.M. (1972) *The Mountain People*. New York.

UN/UNESCO/UNEP (1982) 'Marine and coastal area development in the East Africa region'. *UNEP Regional Seas Reports and Studies, No 6*.

UNEP (1982a) *Environment and Development in Asia and the Pacific: Experience and Prospects*, Geneva, UNEP reports and proceedings Series, no 6.

UNEP (1982b) 'Environmental problems of the East African region'. Geneva, *UNEP Regional Seas Reports and Studies, No 12*.

UNEP (1983) 'Action plan for the protection and development of the Marine and coastal areas of the East Asian region'. Geneva, *UNEP Regional Seas Reports and Studies, No 24*.

UNEP (1984) 'UNEP Regional Seas Programme: the Eastern African experience': Geneva, *UNEP Regional Seas Reports and Studies, No 53*.

UNEP (1985) 'Action plan for the protection, management and development of the marine and coastal environment of the Eastern Africa region'. Geneva, *UNEP Regional Seas Reports and Studies, No 61*.

UNEP (1987) 'Environmental management of small and medium size industries'. Geneva, *Industry and Environment* **10** (2).

United Nations Centre for Human Settlement (Habitat) (1984a) *Human Settlement Policy Issues in the ESCAP Region*, Nairobi.

United Nations Centre for Human Settlement (Habitat) (1984b) *Land for Human Settlements*, Nairobi.

Waddell, E. (1972) *The Mound Builders, Agricultural Practices, Environment, and Society in the Central Highlands of New Guinea*, University of Washington Press.

Wagar, J.A. (1974) 'Recreational carrying capacity reconsidered'. *Journal of Forestry* **72**: 274–8.

Walter, H. (1977) 'Climate'. In Chapman, V. J. (ed.) *Ecosystems of the World: Wet Coastal Ecosystems* **1**. New York, Elsevier.

Watters, R.F. (1971) *Shifting Cultivation in Latin America*. Rome, Food and Agriculture Organization of the UN.

Webster, C.D. and Wilson, P.N. (1966) *Agriculture in the Tropics*. London, Longman.

Weiss, R.S. and Rein, M. (1970) 'The evaluation of broad-aim programmes: experimental design, its difficulties and an alternative'. *Administrative Science Quarterly* **15**: 97–109.

Winiger, M. (1981) 'The thermic-hygric differentiation of Mt. Kenya' *Erdkunde Bd.*, **35**.

Winiger, M. (ed.) (1986) *Mount Kenya Area: Contributions to Ecology and Socio-economy*, Institute of Geography, University of Berne, Switzerland.

World Bank (1975) *The Assault on World Poverty*. Baltimore, Md and London, Johns Hopkins University Press.

World Bank (1980) *World Development Report 1980*. Oxford, Oxford University Press.

World Bank (1982a) *World Development Report 1982*. Oxford, Oxford University Press.

World Bank (1982b) *Uganda: Country Economic Memorandum*.

World Bank (1983a), *Learning By Doing: World Bank Lending for Urban Development, 1972–1982*, Washington, DC. The World Bank.

World Bank (1983b) *World Development Report 1983*. Oxford, Oxford University Press.

World Bank (1984) *World Development Report 1984.* Oxford, Oxford University Press.

World Commission on Environment and Development (1987) *Our Common Future.* Oxford, Oxford University Press.

Zimmermann, E.W. (1933; 1951 revised) *World Resources and Industries.* New York, Harper and Brothers.

Zimmermann, E.W. (1964) *Introduction to World Resources.* New York, Harper and Row.

Index

Note: Most references are to developing countries, unless otherwise indicated.

Abidjan 170–2
Africa
  East: marine ecosystem 123, 129–43
    conservation 144–51
    protected areas 146–7, 148, 150
    resource management 132–43
    threatened species 148–50
    wildlife management 10–13
agriculture
  cash crops 8–9, 106–7, 116
  contribution to economy 66–8, 89, 182–3
  dry farming techniques 30, 47
  on East African coast 129–30
  and education 195–6
  green revolution 84–5, 176, 194
  inputs 30, 88, 181
  investment in 87
  modernization 86–7, 174–5, 183, 185–7
  in mountain regions 106–7, 116–18
  patterns of land use 68–70
  productivity 59, 61, 72–4, 77–9, 85–90,
    117–18, 182–3
  research 86–7
  systems 70–84
  in Uganda 56, 57–8, 59, 61–2
agro-chemical pollution 141
agro-forestry 21–2, 114
air rarefaction 93, 98–9
allogenic succession 20
altitude 93, 98–9
animals *see* fauna
anthropogenic climax 22, 37
arable land 59, 61, 68–70
Asia
    mountain resource management in 106–8
    Western: industrial investment 165–6
attitude scaling technique 36
autogenic succession 20

banking, land 157
benefit-cost analysis 29–30
biological oxygen demand (BOD) 139
Brundtland report (1987) 178
building standards 160
bureaucracy 188–9

carrying capacity 24, 71
cash crops 8–9, 106–7, 116
cereals: high-yielding varieties 84–5
citizen participation technique 36
climate, mountain 95–100, 109–11
climax community 21–3
coastal ecosystems 28, 122–8
    East African 123, 129–43
    erosion 142
    flooding 126
    habitat destruction 141–2
    resource management 144–51
    see also marine resources
colonial administration 8–14
    pre-colonial period 6–8
    post-colonial period 14–16
commercial exploitation 8–9, 106–7, 116
communal land 10
community
    concept of 19
    mangrove 125–8
community upgrading schemes 163–4
compensation, land 157
conservation 4–5, 116–17, 118, 174
    government policies 177–8
    holistic approach 179–80
    international programmes 175–7
    marine and coastal 144–51
consumption patterns 41, 43–4, 46
content analysis technique 37

Index

contingency evaluation 28
continuous rain-fed agricultural systems 75–9
conventions: marine resources 145, 148
coral reefs 131, 141–2
corruption 188–9
Costa Rica 177
cultivation systems *see* agriculture
cultural consistency 35
culture
  and agricultural modernization 185–7
  and resource management 34–7
  and technology 7, 31, 32, 33

deforestation 15, 62, 100–1, 134, 175
domestic pollution 139–41, 143
dry farming techniques 30, 47

ecology
  concept of 19
  and resource management 18–27
economy
  agricultural prices 87–8
  consumption patterns 41, 43–4, 46
  contribution of agriculture 66–8, 89, 182–3
  developing countries 40–7, 177, 182–3
  international 15, 41–3, 89
  and resource management 27–30
education 35–6, 195–6
employment 46
environmental deterioration
  coastal 132–43
  and farming techniques 89–90
  marine 188
  mountains 105–6, 119
environmental impact accountability 25–6, 184
environmental impairment 23
erosion 7–8, 10, 28, 116–17
  coastal 142
  mountain 99, 100–1
  run-off 89–90, 100
  and sedimentation 133–4
  slope 94
estuaries: ecosystems 122–8
  see also coastal ecosystems
ethnology: and resource management 34–7
eutrophication 139, 141
expropriation, land 158–9
extended family system 160
extinction
  threatened species 63, 148–50
  universal 179

fallow period 70–1
families: extended 160
family planning programmes 192
fauna
  coastal 124, 128, 130–1
  mountain 102
  protection 10–13

threatened species 63, 148–50
fisheries: in Uganda 63
fishing 120–1, 132, 148
  habitat destruction 141–2
flooding, coastal 126
flora 21–2
  coastal 125–8
  mountain 95, 101–2, 111–13
  protection 10–13
  see also forest
Food and Agriculture Organization (FAO) 176
forest
  management 113–16
  re-afforestation 114–15, 177
  removal 15, 62, 100–1, 134, 175
  reserves 12–13
  in Uganda 62
frost: mountain 99
fuelwood 62, 134, 193

game reserves 11–12
grazing land 9, 61–2, 68, 134
green revolution 84–5, 176, 194
group farms 175

high-yielding varieties (hyv) 84–5
housing
  community upgrading 163–4
  policies 161–4
  schemes 163–4
  site and service 163
  in urban areas 159–64

India 178
  Mandi Project 106–7, 108
industrial period 8–14
  pre-industrial period 6–8
  post-industrial period 14–16
industrialization 164–73
industry
  and agriculture 90
  development of 164–8
  growth 166–8, 182–3
  habitat destruction 142
  investment in 165–6
  pollution 136, 139, 168–73
  waste products 170–3
institutions 35
  conservation policy 144, 148, 150–1, 175–7
  decentralization 45–6
  international 175–7
  need for reform 187–90
international
  organizations: conservation programmes 175–7
  relations 196–7
  trade 15, 41–3, 89

International Union for the Conservation of
    Natural Resources (IUCN) 178
investment
    agricultural 87
    industrial 165–6
irrigation 4, 7–8, 68, 80–4
    definition of 80
Ivory Coast
    industrial waste 170–2
    industry in 168, 169, 170

Jua Kali 193–4

Kariba Dam 3, 31, 36–7
Kenya 36, 125
    alternative technology 193–4
    conservation 175, 177
    game reserves 11–12
Kenya, Mount
    agricultural land management 116–18
    climate 96, 98, 109–11
    ecological zones 95, 102, 111–13
    forest management 113–16
    resource development 109–18

lakes, human-made 3, 31, 36–7
land
    communal 10
    patterns of use 68–70
    public acquisition policies 117–18, 155–9
    reform 90, 153
    in urban areas 152–9
    see also agriculture
landslides 93, 94, 100–1, 103
leasehold, land 156–7
legislation 35
    conservation 144, 148
    land 156, 159
    marine 188
livestock 61–2, 134, 186

malnutrition 88–9
Man and Biosphere (MAB) programme 176
Mandi Project 106–7, 108
mangrove swamps 125–8, 130
marine resources 120–51
    in East Africa 123, 129–32
    ecosystems 121–8
    resource development 129–32
    resource management 132–51
    threatened species 148–50
Mekong Valley Project 4, 107–8
Mexico 189
mountains 28, 34, 91–119
    biota patterns 101–2
    climate 95–100, 109–11
    commercial use 104–5
    ecosystems 92–103
    morphology 93–5
    resource management 102–19

in Asia 106–8
    in Mount Kenya 109–18
    soils 100–1
mulching 89–90
multiple cropping 74–5

national
    boundaries 9
    parks 10–11
    reserves 12
nationalization, land 158–9
natural resources 5, 57–9
Nepal 178
nomadism 7–8, 28
nutrition 8–9
Nyayo Tea Zone 117

oceanic subsystem 122, 132
oceans 120, 121
oil 41, 42
    pollution 136, 137–8

Pacific Islands, South 16
Papua New Guinea 2
pests and diseases 72–3
political instability 58–9, 60, 87
pollution 14, 135–41
    domestic 139–41, 143
    industrial 136, 139, 168–73
    oil 136, 137–8
    and technology 31–4
population
    growth 76, 77–8, 144, 154–5, 190–2
    mountain 97–8
    in Uganda 64
poverty 40–65, 177, 180–1
    alleviation 44, 45–7, 57, 58
    causes 41–5, 56–7
    and housing 159–64
    indicators 55–6, 181
    and international relations 196–7
    and land availability 152–9
    rural 44–7
    syndrome 43, 44, 181
    in Uganda 47–65
precipitation, mountain 97, 98, 99, 102,
    110–11
producer prices 87–8
productive forests 114–16
public involvement: in resource management
    14, 34–7, 46

readjustment, land 157–8
re-afforestation 114–15, 177
religion: and agricultural modernization
    185–6
research, need for 64–5, 194–5
    in agriculture 46–7, 86–7
    in irrigation 82
    in mountain regions 108

Index

resettlement schemes 113–14, 117–18, 134
resource
  allocation 3
  concept of 1–3
  conservation *see* conservation
  see also resource development; resource
    management
resource development
  concept of 3–4
  marine 129–32
  in mountain areas 103–8
  sustainable 183–4
  see also resource management
resource management
  agricultural land 66–90
  colonial period 8–14
  concept of 4–5
  critical issues 178–84
  ecological approach 18–27
  economic approach 27–30
  ethnological approach 34–7
  evolution of 5–16
  future prospects 184–97
  integrated approach 37–9, 184–5
  marine and coastal areas 132–51
  in mountain regions 102–19
  post-colonial period 14–16
  poverty 57–65
  pre-colonial period 6–8
  problems 185–97
  technological approach 30–4
  trends 174–8
  in urban areas 152–73
rural areas
  land availability 153
  poverty 44–7
rural to urban migration 154–5, 183

salinity 83, 126–7, 128
sedimentation, coastal 63, 133–5
settlement schemes 113–14, 117–18, 134
settlements: in mountain areas 103–5
  see also housing
sewage 139–41, 143, 172
shifting cultivation 7–8, 28, 70–5, 133–4
  environmental implications 72–4
  management techniques 74–5
site and service housing schemes 163
slope
  erosion 94
  geology 103
  morphology 93–5
slums 161–2, 163–4
social change
  and agricultural modernization 185–7
  and technology 7, 31, 32, 33
social impact assessment 36–7
soft bottom habitats 124–8, 130–2
soil
  composition 79

mountain 100–1
  nutrients: decline in 72
  see also erosion; sedimentation
species
  diversity 22–3
  endangered 63, 148–50
  see also fauna; flora
squatters 143, 154–5, 161–2, 163–4
subsistence crops 8–9
succession
  concept of 20–1
  mangroves 126–7
sustained yield, concept of 23–4
swamp reclamation 3, 63

tea plantations 117
technology 8, 192–4
  in agriculture 86–7
  alternative 193–4
  and pollution 31–4
  and resource management 30–4
  social effect of 7, 31, 32, 33
  traditional 15–16, 160, 193
  transfers 15, 194
temperature, mountain 96–7, 109–10
terracing 7–8, 116
tourism 11, 13, 131, 143
trade
  international 15, 41–3, 89
  producer prices 87–8
tradition: and agricultural modernization
    185–7
training 195–6

Uganda 2, 3, 10, 34
  agriculture 56, 57–8, 59, 61–2
  fisheries 63
  forest resources 62
  industrial growth 167
  population 64
  poverty in 47–65
  resource management 57–65
  water resources 63
United Nations Development Programme
    (UNDP) 176–7
United Nations Environment Programme
    (UNEP) 175–6
urban areas
  housing 159–64
  land issue 152–9
  resource management in 152–73
  see also industry
urbanization: on East African coast 142–3

value-freezing, land 159
value judgement 24–5
vegetation 21–2
  burning 72
vegetation zones: mountain 95, 101–2,
    111–13

villagization programmes: in East Africa 134
  see also settlement schemes

Wangu Embori farm 117–18
waste
  domestic 139–41, 172
  industrial 170–2
  management 172–3

water resources: in Uganda 63
  see also irrigation
weeds 72–3
welfare economics 14
wildlife management: in Africa 10–13
  see also fauna; flora
willingness to pay technique 28
World Health Organization (WHO) 176